ABOUT ISLAND PRESS

HUMAN ECOLOGY

HUMAN
ECOLOGY

Following Nature's Lead

FREDERICK STEINER

ISLAND PRESS

WASHINGTON · COVELO · LONDON

Library of Congress Cataloging-in-Publication Data
Steiner, Frederick.
Human ecology : following nature's lead / Frederick Steiner.
p. cm.
Includes bibliographical references and index.
ISBN 1-55963-995-4 (hardcover : alk. paper)
1. Human ecology. 2. Human ecology—Philosophy. I. Title.
GF41 .S73 2002
304.2—dc21
2002009834

British Cataloguing-in-Publication Data available.

Printed on recycled, acid-free paper ♲

Manufactured in the United States of America
09 08 07 06 05 04 03 02   8 7 6 5 4 3 2 1

What does it mean, anyway, to be an animal in human clothing?

—Barbara Kingsolver
High Tide in Tucson

The story of man may be found in the palm of his hand,
in the leaf of life impressed in his palm.
The cohesive force between molecules in a drop of water is the start
of identity in our body.

—Giuseppe Penone
Giuseppe Penone

CONTENTS

Foreword xi

Preface xv

INTRODUCTION: THE SUBVERSIVE SUBJECT 1

1. FUNDAMENTAL PRINCIPLES 19
OF HUMAN ECOLOGY

2. HABITAT 39

3. COMMUNITY 57

4. LANDSCAPE 77

5. THE ECOLOGICAL REGION 95

6. NATION, STATE, AND NATION-STATE 125

7. THE GREEN CHAOS OF THE PLANET 145

8. FOLLOWING NATURE'S LEAD 167

Acknowledgments 177

Notes 181

Bibliography 209

Index 229

ix

FOREWORD

THE FUTURE? THAT'S WHAT LIES AHEAD. OR IS IT WHAT WE CREATE? Suppose nature and people were each working independently to mold the future. Or even imagine a future with human ecology at its core.

I recently heard of two prominent environmental leaders being separately asked by the press what they had accomplished in their careers. After a thoughtful pause each made essentially the same comment, "I believe I helped slow the rate of environmental (or land) degradation." The response was right on target. I was stunned by the answer. If leaders only slow the downward spirals so visible around us, there must be a more promising route.

Many of us spend our life trying to make the world we are given a little better. Yet an alternative exists that might accomplish far more. Try sketching out a vision, a goal for the future. Highlight its key principles and foundations. Give it tangible spatial outlines so that people can relate personally to it. Of course the vision will be partially shrouded. It will provide only glimpses upon which to construct a future. Over time, alternative visions, and the alternative trajectories to attain them, will emerge. Fine. Evaluating and choosing among visions and trajectories should be our bread and butter. People with vision get leaders and the public engaged.

Let me briefly illustrate. Consider a future where both nature and people thrive over the long term. To portray this vision, we accumulate state-of-our-knowledge principles and outline a framework or rough design that arranges nature and people to accomplish the core objective. This vision, as schematically portrayed below, first appears embryonic and shrouded, then slowly materializes. I see it as a ray of hope, a rare concrete basis for optimism.

Think of a large landscape bathed in swirling mist. We see only glimpses, vignettes. A few large blobs of natural vegetation. Strips of greenery along major streams. Connections between the large green blobs. Bits of nature scattered across a matrix of human activities and concentrated near the large green blobs. Major land uses mainly aggregated into large patches. Small sites of human activity concentrated along major land-use boundaries. Hermits, plus isolated human land uses, present but rare. Strategic points ringed by conspicuous planning and management activity. Road networks that facilitate walking and the natural movements of water and wildlife across the landscape. Traffic flows quiet enough for wildlife and people to thrive nearby. A coarse-grained land of large patches, but with fine-grained areas present. The overall framework or puzzle hierarchically organized yet tied together with loops, feedback loops.

Individual puzzle pieces also come into focus. Some exhibit natural processes; others, human activities; and many effectively mesh both. Buildings placed to avoid disturbing natural areas, and arranged for environmental and social benefits. Local and regional cultures manifest in the aesthetics and treasured heritage of places. Ecological flows and processes across the land little interrupted by human structures. Built areas with an abundance of natural forms and peppered with bio-rich spots. Buildings, routes, and green areas arranged for the daily uses in a person's home range. An imprint of walking routes and meeting places in built areas. Compatibility of adjacent puzzle pieces for both people and nature. Each patch sustained by links to a constellation of neighboring puzzle pieces.

This shrouded vision also hums right along and evolves over time. Water, soil, nutrients, and species moving, balanced by the flow of people, goods, money, and information. A changing landscape, not at the "overnight" rate of economics and politics, but sustainably at the rate of local and regional culture. Individual puzzle pieces transformed in harmony with broad keystone land-use patterns. These are but glimpses of a vision for a sustainable nature and people.

In contrast, the book in your hand provides substance and a welcome new perspective on human ecology. Frederick Steiner offers an impressive array of insights and vision. Every chapter bulges with principles and information. His syntheses provide new understanding but also address persistent societal challenges involving ecology and culture, nature and humans, land and people.

With foundations in anthropology, sociology, ecology, landscape architecture, and planning, human ecology not only plays an important role in each field but also increasingly manifests its own attributes. Two highlights very much on Steiner's palette—landscape ecology and landscape architecture/planning—add valuable new dimensions to human ecology. Combining a perceptive mind and a skilled hand, Steiner deftly unravels these fields. Furthermore, in concert with familiar human ecology perspectives, these new dimensions provide a solid yet creative foundation for action.

Delightful images appear throughout the pages ahead. Steiner leads us to discoveries in our own home and yard as well as in neighborhoods, cities, and the countryside. He opens our eyes to special places across the entire United States. The creative hands of Vitruvius, Jefferson, Penn, and Powell come alive. In a magical descent over Mexico City, he elucidates patterns spread out below. From Poland to Dubai, from Spain to Australia, and in every continent and in many eras, we take home vibrant human ecology messages. And imagine the proverbial cab ride across Rome: the perceptive author uncovers layer after delightful layer of insight into the intertwining arms of nature and people.

Steiner repeatedly poses important questions, many of which are the grist of discussion with family and friends, and others that are of a cosmic nature. Some are answered directly; many are addressed with salient principles and examples. Perhaps most make us ponder. In the hierarchy from home to globe, which level is most promising for a sustained human ecology? What would the human and the ecology components look like? Does regional planning have a chance? Do state departments of transportation create and eliminate communities? Is Gaia, ethics, or religion an essential cohesive force here? How can we best put our impressive knowledge of human ecology to work for society—and for nature?

With appealing prose, Frederick Steiner lucidly links science and art. The scholar, the student, and the educated public will learn much, and may experience an epiphany, in the pages that follow. Dig deeply; herein lies a treasure trove of wisdom.

RICHARD T. T. FORMAN
Harvard University

PREFACE

THE SUBWAYS OF SEOUL BURROW THROUGH THE STRATA BENEATH a complex, urban matrix. Every once in a while, the trains come up for air, as they cross the expansive Han River or roll to a new town on the periphery of the city. I'm a stranger to this hemisphere. My companions on the train are not.

We're traversing Seoul. My new students know this place. I'm trying to learn. They direct aboveground students to the location of our rendezvous. Cell phones connect us to each other and to the weather on the surface.

A cold front entered Seoul the night before, bringing with it strong winds and snow. Will we be able to conduct our charrette, or will it be snowed or rained out? Reports from the students outside the train indicate improved conditions.

From an earlier visit, I've selected an appropriate place for our daylong charrette, the Insa-dong neighborhood. I like this district because remnants of traditional Korean culture persist in the design of the windows and roofs. Its original builders designed with nature. The students and I are going to Insa-dong to learn about human ecology.

We have already spent an hour or so back at the conference center reviewing the history of Insa-dong. A translator had been provided even though all twelve students speak some English. They come from several disciplines—architecture, planning, landscape architecture, graphic design, interior design, and geography—and represent four universities.

Some of the students dress rather conservatively, others quite trendily. One young woman wears beautiful, layered grays and black. Several students sport Nikes. Two male architects present themselves in gang-banger costumes and have dyed their long hair blonde, well, sort of blonde.

The conference organizers have provided us with maps that present broad information about Seoul—its geology and hydrology, the road and park networks—as well as site-specific data for Insa-dong, including topography and soils, land use, and structures of the neighborhood. We review these maps in the subway. Upon entering the main street, Insadong-gil, we will attempt to read the text of the city among the art galleries and handicraft shops.

The students huddle in the cold.

The snow has turned to light rain.

We share umbrellas and seek refuge under storefront roofs.

I take a picture of some soggy leaves on the sidewalk. I don't know these leaves, and I wonder from what naked branch they fell. I also ponder who built this street, this city, this nation, what forces needed to be understood and harnessed before safe and healthy settlement could occur.

My charge to the students: Tell me how nature and culture interact here.

We walked and talked. We sought to understand the ordinary, but this was no ordinary place. Perhaps no place is truly ordinary. Every spot on Earth has its own tale to tell. So we sought the story of Insa-dong.

Shoeless and sitting on the floor, we ate lunch in a restaurant in a traditional Seoul courtyard house. Over *yukgaejang, kimchi, bulgogi,* and *poricha,* we discussed the students' interests and backgrounds. One student spoke in a rural dialect, and the others poked fun as she blushed.

After lunch, the students sketched and I took pictures. We studied walls and doorways, gutters and paving, paintbrushes and handmade paper, storefronts and street trees. The sun broke through the clouds for a while, but then the rain returned. We retreated to the conference center where I gave the students a second task: based on the nature and the culture of Insa-dong, suggest one intervention.

The architects designed a building for a vacant lot, the landscape architects proposed some trees and street improvements, the planners had ideas about how to make the circulation more effective. The graphic designer presented the most poetic proposition: she suggested a scheme of basic colors—blues and greens—to call attention to the current drainage patterns of the neighborhood and to retrace those of the past.

At the end of the charrette, we had a group photograph taken of our community-for-a-day. A couple of the students have stayed in touch with me via e-mail. They tell me how their studies are progressing and seek my advice about graduate school. Through them, through our electronic interactions, I remain connected to a place many time zones away.

My quest in this book parallels the two charges I gave to the students in Seoul. First, I seek to explore how nature and culture interact in human settlements. Second, I'm interested in how an understanding of such interactions informs how we shape our homes, neighborhoods, landscapes, city-regions, and nations.

INTRODUCTION:
THE SUBVERSIVE SUBJECT

Chaos is the law of nature,
Order is the dream of man.

—HENRY ADAMS

WE INTERACT WITH EACH OTHER AND WITH OUR PHYSICAL environments. We are biological creatures who depend on the living landscape to sustain us. Plants and animals are affected by our actions, and our existence is impacted by plants and animals. We exist within complex sets of interactions—that is, we live in an ecological world.

Learning to perceive the world as a never-ending system of interactions—that is, to think about our surroundings and our relationships with our environments and each other ecologically—is challenging. Such thinking forces us to rethink our views of economics, politics, and business. It suggests different ways to plan and design. In economics, for example, an ecological view suggests a much more complex set of relationships than supply and demand: supply of what and where from and at what cost, not only in dollars but to other species and other generations. Ecological understanding can also confront our values and religious beliefs, although most faiths address human connections to the natural world and stewardship responsibilities for future generations. The ecologist Paul Sears, in 1964, was the first to call ecology a subversive subject. He speculated that if ecology were "taken seriously as an instrument for the long-run welfare of mankind, [then it would] endanger the assumptions and practices accepted by modern societies, whatever their doctrinal commitments."[1]

1

Ecology is, by definition, the reciprocal relationship among all organisms and their biological and physical environments. People are organisms. As a result, we can ask, Is the use of "human" as a modifier to "ecology," as in the title of this book, necessary? Many overlaps between the social and biological sciences existed at the end of the nineteenth century and during the early twentieth century. Ecological concepts were prominent in both sociology and geography. For example, "environmental determinism" suggested that our surroundings shape everything from skin color to behavior. However, these concepts led to rather simplistic, and even racist, notions about how environments shaped cultures, and environmental determinism was discredited by the 1920s.

Increasingly, the social sciences became disconnected from the physical sciences and, by extension, from the material world. The focus of the social sciences shifted from ecological models to the embrace of economic, political, and demographic approaches where the role of natural forces was more subtle. In order to bolster the validity of their science, some researchers emphasized quantitative analysis that favored data about people over the observation of the human condition. Meanwhile, ecologists, especially those in North America, concentrated on the study of natural, nonhuman environments. Some one-third of the land in the United States was in public ownership, enabling wildlife and vegetation research on vast expanses with little human interruption.

There are many ironies in this disconnection. For example, the Greek root for both ecology and economics is the same: *oikos*. Both disciplines involve the study of the household. Ecology is the "study of the environmental house, including all its inhabitants, in which we live and in which we place our human-made structures and domesticated plants and animals."[2] Economics is the study of the household of money. As we can track the flow of money, we can also illuminate other movements in the places where we live. But beyond their common Greek root, economics and ecology diverged with few clear connections persisting.

"Human" with "ecology" helps reinforce the reality of our place in environments. Human ecology, then, is "an attempt to understand the interrelationships between the human species and its environment."[3] According to Paul Shepard, "Human ecology may not be limited strictly to biological concepts, but it cannot ignore them or even transcend them."[4]

Since the first Earth Day in April 1970 and the rise of the modern environmental movement, social scientists have rediscovered "the environment" while biologists have probed social interactions.[5] Meanwhile, several ecologists have addressed human communities, and planners and designers have attempted to provide syntheses to shape human communities.[6] In addition to the stimulus from popular culture, as expressed in wide-ranging areas from politics to music, advances in theory through computing technologies, urban morphology (the study of how cities are structured physically), landscape studies, and ideas about chaos and complexity have contributed to this renewed interest in the environment by social scientists. From within the biological sciences, research has altered conventional views about organism-environment interactions.[7] Increasingly, ecologists consider human influences on their environments.[8]

This new human ecology emphasizes complexity over reductionism, focuses on changes over stable states, and expands ecological concepts beyond the study of plants and animals to include people. This view differs from the environmental determinism of the early twentieth century. The new ecology addresses the complexity of human interactions rather than how a specific physical environment shapes human anatomic variations. Because people form part of its scope, new ecology may be viewed as human ecology, or the evolution of traditional ecology to reconsider human systems.

The geographer Karl Zimmerer notes that the "'new ecology' offers a sort of shorthand for a significant reorientation that has occurred in the field of biological ecology. . . . The 'new ecology' accents disequilibria, instability, and even chaotic fluctuations in biophysical environments, both 'natural' and human-impacted."[9] Pulliam and Johnson identify two primary changes in new ecology, differentiating it from its traditional progenitor:

> (1) a shift from an equilibrium point of view where local populations and ecosystems are viewed as in balance with local resources and conditions, to a disequilibrium point of view where history matters and populations and ecosystems are continually being influenced by disturbances; and (2) a shift from considering populations and ecosystems as relatively closed or autonomous systems independent of their surroundings, to considering both populations and ecosystems as "open" and strongly influenced by the input and output or "flux" of material and individuals across system borders.[10]

Traditional ecology relied on the assumptions that nature could achieve balance and that ecosystems functioned as closed systems. Natural plant communities evolved through several stages, climaxing in a steady state, according to traditional theory. Since ecologists studied plants and animals in

forests, deserts, and other environments relatively removed from human settlements, their interactions could be isolated for study within closed systems.

New ecology challenges both assumptions. Living systems are viewed
as changing and complex rather than stable and balanced. In addition, the
boundaries between communities blur. Open systems possess fluid, overlapping boundaries across several spatial scales from the local to the global.

IDEAS CONTRIBUTING TO A NEW HUMAN ECOLOGY

Ecology lends itself to reinvention, to reinterpretation. Relationships link
things, and how we view connections among elements changes. As early as
the 1950s, anthropologists called for a "new ecology."[11] This (now old) new
ecology advocated "populations as referent units in ecological formations"
instead of the then more prevalent "cultural ecology . . . , in which cultures
are taken to be the environed units."[12]

The ideas leading to the more recent, expanding view of ecology have
come from many sources and a variety of disciplines, including anthropology.[13] The catalysts for change include advances in technologies, the study
of urban morphology, the evolution of landscape studies within the humanities, social criticism, the emergence of the science landscape ecology,
a broader understanding of chaos theory, and increased interest in issues of
sustainability. The emergence of urban ecology exemplifies a beginning
synthesis of these sometimes divergent catalysts. Urban ecology focuses on
organism-environment interactions within cities and other human settlements. By concentrating on urban areas, the interests of the new ecological
perspective are woven closer together.

Fresh ways to observe nature, primarily as a result of computer and remote-sensing technologies, have altered our understanding of functions,
structures, and patterns. These new (and evolving) technologies are yielding
a "deeper perspective," a "new mythology," according to the ecologist Daniel
Botkin who identifies two key aspects of this new view. First, many events
can be "considered simultaneously in a connected network," and, second,
chance can be included "as a fundamental aspect of life and death."[14]

A computer technology especially valuable for revealing complex, ecological relationships is geographical information systems, known by its ab-
breviation GIS. These computer software programs allow analysts to study
overlapping spatial data and map the results. For example, the home range
of a tiger beetle species can be mapped then compared with a similar map

for a species of brown bear. In turn, both can be overlaid on the migration routes of Canada geese and the extent of a coniferous forest and so on.

GIS originated in the 1960s and 1970s as much or more from within planning and landscape architecture disciplines as from within geography.[15] Many of the contemporary innovators in GIS development are geographers as well as planners and landscape architects such as Jack Dangermand and David Sinton.[16] In the 1960s and 1970s, when GIS originated, the cartographers within geography had been largely marginalized, leaving a gap in spatial representation expertise. Geography was undergoing a quantitative revolution, and those who worked with paper maps were viewed as somewhat quaint relics. Mapped information forms the basis for GIS. As a result, GIS has emerged as a largely multidisciplinary way of viewing landscapes with significant contributions from a broad spectrum of disciplines in the environmental design arts, the environmental sciences, and the social sciences. GIS technologies offer new ways to describe, analyze, plan, and design the complexities of human settlements. GIS emerged concurrently with new ways to see and to record the surface of the planet, such as remote-sensing technologies. Whereas GIS programs map information, remote sensing creates imagery of phenomena on the surface of Earth.

As the Apollo astronauts approached the moon, they relayed images back to Earth unlike anything previously seen. The hypnotic pictures of the moon riveted our attention, of course, but the photographs of the blue-green orb of Earth were perhaps even more profound. Continents and water bodies were clearly visible beneath swirls of clouds, but borders had disappeared. No longer would we see Earth in the manner of the little globes in our classrooms. NASA continues to produce images of the planet, as do other governmental and private remote-sensing groups. In fact, NASA broadcasts continual images of our planet on its own television network.

Remote-sensed information is collected through satellites or high-flying aircraft. The images can be enhanced with computers to reveal specific phenomena, such as land cover, land use, and fault lines. Climate patterns can be tracked and future weather events forecasted. Remote sensors can also be linked to on-the-ground monitoring stations. Such connections allow phenomena to be observed through time. For example, a drainage basin can have several stream-monitoring gauges, which may be linked to a central data collection center. In turn, satellites may be able to collect rainfall and snowpack information daily that can be combined with the field data to predict future water supplies.

The use of GIS and remote-sensing technologies has spread like wild-fire among scientists during the past few decades. A geologist can overlay a map of bedrock on an aerial photograph to determine where a fault line intersects with settlement. An ecologist can map wildlife corridors on a re-mote-sensed image, enter that information into a GIS, then compare it with the geologist's map. Additional technologies likely will open more possibilities. For example, visualization techniques present three-dimensional representations of objects. Such visualization can be combined with GIS to show places more holistically. For example, the maps of the geologist and the ecologist can be rendered in three dimensions to illustrate the relationships among phenomena such as bedrock, wildlife corridors, and land use. The Internet opens opportunities, too. For instance, a team of American students can work with a group of Italians in a "virtual studio," and share GIS maps and photographs of a place, say, in Africa.

Do we live in an Information Age or a Computer Age or an Ecological Age? We live in all three. Information stored and communicated via computers reveals more and more about our interactions, with each other and with our worlds. GIS combined with real-time satellite images and the Internet provides the equivalent of a central nervous system for the planet. Humans can aspire to provide the brain for that system. How we apply our brains to use these technologies and this information will transform how we live and, therefore, the patterns of our settlements.

As the information landscape advances, we can gain a better under-standing of human ecology. For example, satellite imagery can produce daily climate information for settlements. Such information can be mapped through GIS over time. GIS can be used to overlay climate data on land-use and land-cover maps. This process reveals how we use the land and how what we plant on its surface affects urban climate. In this way, GIS and remote-sensing technologies enable us to visualize relationships. Since human ecology is essentially about relationships, our ecological un-derstanding advances as we reveal previously unseen connections.

We especially gain insights into urban places. Urban morphology is the study of human settlement patterns. People create non-urban settle-ments ranging from farmsteads and rural villages to mines and ski lodges. Suburbia lacks urbanity but is often classified as urban by geographers. Population trends indicate that the world is becoming more urban. For the first time in human history, over half the world's population lives in met-ropolitan regions. As the planet has urbanized, the structure of urban areas has attracted the attention of scholars.

According to Anne Vernez Moudon, a professor of architecture, landscape architecture, and planning at the University of Washington (1997), urban morphology evolved primarily in geography from the work of M. R. G. Conzen in England and in architecture through the work of Saverio Muratori in Italy. They promoted the rigorous and thorough mapping of the physical structure of cities. Conzen and Muratori prepared detailed maps of what the Italians call *tessuto*, or the tissues of the city—that is, clusters of structures, vegetation, and roadways that hold the urban body together.[17] Their influence has spread among geographers, architects, and planners in Europe and North America. Moudon notes that "*form, resolution* [or hierarchy], and *time* constitute the three fundamental components of urban morphological research."[18] Urban morphologists advocate reading the city as a text to reveal culture. Moudon notes that the city has "unique mnemonic powers as a cultural palimpsest."[19] For others, landscapes possess such power as both a cultural *and* a natural palimpsest.

Landscapes offer a scale where social and physical processes and patterns can become evident. We see landscapes and all our senses react to their well-being. Landscape is a word and a concept with growing intellectual currency. As a result, it is a topic of growing interest and study in the humanities, sciences, and the fine and applied arts.[20] Several prominent historians have discovered landscape and used it as a focus of their work. Simon Schama has written of "landscapes and memory," John Stilgoe has traced the history of landscape in America, Stephen Pyne has explored the "cultural history" of fire, and William Cronon has used landscape to explain the history of Chicago as well as Native Americans and colonists in New England.[21] John Opie rewrote the history of the United States from an environmental perspective.[22] American historians are indebted to the French *Annales* school of historiography, which focuses on the landscapes of everyday life.[23] In addition, histories and archaeology of landscapes are being constructed or perhaps deconstructed.[24] Writers, especially those of the American West, from Wallace Stegner to Barbara Kingsolver, use landscape prominently in their essays.[25] Landscape is almost elevated to a character in the work of mystery writer Tony Hillerman, and the land is one of the most important characters in both Alan Paton's *Cry, The Beloved Country* and Knut Hamsun's *Growth of the Soil*.[26] The wonderful, quirky Mike Davis uses landscape for his dark, humorous explorations into the cultures of southern California.[27]

Natural cycles intersect with human intentions in the landscape. For example, in *Refuge*, Terry Tempest Williams tracks the natural rise of the

Great Salt Lake, its impact on bird populations, and the attempts by people to thwart its flooding.[28] The water rise and fall is "natural," as perhaps
are the human and bird responses, but the people are not content to adjust
to the nature of the lake, and their actions seem to exacerbate the problem.
Against this landscape, other human manipulations result in unnatural disturbances in the lives of Williams's family.

Nuclear tests in the "uninhabited" deserts of Nevada and Utah have
resulted in deadly cancers. Terry Tempest Williams recounts the deaths of
both her mother and her grandmother as natural occurrences caused by unnatural tampering. The landscape Williams sought as a refuge turned
deadly to her other sanctuary, that of her family.

Critiques of the idea of nature, of the social construct of nature, notably,
that by the Canadian environmental theorist Neil Evernden, have also expanded the discussion of ecology and especially the human role in/with nature. Evernden notes: "To say that there is a natural element in humans may
be a compliment, linking us with the greater sphere of nature. Or, it may be
a criticism, implying some lingering aspects of bestiality that must be over-
come through civilization."[29] And further, "we resist the possibility of there
being anything 'human' in nature, including purpose and meaning, but then
we proceed to use nature as a refugium for social ideas."[30]

Nature and culture, or rather natures and cultures, are inseparable.
Thinking about the nature of natures, the culture of cultures, the nature of
cultures, and the culture of natures is a natural impulse for humans, but nature may indeed be more complex than we *can* think, as the ecologist Reed
Noss and the ethnobotanist Gary Paul Nabhan assert.[31] As ecological
thought has matured from philosophical critiques, scientific knowledge has
also deepened.

Landscape ecology focuses on the ecological relationships at the landscape scale. According to ecologists Richard Forman and Michel Godron,
landscape ecology is "a study of the structure, function, and change in a
heterogeneous land area composed of interacting ecosystems."[32] European
scientists advanced landscape ecology before their American counterparts.
The landscapes of Europe have been more densely settled than in North
America, and, as a result, the human influence was recognized quickly by
European scientists. American ecologists are more accustomed to studying
relatively pristine landscapes. The refinement of the landscape ecology discipline, coupled with increased suburban sprawl nationwide, has changed
this situation as more American ecologists acknowledge human interactions with natural systems. As landscape ecology has evolved through mul-

tiple interactions among European, American, and Australian contributors, it has crystallized into something new and powerful. Richard Forman observes that human settlements form mosaic-like patterns on landscapes and that this land mosaic vision makes the landscape readily accessible to scientists, especially ecologists.

We can see change and interactions in landscapes. Edges—or interfaces—between land uses can be especially sensitive and rich. In rapidly growing regions, edges are unstable and conflicting. New homes replace farmland. The land sells relatively cheaply. The open land provides an attractive backdrop. Agriculture practices create dust and noise. Farming often depends on chemicals that have consequences for human health. Suburbanites possess different lifestyles and expectations that vary dramatically from those of their rural neighbors. Large John Deere tractors and combines are replaced by small John Deere riding lawnmowers. Such landscape change lends itself to scientific analysis. For example, ecologists can ask, What interactions are driving the change and what patterns are resulting?

Landscape ecology has influenced the applied arts. Landscape architecture is one profession where such an influence should be obvious.[33] Planning is another applied discipline affected by landscape ecological research.[34] The growing field of conservation biology has also been strongly impacted by findings from landscape ecology.[35] These disciplines, or at least ideas from them, come together for planning specific projects, such as greenways.[36]

As we explore the ecology of landscapes, the knowledge gained can help us guide our actions as well as constrain them. According to architect Ken Yeang of Kuala Lumpur, four aspects must simultaneously be considered in ecological design. In addition, how these aspects relate with one another needs to be understood.[37] The first two aspects are the "external and internal interdependencies of the designed system."[38] The first aspect addresses external interdependencies, that is, processes and activities in the environment. What are the landscape processes and activities, we may ask, that will interact with what we design? The second aspect refers to the processes and activities within, or internal to, the designed system. What new sets of processes and activities, we can ask, are we creating within this design? With the first two aspects, we seek to understand the context and the internal workings of what is being designed.

The next two aspects address the "external-to-internal and the internal-to-external exchanges of energy and matter," according to Yeang.[39] In these cases, environment influences to the designed system are considered, and vice versa. By employing such an analysis in design and planning, individual designed objects, be they buildings or gardens, are not viewed independently but rather as parts of dynamic landscape systems.

Artists as diverse as Robert Smithson and Nancy Holt from England, the Americans Mary Miss and Michael Singer, as well as Giuseppe Penone of Italy have made landscape central to their art. Nature, it can be and has been argued, underlies all art, so landscape as a visualization of nature and culture "naturally" attracts the attention of artists. Architecture theorists, such as George Hersey and Grant Hildebrand, have also explored the "biological roots" of buildings.[40]

"Art's about life and it can't really be about anything else. There isn't anything else," the artist Damien Hirst proclaims.[41] We need art for life's sake, lives for the sake of art, arts that enliven our senses to nature. In Phoenix, the artists Michael Singer and Linnea Glatt created a solid waste management center adjacent to a landfill.[42] Engineers and architects had earlier designed the facility as a nondescript big box. Glatt and Singer restructured its form with a series of heavily planted terraces. Views to the recycling activities within and to the mountains and city around were facilitated. The activities in and around the facility became transparent and the focus of environmental education. "Where's the art?" visitors accustomed to object-centered creations ask. The art is everywhere.

Yet another body of thought influencing how people and nature interact is chaos theory, which asserts, "Our universe has a pluralistic, complex character."[43] Chaos theory addresses the complexity of systems. According to the authors of *Order Out of Chaos*, Ilya Prigogine and Isabelle Stengers, "nature is undergoing a radical change toward the multiple, the temporal, and the complex."[44] Furthermore, they explain that "irreversibility is a source of order at all levels. Irreversibility is the mechanism that brings order out of chaos."[45]

Chaos was once thought to have been that infinity of space and formless matter preceding the existence of an ordered universe. But is the universe ordered? For a system undergoing spontaneous change, entropy increases—that is, the amount of energy available for work decreases. If spontaneous change is the norm, then the universe is in perpetual disorder. But if this is the case, all energy would be lost, and entropy would reign. It seems as though chaos creates a certain order, through negentropy, that restores energy to systems that would otherwise be lost. Landscape architect Laurie Olin contends that while nature is not disorderly, it is certainly "rambunctious."[46] Chaos theory can enable us to wend our way through nature's exuberance. The theory helps reinforce and inform ideas about change and complexity in new ecology.

A growing interest in the ecologies of urban areas provides evidence of a coalescence of these catalysts for change.[47] In the United States, the National Science Foundation (NSF) established two Long Term Ecological Research (LTER) projects in 1997. Before setting up these projects in the Baltimore and Phoenix metropolitan regions, NSF located LTERs in nonurban places. Remote locations presented ideal places for ecologists to explore the traditional concept of stable states in relatively closed systems. Increasingly, influential American ecologists began to urge NSF to consider the ecology of metropolitan regions too in order to pursue the study of more complex systems. "Urban ecological systems present multiple challenges to ecologists," the biologist Nancy Grimm and her colleagues assert, including "pervasive human impact and extreme heterogeneity of cities, and the need to integrate social and ecological approaches, concepts, and theory."[48]

The Baltimore and Phoenix LTERs offer contrasting urban conditions. Baltimore, located in the northeastern region of the United States, is an older city than Phoenix and has a more dense urban fabric. The Sun Belt location of Phoenix offers a city developed as a result of automobile, airplane, air conditioning, and refrigeration technologies. Whereas growth in Baltimore is rather slow, population expansion in the Phoenix metropolitan region leads the nation. The humid Chesapeake Bay contrasts the arid Sonoran Desert. As a result, the Baltimore and Phoenix LTERs can help us understand constants in urban conditions as well as specific variations resulting from the natural surroundings and from the period of settlement.

Thus far, there has been relatively little interaction between the "urban ecology" camp dominated by scientists and the "urban morphologists" led by architects and planners. Geographers are present in both groups and likely will form bridges. The substance of such spans can be provided through better understanding human ecology.

Human ecology is important if we are serious about sustainable development—that is, "economic progress that meets all of our needs without leaving future generations with fewer resources than those we enjoy. A way of living from nature's income rather than mining its capital account."[49] Or, as defined by the planner Jill Grant and her colleagues, "Sustainable development implies adaptation and improvement in a context in which communities seek to protect natural processes and landscape function, and to conserve resources for future generations."[50] We must understand the organization—the function, structure, and processes—of the communities that we inhabit in order to lay the foundations for the future.

Perhaps the growing interest in sustainable development—in seeking to make communities more livable—derives from a sense that we are living in places where something is out of whack. Perhaps the creative impulse derives always from a dread of the future, the feeling that the world may not improve for our children, and our desire to fend off doom to improve things for those who follow. To sustain things, we must keep them from falling apart, now and in the future. All around us, things indeed appear to be coming apart at the seams. Where once was a farm field, now stands a convenience store. Where once children played in the park, now homeless people sleep. Where there was once a vibrant downtown, there are now vacant lots.

The farm field, the park, the downtown; the convenience store, the homeless people, the vacant lots form pieces in larger mosaics, larger processes. In itself, the field or the convenience store is neither good nor bad. Both, however, are part of larger systems that may be either healthy or sick, that is, either capable of sustaining themselves or not. The individual farm field contributes to a regional agricultural system. The crops produced in the field help sustain the regional economy. The crops support not only the farm family that produces them, but the local co-op that processes the crop for the market and the tractor dealer as well. The convenience store has an asphalt parking lot. Its impervious surface contributes to regional drainage and flooding problems because of increased runoff. Because the parking lot is black, it adds to the urban heat island effect resulting in summer discomfort among nearby residents. The understanding of how living systems are organized from the local to the regional provides a means for assessing their capabilities to adjust to change.

NESTED NETWORKS

Living systems are organized hierarchically and communicate through feedback networks. Sheila Peck mentions that the concept of biological hierarchy "involves a series of levels of structural complexity."[51] That is, what is whole at one level of organization is a part at another. A cell is a complete entity, but only part of an organism. Individual organisms are both simple and complex: members of larger species and variegated communities, which form landscapes and regions that are part of global systems and processes. Levels of organization are convenient ways to understand complex systems. Levels of biological organization range from the organism to the biosphere.[52] Feedbacks cycle energy and information through systems within and between various levels of organization.

The elements within a system may vary greatly in organization. According to urban morphologists, "urban form can be understood at different levels of resolution. Commonly, four are recognized, corresponding to the building/lot, the street/block, the city, and the region."[53] A building may be tall or short, with a pitched roof or a flat one, brick or wood or adobe. A lot, a street, or a block may be narrow or wide, straight or curved. A city may be densely settled or spread out. A region can be defined by a river or a mountain or a coastline or all three and by other factors.

Hierarchies help us understand how people are connected with one another—the basic idea of community. The hierarchical structure of human societies and community are ancient topics. For example, Marcus Tullius Cicero wrote in the century before the birth of Christ:

> Then, too there are a great many degrees of closeness or remoteness in human society. To proceed beyond the universal bond of our common humanity, there is the closer one of belonging to the same people, tribe, and tongue, by which men are very closely bound together; it is still closer relation to be citizens of the same city-state; for fellow-citizens have much in common—forum, temples, colonnades, streets, statutes, laws, courts, rights of suffrage, to say nothing of social and friendly circles and diverse business relations with many.[54]

Three centuries before Cicero, and on a more cosmic level, Plato imagined the universe in *Timaeus* as "a single visible living being . . . a whole of complete parts . . . a single complete whole, consisting of parts that are wholes. . . . "[55] We view ourselves as a whole, but are incomplete without our connections to others. We define ourselves internally but also through our relationships with others.

To understand human ecologies, the most relevant levels of organization include habitat, community, landscape, region, nation and state, and earth or ecosphere. These levels present different, yet interconnected, scales of analysis. Each level possesses a history and a literature of analysis and debate. The habitat includes the building and lot. The community is comprised of buildings, lots, streets, and blocks. Landscapes can be urban, suburban, rural, and wild. Regions are hodgepodges of landscapes, while the distinctions between regions, and often those between states and nations, are even more blurred. But there is less ambiguity about the ends of the Earth.

Planners are one group who conceptualize the world hierarchically. Often "community" and/or "region" or perhaps "city" is added to planning in academic program and degree title names. The discipline's planning unit (nation, state, region, county, or city) is "an element in a larger system, but is also comprised of smaller geographic units like neighborhoods [or communities], which are, in turn, collections of single households [or habitats]."[56] Drawing on work by psychologists, the planner Alice Jones speculates that the average citizen conceptualizes these units differently, that is, "each scale unit is thought of as a distinct entity that is separate from other units."[57] She notes that the individual tends to regard the units "most relevant or important" as those "that are closest to the individual's personal experience: his or her own household and his or her own personal referent communities—a relatively tiny sphere of friends, family, neighbors, and co-workers."[58] This focus on our immediate sphere presents an important hurdle in our ability to connect individual relationships and actions to broader consequences.

In numerous publications, Washington State University professor of environmental science Gerald Young identified a fundamental challenge for the wider acceptance of human ecology to be understanding the relationship between the unit and the whole.[59] Professor Young poses the question, "How real is the notion of hierarchies? Do they exist or are they simply structures of the human imagination, created to make us more comfortable with a fearful and chaotic universe?"[60] Like other structures created in our imaginations, hierarchies exist because we say they do. But, with the exception of the planetary scale, these hierarchies are not fixed.

Hierarchy may be seen as a framework, a system of nested networks. Hierarchy theory offers a useful way to conceptualize the organization of both natural systems and human cultures. The challenge becomes how to connect individual households and specific neighborhood actions to community, region, nation, and globe.

A critical feature of these nested networks "is the asymmetric interactions in between levels."[61] As the ecologist C. S. Holling explains, "the larger, slower levels maintain constraints within which faster levels operate."[62] There are, however, circumstances when "slower and larger levels in ecosystems become briefly vulnerable to dramatic transformation because of small events and fast processes."[63] Large, slow levels tend to keep things in place. Small, fast levels initiate changes when the larger levels are not functioning effectively.

Viewing the world hierarchically does not necessarily imply viewing it through a machine-like lens. Rather, it is to suggest components of a vocabulary to read our surroundings, our world. As Evernden speculates, "It is an amazing prospect, to dwell in a world in which each element is potentially meaningful, and which must be read like a book, not dismantled like a machine."[64]

Human Ecology takes on the challenge of helping its readers to understand the texts of their surroundings. The language of ecology helps us read our relationships and interactions with our environments.

In pursuit of challenge, this book links concepts from new ecology to human ecology. Traditional ecology was commonly grounded in the assumption that somehow nature is in balance. Even the most casual observation of the human condition indicates that we are seldom balanced in our affairs. As the ecologists Jianguo Wu and Orie Loucks note, the term "balance of nature" implies that "undisturbed nature is ordered and harmonious, and that ecological systems return to a previous equilibrium after disturbances."[65] They furthermore note that "theories and models built around these equilibrium and stability principles have misrepresented the foundations of resource management, nature conservation, and environmental protection."[66] Such "misrepresentation" has serious consequences for how we plan and design our environments.

Nonequilibrium represents an important change in thinking. An equally, or perhaps even more, important change derives from viewing environments at multiple, interacting scales. Landscape-level ecology, in particular, provides spatial form and function to nature's flows and human activities. New ecology, a deeper understanding of interactions at various scales, holds the prospect for better, although more complex, approaches to resource management, nature conservation, and environmental protection as well as the arts of environmental design and planning.

WHAT LIES AHEAD IN THE REST OF THE BOOK

The book explores the ecology of people. This introduction and the first chapter summarize the development of "new ecology" and the theory of human ecology. The major elements of human ecological theory (language, culture, and technology; structure, function, and change; edges, boundaries, and ecotones; interaction, integration, and institution; diversity; adaptation; and holism) form the organization for the subsequent chapters. Those chapters are organized hierarchically from the smallest scale to the largest—that is, habitat, community, landscape, region, nation-state, and globe. The final chapter addresses the ethical implications of human ecology. The book fits within a larger context of what's been called a "new ecology."

The emerging new ecology grows out of a recognition that (1) people engage in ecological relationships and (2) urban and suburban environments provide laboratories for ecological inquiry. A basic assumption of this new human ecology is that human interactions can be studied by using hierarchy as an organizing device. That is, interactions that occur at one level, the habitat, for instance, are nested in other "higher" groupings, such as the community.

A rather vast, multidisciplinary literature underscores this thesis. However, the work of these diverse, sometimes divergent, scholars needs to be coalesced to illustrate how hierarchy can be used as a critical device to help understand the ecologies of people.[67] My goals with this book are, first, to bring together the scholarship from the social and natural sciences as well as the environmental design arts on this topic, and, then, to show how we might use that knowledge to envision our futures.

I sought to explore and explain these two goals. There is no comparable work on human ecology, a subject that is important because there is a growing interest in urban ecology and it is impossible to explore the ecology of cities without including how humans interact.

The book presents a theoretical perspective, which I believe has broad policy and practical implications. I seek to shed new light on how people are engaged in ecological relationships. People are commonly regarded as existing outside of nature, or, alternately, ecology is studied in "pristine" wilderness areas, far away from human settlements. My position is potentially controversial. It is obvious, however, that we humans interact with each other as well as with other organisms and with our surroundings. I explore this point both analytically and historically.

We can learn much from history and the analysis of physical phenomena. Much more lies beyond our reconstructions of the past and our representations of the built and natural worlds. Experiential learning can help us connect the intangibles in the web of life. Human interactions can resemble the variabilities of climate. A careful observation of weather reveals that temperature, winds, and precipitation possess cycles and patterns. People, too, are bound to processes that repeat themselves and that form the structures of their lives.

FUNDAMENTAL PRINCIPLES
OF HUMAN ECOLOGY

*The eye is the first circle; the horizon which it forms is the second; and throughout na-
ture this primary picture is repeated without end. It is the highest emblem in the cipher
of the world.*

*Our life is an apprenticeship to the truth that around every circle another can be
drawn; that there is no end in nature, but every end is a beginning; that there is always
another dawn risen on mid-noon, and under every deep a lower deep opens.*

—RALPH WALDO EMERSON

FLYING INTO MEXICO CITY, I SEE AN ECOSYSTEM, AN URBAN SYSTEM
sprawled below the yellowed cloud layer. Green boulevards radiate un-
evenly like broken spokes of a wheel. Canals follow some of these green
swathes, commuter rail lines others. Mountains formed by volcanoes ring
the city, a city built from volcanic rock—red, gray, black. The remnants of
what was once a much larger lake form odd-shaped geometries, hemmed
in by dikes, bled dry by ditches. A cluster of skyscrapers marks the heart of
the metropolis. As the AeroMexico jet lowers, houses and businesses,
painted with bright primary colors, come into focus. Human systems ram-
ble to all horizons. Natural systems expand as far as the eye can see.

It is tempting to think that all principles from ecology apply to humans, but people differ significantly from plants and other animals. Plants
are more fixed to place, for example, than either people or most other animals. Humans possess culture, which perhaps only a few other species of
animals have, and even then in rather rudimentary forms. As the Rutgers
University cultural anthropologist Yehudi Cohen explained:

> Culture is man's most important instrument of adaptation. A culture is made
> of energy systems, the objective and specific artifacts, the organizations of
> social and political relations, the modes of thought, the ideologies, and the

19

range of customary behaviors that are transmitted from one generation to another by a social group and that enable it to maintain life in a particular habitat. Although a capacity for culture is not the exclusive property of *Homo sapiens*, only human culture evolves. Correlatively, as far as we know, man is the only animal capable of self-consciousness with respect to his cultures—the only animal able to blush, laugh at himself, and think of himself as a culture-bearer in third-person terms.[1]

Roy Rappaport, also an anthropologist, defines culture as "the category of phenomena distinguished from others by its contingency upon symbols. A culture consists of the cultural phenomena distinguishing a particular group or category of people from others."[2] In biological terms, culture involves the act of cultivation as well as what is yielded from such cultivation. Culture is what we create and pass on to others. Cultural creations surround our being and accumulate through our being.

Culture provides mechanisms to help us organize the complexity that surrounds us. We inhabit a world with an explicit spatial dimension. It is a world we seek to order, predict, and even dominate. Ordering is an ongoing human enterprise in all environments.[3] We seek to order things as an attempt to make some sense of our surroundings, our interactions with those surroundings, and our interactions with each other.

Hierarchy provides a theoretical organization to order these relationships at various scale levels. Across those scales, eight concepts assist us in understanding human settlement in terms of variability, time, and complexity. These concepts, suggested mostly by Gerald Young and followed by others, include systems thinking; language, culture, and technology; structure, function, and change; edges, boundaries, and ecotones; interaction, integration, and institution; diversity; adaptation; and holism.[4]

Each of these eight concepts can be best understood by considering settlements hierarchically, that is, from a more immediate scale to the global. The specific scales of habitat, community, landscape, region, nation-state, and the planet are addressed in the following chapters. Each of the eight concepts takes on different forms, depending on the scale. For example, the boundary of one's habitat, one's home and workplace, differs from the boundary of a nation-state.

The concepts also relate with each other in various ways, again with additional differences depending on the scale. The boundary of a nation-state will probably be linked to language. Most often, little language diversity exists at the level of the habitat or even a community. More diversity is likely at the regional level and is frequently found in nation-states. Before moving through the scale hierarchies, it is important to understand each of the eight concepts associated with human settlement.

SETS OF CONNECTED STUFF

A system is a complex whole, a set of connected things or parts. Botkin and Keller define a system "as any part of the universe that can be isolated for purposes of observation and study."[5] Systems are organized and arranged through networks. For a system to exist, there must be ordered, connecting channels of communication, the essence of the interaction process. Human societies add up to more than the sum of their parts; that is, interactions among elements create something larger. Ecosystems can be described as interacting wholes.[6]

In 1866, the German scientist Ernst Haeckel invented the term *oekologie*, which has come to be ecology.[7] The study of interacting systems provides a central pillar of ecology. The ecosystem then is an organized set of connected relationships. In an ecosystem, habitat, plants, and animals are "all considered as one interacting unit, the materials and energies of one passing in and out of the others."[8] In human ecosystems, we create many of the interactions.

General systems theory attempts to link the parts to the whole, to be holistic rather than reductive. In general systems theory, control is maintained through the feedback received by what is dubbed the "control mechanism." The control works like a homeostat,[9] and the result is a regulatory action[10] that keeps the system in a dynamic equilibrium. Members of the community monitor their environment in this manner and adapt to changes, in much the same way James Lovelock asserts biological processes regulate the conditions for life on our planet.

Following Julian Steward, the assumption can be made that the institutions associated directly with resource exploitation are the "core" of the social system.[11] Steward and Clifford Geertz described the "cultural core" as "that series of economic, political, and religious social relationships most closely connected with the exploitation of a relevant environment," and a "relevant environment" as "those natural factors the users deem relevant to their survival."[12] The institutions at the cultural core of most traditional rural communities include the extractive industries' institutions, such as agribusiness and mining, which are developed to free energy and material for societal use.

In urban regions, information is increasingly the key resource being exploited. Arizona State University president and science policy guru Michael Crow observes that urban regions in the future will be either "knowledge importers" or "knowledge exporters." Innovation and creativity are necessary for city-regions to maintain or advance their competitive edge in the global economy. As a result, those institutions involved in information collection and transformation form the core of many urban cultures.

The local political economy—agribusiness, banking, real estate, and government—can be viewed as a set of interactive institutional structures adapted directly to the local natural environment. These political economic institutions contain an ecological adaptive-control mechanism. Control over the ecological system is located in the community power structure.[13] Sometimes local power structures appear evident with control in the hands of the few. In other cases, the parties in control are less clear, and power is spread more diffusely. Whether centralized or more diffuse, the most successful power structures adjust to change through time.

For instance, Via Tiburtina between Rome and Tivoli is well traveled. Emperors and popes have trekked to the higher elevations of Tivoli to seek refuge from the summer heat that engulfs Rome. Along the way, the traveler passes through a strong sulfur smell. The smell originates from hot springs charged with sulfuretted hydrogen said to be beneficial for skin, throat, and urinary infections. Called "Aquoe Albuloe" in Roman times, the hot springs have been controlled by many parties over the past two thousand years. Throughout that time, the economy of the local town, Bagni di Tivoli, has been sustained.

Further along, Via Tiburtina passes through an area of travertine quarries. The *lapis tiburtinus* stone hardens after cutting. For generations, Italian architects and master builders have used this stone to construct both ancient and modern buildings, for example, the Colosseum and St. Peter's Church in Rome. Like the hot springs, control of the quarries has shifted through the centuries.

During the Roman Empire, the travertine quarries opened only when a monumental building was to be constructed. The travertine was then used primarily for structure—that is, the bones of the building, not its skin. Noble families probably owned the mines, but the government controlled the mining.

After the fall of the empire in 476, the quarries were rarely worked until about the seventeenth century. During that long period, the travertine was mined from existing Roman structures and reused. When the mines reopened, noble families continued to own the land, but entrepreneurs operated the mines. A *mastro* acted as a sort of purchasing agent between an artist or an architect who needed the stone and the mine owner or operator. Since the seventeenth century, the travertine has been used for the skin of the building.

With the formation of the Italian nation-state in the late nineteenth century and the elevation of nearby Rome as its capital, the travertine quarries experienced a boom. A shortage of skilled labor in Rome spurred workers to emigrate from San Marino and Carrara to the privately owned quarries. From the Fascist era on, the extraction of the travertine has been regulated by a variety of national and regional laws. Since the 1970s, travertine has been marketed worldwide.

As with the ancient Aquoe Albuloe, the travertine quarries sustain a local economy. Local and regional elites have kept stone flowing from the quarries and visitors submerging themselves in the hot springs.

In general systems theory terms, the local political economy, governed by the local elite, is an adaptive-control feedback mechanism.[14] Their decisions over land use and resource allocation affect the supply of natural resources. Changes in natural resources inform the elite's decisions, thus closing the feedback loop. The elite exercise power through local control over exchanges of information, personnel, goods and services, and money that are linked with the rest of the relevant national and international capital, commodity, and extraction systems. A region's political economy is neither completely independent from nor completely dominated by exogenous forces or resources. As a result, local and regional elite must maintain linkages with higher-level power brokers to maintain control.

There is an accelerating evolution of ecosystem approaches that employ both human and natural environments. Like many others, the political scientist William Ophuls recognized the massive world degradation by industrial economies: "The radically different conditions prevailing today virtually force us to be ecological theorists, grounding our analysis on the basic problems of survival on a finite and destroyable planet with limited resources."[15] Accordingly, ecosystems should be understood in the larger systems theory context.

As the ecologist Frank Golley clarifies, a system is "an object that is made up of subsystems or components which interact in such a way that they have, collectively, a recognizable wholeness."[16] "An object," according to Golley, "is defined as a separate entity with visible boundaries" but the system boundaries "are fuzzy."[17] The ecosystem, Eugene Odum noted, is "an interactive system composed of biotic communities and their abiotic environment interacting with each other. A lake could be regarded as an ecosystem; so could a marshland; and so could the earth. To understand nature in terms of ecosystems was to see its diverse 'parts' as interconnected and independent."[18] I regard habitat, community, landscape, region, nation-state, and planet as ecosystems.

Systems thinking also appeals to management and planning theorists. For example, the Southern California University planning theorist Niraj Verma concludes that systems reasoning "is teleological; it promotes integration and denies the quest for rigor when that rigor is achieved by partitioning our terrain. The defining characteristic of this tradition is its recognition of the epistemological necessity of comprehensiveness."[19] Human ecology helps to bridge the systems' views from natural sciences with those of planning and management theorists. Both ecology and planning address interrelated systems. *Human* ecology extends how relationships occur in nature to human systems, such as those concerned with managing and planning human affairs.

INTEGRATIVE TRAITS

Language, culture, and technology comprise the second set of concepts for understanding the variability and complexity of human settlement. These three "integrative traits" help distinguish human ecology from the more traditional ecology that focuses on plants and animals. These characteristics "include the development and use of language and signs, the presence of culture, and the creation of technology."[20]

Language represents a universal property of humans, but one that also divides us. We communicate with symbols and through our body motions as well as our voices. Culture is, according to Golley, "a collective sense of a social whole."[21] A fundamental element of culture is education, that is, how one generation passes knowledge to the next. Learning and feedback between the human and natural elements represent key attributes of urban ecosystems.[22] Other species construct habitats—bird nests, bee hives, and beaver dams, for example—but only "humans have produced a technology that has permitted them to create a new kind of environment and reshape humanness itself."[23]

Bodies of words combine to form languages, as do agreed upon systems for their use. Conventions exist for verbal use as well as for the formalized application of symbols, signs, and gestures. Initially, at least, languages derive from common geographical areas. Words, their symbols, and the rules for their use define communities and nations—they define common cultures. The use of words may differ within a nation and become a dialect or a regional vernacular.

Languages can transcend nationalities; for example, scientific communities have their own bodies of words, their own jargons, as do communities of artists. Many scientists still use Latin, or terms derived from Latin, for certain forms of communication, such as for the taxonomy of flora and fauna. Scientists also rely on equations that transmit messages beyond words. Paintings and photographs possess certain vocabularies for artists that can often communicate to the broader public as well as across nations. Music relies on formalized systems—scores—for communication. While the arts and sciences can transcend cultures, they are also grounded in culture.

We employ technology to transform matter into useful stuff. The most basic transformations involve energy and information. Coal is a lump of rock, which, when burned, can heat our homes. In the process, wastes are created that must be disposed of. Thus, the environment is both a source and a sink for technological transformation. Information—that coal can be burned to heat homes and that its combustion can create pollutants—is necessary for the process.

Technologies consistently alter our relationships with the planet and with each other as well as how we settle places. When people relied on their feet and horses to travel, cities took on certain characteristics. For example, buildings clustered together and distances to the market and to places of worship were short. These elements evolved different forms as people needed to defend themselves. For example, homes could not be higher than city walls, and roads needed to pass through city gates. Technological changes in warfare, from the cannon and rifle through airplanes and guided missiles, have influenced the shape and form of cities. Defensive walls defined the city through much of history, but such defenses were rendered obsolete not only by artillery that could break down armaments or lob shells over defensive shields, but also by jets and missiles, which strike from the skies. As the walls came down, city limits changed.

Currently, roads and transit shape human settlements. Some cities, like Seoul and Phoenix, are largely creations of the automobile culture. Other cities evolved more hybrid forms. Rome inside the Aurelian Wall is a different place than the periphery where most modern Romans live. Inside the wall, amid the ruins of the ancient city, Rome is a medieval maze punctuated by Renaissance streets and Baroque churches. Outside the wall, Italian suburbia sprawls, only more vertical than its horizontal American cousins. Across the Atlantic from Rome, in Mexico, Guadalajara's center retains the influence of its Spanish colonizers, but the city expands out into its lush green surroundings with ever wider streets.

Chicago's center, "The Loop," reflects its railroad heritage, but the newer suburbs mirror the development of internal combustion technology. Location, location, location—the real estate agent's mantra helps explain Chicago's boom as railroads expanded westward. Its strategic location at the edge of Lake Michigan, relatively close to the Mississippi River across a flat prairie, fueled Chicago's rise. Rail lines connecting east to west, north to south, converged in its city center. The same flat prairies that were advantageous to railroads proved equally accessible to highway development.

Technology, as an integrative trait of people, alters how we live. We constantly seek to improve our mobility—our ability to transport people and materials—and in doing so this technology, among others, influences how we live.

THE SCAFFOLDING OF PLACE AND CHANGE

The third set of concepts for understanding human settlements includes function, structure, and change. Functionalism provides one way to address parts and wholes in a system's framework. The functionalist approach studies how the parts of a whole or a system interrelate.[24] In social systems, interrelationships may be considered as a product of connectivity. Interactive processes, such as communication and transportation facilities, provide the glue that holds the parts with an interacting whole into a system, a community, or a region.

These systems can be viewed in structural terms. The form of a human system—habitat, community, landscape, region, or nation-state—is described by its structure, the scaffolding of parts that come together to comprise the whole. Elements of biophysical scaffolding include the geology, physiography, hydrology, climatology, pedology, and biology of a place. A place can be partly understood by studying its rocks, terrain, water flows, weather, soils, plants, and animals. How humans use land may also be viewed as an element of biophysical scaffolding. For example, airports use land in a manner that imposes physical structures on natural and human systems. Life abounds at airports—from grass growing in the medians between runways to travelers logging in at cybercafés.

Light distinguishes place as much as do boulders, shrubs, and settlements. Light varies with the times of the day, the seasons of the year, and the dew points of water in the air. Smells follow seasons as well, like the aroma from a creosote bush in the desert after the rain or from dairy cows during the Dutch spring. Winds shape places—the tropical storm, the tornado across the prairie, an afternoon thunderstorm in Denver. Light, smell, and wind help structure a place and also demonstrate change and how changing processes shape places.

Human structural components include economic and sociocultural processes. A place functions through its use of resources, products of labor, markets, capitalization, and consumption. The demographic aspects of population size and density, age, ethnicity, education, and occupation form structures as do the cultural aspects of values, beliefs, attitudes, knowledge, information, technology, literature, and aesthetics.

Forman and Godron offer a framework for landscape ecology that can be extended to human ecology. It is based on three ecosystem characteristics: function (flow relationships), structure (spatial relationships), and change (dynamic relationships). Function, in landscape ecology terms, means examining how energy, water, mineral nutrients, animals, and places move through space.[25] For a human ecosystem, energy flow may be understood as a function of transportation or of heating systems.

These functions are revealed in various structures: highways, gas stations, power lines, and energy generation plants, for example. Urban morphologists focus on "three fundamental physical elements: buildings and their related open spaces, plots or lots, and streets."[26] Such elements accommodate a variety of functions. Forman and Godron use the terms patch, corridor, and matrix to describe landscape structure.[27] Again, these landscape structures accommodate many functions. Patches piece together places, corridors connect places, and matrices mold places to one another. The Swiss landscape planner Anna Hersperger notes that these structural "elements—patch, corridor, and matrix—can be described and characterized according to the following criteria: origin, shape, size, connectivity, porosity, boundary shape, edge, configuration, contrast, heterogeneity, and mesh size."[28]

Hersperger furthermore observes, drawing on Forman and Godron, that change "is the product of the interaction of function and structure over time. The study of change is therefore a temporal analysis. Change can be measured as alteration of either structure or function."[29] In ecology, change unifies theory. Change connects all life-forms. Traditionally, change tended toward a steady state where objects and lives existed in balance. In new ecology, change is constant; objects and lives exist in constant flux.

Natural disturbances, such as fire, tornadoes, earthquakes, and pest infestations, as well as human activities ranging from farming to city building, result in spatial changes.[30] We call human change "history" (the study of past events) and "planning" (the arrangement of a possible future). According to Moudon, "urban form can only be understood historically since the elements of which it is comprised undergo continuous transformation and replacement."[31]

History and planning may thus be viewed as the scaffolding of change. What was and what may be help us function in the present. Our homes, even new ones, harbor histories. Before a family can move in, a house has to be designed then approved by local authorities, constructed, and sold. We possess plans for our homes, a kitchen or a bathroom to be remodeled, a new path around the side of the house, a wall to be painted. Likewise, plans and histories accompany our communities and landscapes.

LAMINATIONS

Edges and boundaries form the fourth set of concepts for understanding human settlements. We often cross natural boundaries. When flying, we frequently encounter turbulence. As the jet ascends or descends, it penetrates different atmospheric layers, resulting in a "bumpy" ride. The boundaries between these layers cause the turbulence. As the plane glides across the sky, it also encounters weather fronts, another cause of "bumps." Weather fronts and complex atmospheric layers are especially common as the landscape below changes, for example, between the Great Plains and the Rocky Mountains in North America. Boundaries and the edges between places are dynamic. In some places, distinctions are less sharp and characteristics from one merge with those from another. In ecology, such places are called ecotones.

Ecotones occur as transitional zones between two ecological communities. These are areas of integration. An ecotone frequently displays greater biological richness than either of the communities it separates. An ecotone, according to Eugene Odum, "is not simply a boundary or an edge; the concept assumes the existence of active interaction between two or more ecosystems (or patches of ecosystems), which results in the ecotone having properties that do not exist in either of the adjacent ecosystems."[32]

According to Dramstad and her colleagues, an edge "is described as the outer portion of a patch where the environment differs significantly from the interior of the patch. Often, edge and interior environments simply look and feel different."[33] Ecologists refer to the differences between the edge and the interior of an ecosystem as the "edge effect" and note differences in vertical and horizontal structure, width, and species composition and abundance.[34] With people, to be "edgy" is to be different, to take risks, to stretch boundaries.

Boundaries are real or notional lines that mark the limits of an area or territory. As Dramstad and her collaborators note, boundaries may be natural and also "political" or "administrative."[35] Political boundaries may or may not correspond to natural edges. "The concept of *boundaries* is essential to systems thinking," and, furthermore, they "demarcate the system and represent the interface between the system and subsystems, suprasystems, and the environment, that which is external to a system."[36]

MIT planning professor and urban theorist Kevin Lynch stressed the value of edges and borders in the design of human environments.[37] Edges can help define open space systems, because of the contrast created between buildings and places without structures. Central Park in the heart of Manhattan provides a dramatic example of such contrast. One walks north on Broadway to 7th or 6th Avenue—the Avenue of the Americas—and is confronted by a forest. But, at 59th Street, which has become Central Park South along the park's southern edge, one must step down to engage the woods set across a small lake, called The Pond. Further north, a sheep meadow, an ice rink, and a children's zoo welcome the visitor—all in the heart of one of the busiest, most built-up places on Earth. Around the world, from the central park north of downtown Nairobi to the central park of the Pundang new town on the current periphery of Seoul, to the former Olympic park of Amsterdam, similar places form human ecotones where the built-up and open areas intermingle and yet provide vivid contrasts.

We use maps, among other devices, to indicate the boundaries between us. Maps and mapmaking differ from plans and plan making. Maps seek to represent what is; plans posit what might be. Maps distort and simplify what is or what was. Plans project and amplify what might be. Both have to do with how we perceive and interact with the distinctions in, and the boundaries and edges of, our surroundings.

The mapping of soils provides an example. In the United States, soil scientists from the Natural Resources Conservation Service and its predecessor, the Soil Conservation Service, have diligently mapped soils at the county level since the 1930s. Aerial photographs help these scientists map associations based on topographic and vegetation variations. In the field, they dig pits and study the soil profiles. Specific horizons can be identified, layers where organic matter builds up or where minerals are leached. Color matching helps the scientists group soils with like types. The resulting soil maps display jigsaw puzzle combinations, but the lines on these maps represent only approximations where one soil type blends into another.

People use maps to mark boundaries. Maps can be artful representations of human hopes, aspirations, prejudices, and limitations. Mapmakers draw what they believe to be accurate accounts of places, communities, regions, states and nations, and the world. But how do we map the human imagination? James Cowan explores the dreams of mapmakers, the challenges of putting down on paper the complexity and contradictions of our vast interior landscapes.[38]

INTERACTION, INTEGRATION, AND INSTITUTION

The fifth set of concepts for understanding how people settle places includes interaction, integration, and institutions. Interactions and forms of integration occur in nonhuman systems, but only people create institutions. We form institutions, in part, to help protect us from our natural instincts.

Nature is not benign. Woody Allen once described it as a giant restaurant, but restaurants are more polite than nature. In nature, one species eats another or even members of its own kind. Individuals compete with others of their own sex for territory, so that they can control a larger food supply and attract members of the opposite sex. They exclude others in order to more effectively exploit the resources of an area for themselves. The members of a species marginalized by such competition struggle for survival. Competition, exclusion, exploitation, and, ultimately, survival comprise the rough-and-tumble components of the natural world (and, often, of the human world). Survival characterizes a challenging outcome of interaction.

Interaction has more positive consequences, too; competition and survival, while perhaps ugly, can be beneficial. The positive or negative characteristics of nature are human constructions; although from the prospect of any sentient or nonsentient individual, being eaten by another cannot be the most positive experience. Individuals spend considerable energy to avoid being eaten, to survive. Many strategies used to avoid demise involve cooperative interactions with others.

Botkin and Keller identify competition, symbiosis, and predation as the "three basic kinds of interactions between species."[39] They contend that competition, the first kind of interaction, leads to negative outcomes for both groups involved—an observation sure to provoke debate among (non-Marxist) economists. Symbiosis, "which benefits both participants," is the second type of interaction.[40] Third, in predation/parasitism "the outcome benefits one and is detrimental to the other."[41]

Interaction is a concept that has survived the transition from the old to the new ecology. Biologists asserted early that one of the distinguishing features of ecology was its significant emphasis on process. Zoologist Marston Bates and many others have argued that organism and environment should not be thought of as discrete, definable entities, but rather in terms of transactions between processes.[42] Human ecology can be described as the study of processes involving how people interact with each other and their surroundings. According to Gerald Young, the most fundamental of the almost innumerable processes is interaction, which is defined as reciprocal action, the action or the influence of persons or things on each other.[43] Young observes, "Interactions that maintain being and sustain existence, especially the complex existence of human beings, result in functional connections between the living entity or entities and the systems of the earth and life that sustain them."[44]

Integration represents a specific type of interaction, whereby parts are combined to form a whole. The whole in the process becomes distinct from the parts, yet is defined by their interaction. Integration is the process of uniting, unifying, bringing together, merging, mixing, and amalgamating. Integration contrasts many contemporary settlements where groups of people and land uses are separated from one another, where places are designed and built for a single purpose. As the historian Jon Teaford observed, "In the twentieth-century metropolis the parts . . . triumphed over the whole."[45] In Sun City, Arizona, "senior citizens" spend their twilight years cruising around their "city" in golf carts, unencumbered by children playing in the streets.

Integrative interactions are formalized in human societies through institutions. University of Pennsylvania planning theorist Seymour Mandelbaum notes that "institutions often are articulated as systems of rights and obligations."[46] Young states that institutions are "defined and developed *as a consequence of the changing process of interaction in contemporary human groups*."[47] Young further elaborates his proposal of the ecological nature of institutions as follows:

> The process of institutionalization is essentially a response . . . to the human need for order and stability. Humans organize so that relationships can be anticipatory in nature, so that needs, of whatever kind, can be met in a dependable rather than haphazard fashion, so that exchange takes expected rather than unexpected forms: institutionalization is the formation of relationships into dependable systems. . . . Institutions regulate interaction between individuals and community or society and between individuals or communities and their environment. Institutions regulate the flow of goods and materials through the system. . . .[48]

Institutions may be viewed as a form of cultural structure. In human ecology, institutions cannot be separated from the idea of structure (introduced earlier in this chapter) or from function. The idea of change, however, poses a challenge, because institutions resist change.

Young calls institutions a "consequent notion," that is, a concept in human ecology that cannot "normally be found in biological ecology, but [does] help in human ecology to explain some of the characteristics and conditions of human interactions."[49] Institutions are "an organization of social relations," according to Cohen, "the frames within which man spends every living moment."[50] Institutions are our formalized structures for interacting, for achieving purposes from survival to spiritual gratification.

Religion provides a most basic institution. It imbues meaning to our fundamental biological processes of life: mating, birth, and death. Religious rituals—the marriage ceremony, the christening, the funeral service—mark these events. All living creatures reproduce, but religions traditionally provide the ground rules for human procreation. Other creatures die, too, but religions give us hope for an afterlife or reincarnation. Other species also eat, but many religions structure what and when humans can eat.

"Religion," Princeton anthropologist Clifford Geertz asserts, writing about Japanese culture, but clearly with wider implications, "holds society together, sustains values, maintains morale, keeps public conduct in order, mystifies power, rationalizes inequality, justifies unjust deserts, and so on. . . ."[51] Or, as Stewart Brand puts it, "Of all cultural practices, religion is the greatest sustainer and most durable of institutions."[52] Religions outlive most other institutions, from corporations to nations.

Religions bind people together. For instance, in seventeenth-century England, George Fox established the Society of Friends based on the faith that believers receive divine guidance from an inward light. ". . . Friends believe in a continuing revelation of God's will and nature."[53] Their meetings can be silent, interrupted by quaking as believers experience that light or by a proclamation by a member of the meeting. Moderation characterizes the Quaker way of life, moderation in speech and in dress as in all things. They believe in the equality of all people and practice peace. They shake hands with their neighbors to conclude a service.

Religions can also divide people. Although the Society of Friends exhibits remarkable tolerance toward others, their history displays some inflexibility toward their own members. Throughout the nineteenth century, the sect experienced a series of schisms that divided them into liberal and conservative camps. In part, these schisms resulted from protracted debates and discussions. Fox abolished the laity but not the clergy. The whole meeting became the clergy and engaged in group consensus-based decision making. While democratic, the process of making decisions could become cumbersome and lead to unintended consequences. Important private decisions, such as marriage, become a matter of public discussion. A meeting can decide that a couple is not suited for each other and, as a result, not sanction a marriage. A member can be disowned for marrying out of the meeting (roughly the congregation). The refusal to sanction some marriages contributed to a decline in the numbers of Friends over time.

Interactions can integrate people spatially. Such integration of relationships can also be institutionalized. Institutions, such as religions and governments, guide formal interactions. Human interactions, integrations, and institutions assume a broad range of dizzyingly diverse forms.

UNITY IN DIVERSITY

Diversity is the sixth concept to aid with understanding settlement. Diverse ecosystems are generally rich and healthy. Diversity enables natural systems to be resilient, allowing organisms to adjust to change. Less diverse systems, those with few species or single species—monocultures—are notoriously susceptible to deleterious consequences of change. According to Odum, there are two components of diversity: richness or variety and relative abundance.[54] Botkin and Keller identify three concepts of biological diversity: genetic diversity, habitat diversity, and species diversity.[55]

Cultural diversity is even more complex and the topic of ongoing debate within anthropology.[56] More than one culture might be present in a habitat or community; even more cultures are found as we move from landscape to region and beyond to nation-state and around the planet. In summarizing the relationship of culture to nature in this regard, Gary Paul Nabhan states, "Natural diversity and cultural diversity share many of the same patterns of distribution across the face of the earth, and enrich our lives in many of the same ways."[57] That is, we enjoy some combination of trees and flowers, birds and butterflies in our backyards. Our neighbor-hoods are enriched if the people living around us possess differences in the way they look as well as in how they think and what they believe.

Timothy Beatley and Kristy Manning contend that diversity is essen-tial for sustainability: "A sustainable community, then, is one in which di-versity is tolerated and encouraged, where there is no sharp spatial separa-tion or isolation of income and racial groups, where all individuals and groups have access to basic and essential services and facilities, and where residents have equality of opportunity."[58]

A difference is a difference only when it makes a difference. Our ac-tual and perceived differences pose among our most pressing issues as a species. Some differences are necessary for our survival—those between women and men, for example. Differences distinguish one habitat, com-munity, and landscape from another. Differences can help establish identi-ty, but they can also divide people. Thus, it is important to find ways to ac-knowledge and celebrate the diversity of the human species.

Pluralism acknowledges diversity. In philosophy, pluralism is a theory that there is more than one basic principle, which differs from dualism or monism. In human ecology, pluralism involves heterogeneous groups with-in a space. Pluralistic societies achieve unity through diversity.

Health—that is, the ability to recover from disease, injury, and/or in-sult—has been linked to diversity. Aldo Leopold defined ecological health as the capacity of the land and organisms for self-renewal.[59] In a diverse ecosystem, not all the eggs have been placed in a single basket. As a result, more opportunities exist for organisms to heal themselves.

Leopold contributed to the conservation of the Coon Creek watershed in Wisconsin. This watershed remains an exemplar of good soil conservation practices. Plows follow the contours on hilly slopes, the edges of streams re-main lined with trees and bushes, and restored fisheries thrive in the clean waters of those same streams. This healthy landscape exists in part because people recognized the value of its diversity and reinforced that value.

ADJUSTING TO CHANGE

The seventh concept for understanding human settlement is adaptation. Ecologists define adaptation as "a measure of physiological fitness of the organism with respect to one or all the conditions of its environment"[60] and "a pliable capacity permitting a system to become modified in response to disturbance."[61] Adaptation is displayed by "the adequacy of an organism to cope with the conditions of its natural environment and to utilize its resources so as to maintain its ecological position. It is achieved through an adjustment of its requirements and tolerances to the elements of the habitat(s)."[62] Sontag and Bubolz, in their case studies of Michigan families on small farms, observe, "Complex, living systems are . . . capable of *adaptation*, that is, they exhibit behavior that changes the state or structure of the system, the environment, or both."[63]

Humans are perhaps the most adaptive species. Bipedality, manual dexterity, and encephalization separated hominids from our cousins, the apes. Religion, law, politics, planning, architecture, design, and engineering are among our more advanced instruments of adaptation. These instruments of adaptation, or "adaptive strategies,"[64] can be viewed from an ecological perspective. One suggestion for sustainability that California businessman and writer Paul Hawken offers is to "change linear systems to cyclical ones."[65] He elaborates that "cyclical means of production are designed to imitate natural systems in which waste equals food for other forms of life, nothing is thrown away, and the symbiosis replaces competition."[66] Hawken urges "designing for decomposition" because it "is the way of the world around us."[67]

Adaptation permits us to be resilient in the face of change. Yehudi Cohen contends that "adaptation assures the group's survival, reproduction, and efficient functioning, in the sense of 'doing its job in nature.'"[68] Like other species, humans evolve genetically. We also adapt through learning. Increased knowledge about our environments leads (at least theoretically) to more appropriate responses to change.

But humans do more than adapt—we transform and create. The geographer Yi-Fu Tuan observes:

> A human being is an animal who is congenially indisposed to accept reality as it is. Humans not only submit and adapt; they transform in accordance with a preconceived plan. That is, before transforming, they do something extraordinary; namely, "see" what is not there. Seeing what is not there lies at the foundation of all human culture.[69]

The Internet resulted from seeing what was not there. Invented by the military for privileged communication, the Internet now provides a "place" of freedom where anyone with access to a computer can reach information. The Internet evolved from a secret form of communication to an open system through constant innovation. Originally a cumbersome system with long addresses, academics and computer geeks refined its operation, improving its access. Increasingly diverse people, from businesspeople to grandparents, began communicating over the Internet. New ways and protocols for communication followed. Dear Mr. or Ms. So-and-So became Hi Sally or Bob as a greeting. Capitalization and grammar dissipated as streams of consciousness worthy of James Joyce replaced more carefully constructed prose.

HOLISM

The final concept for understanding human settlement is holism. The Hungarian-born British novelist, journalist, and critic Arthur Koestler coined the term *holon* in 1967 to deal with the idea that an entity could be considered both part and whole, and to incorporate its existence or function as part of a larger whole.[70] Koestler's holon concept sheds light on the older, broader notion of holism. Anna Hersperger notes that holism "was formulated as a philosophy by Smuts (1926) and then continued by many ecologically interested scientists."[71] Gerald Young explains Jan Smuts's "philosophic theory" of holism where "the determining factors in nature are organismic wholes which are not reducible to the sum of their parts and that evolution of the universe is a record of the activity and making of these wholes."[72]

Young argues, however, that definitions such as Smuts's are inadequate for human ecology. Young advocates a view of holism that is not deterministic and does not reject reductionism. According to this view, reductionistic inquiries can be helpfully linked to larger synthesis. As a result, Young redefines holism "as any attempt to perceive, or to conceptualize, any entity as a totality, regardless of method, and with no implication of fealty (or indeed opposition) to any predefined philosophy or methodology."[73]

Gerald Young has observed that "holism remains murky and controversial, even in ecology, more a metaphor than methodology."[74] It exists "at the borderline between science and philosophy," according to Hersperger, drawing on the Dutch scholar I. S. Zonneveld.[75] Because of its status as a murky metaphor on the science-philosophy borderline, it is a useful concept for human ecology. The whole cannot exist without the parts; the parts would not be without the whole.

A city forms a whole, an official entity. But the city of San Francisco, for example, would not be San Francisco without its Embarcadero, the Presidio, Golden Gate Park, Steiner Street, its harbor, the cable cars, the fog.

These elements and others also depend on the city. What would the Golden Gate Bridge connect if San Francisco did not exist? Fog would still flow up and down the hills of the peninsula, but it would follow different patterns without the city streets.

THE MULTIPLE, THE TEMPORAL, AND THE COMPLEX

Human culture varies from place to place, yet exhibits certain similarities. There are multiple possibilities for how and where to live, and these options change with time. We are a complex species. Ecology can help us understand this complexity. Like all sciences, ecology is a human construct, or, as Evernden puts it, "The definition and understanding of the natural is linked to that of the human."[76]

Humans construct. We transform spaces into places. We make places to live. We gather with others in neighborhoods, a specific kind of community where informal interactions differ from those in our work environments. We look out from our neighborhoods or our office windows to landscapes where our constructions interact visibly with nature. "I planted that tree," one may say, "and nurtured its growth." Yes, but the planter has no control over the morning sun that illuminates the tree's canopy.

We can chart the courses of the streams of change and even establish new directions through the works of our lives. Even so, the tug of nature, our natures, will pull at our feet with the full power of gravity. We can confront nature, our natures, and even conspire with it, but we cannot trump nature's design. Perhaps we can do our best by attempting to be good humans within that design. We should avoid hurting others and our surroundings while seeking to celebrate and advance beauty.

We are linked to something larger, something we called god or gods in the past (and perhaps in the future). These larger forces can be at least partially illuminated through ecological thinking. While we are connected to bigger processes, we are also what we make ourselves and our settlements to be. We become shadows of our aspirations.

In this chapter I introduced the basic concepts of human ecology, from systems thinking through adaptation, that I have used as building blocks to construct the following chapters. I did not employ holism as explicitly as the other concepts, because the idea, the metaphor, of parts and wholes is integral to hierarchy and thus woven through the various scales. Chapter 2 discusses the ecology of the home.

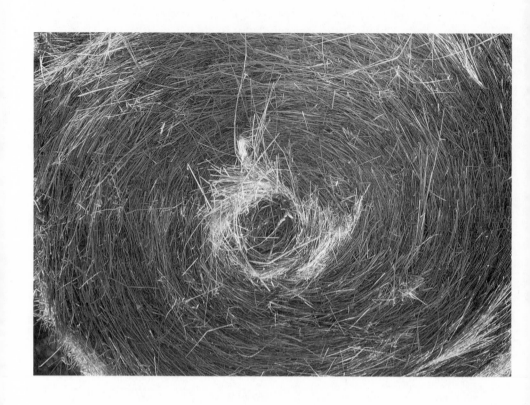

HABITAT

Home is where we start from.

—T. S. ELIOT

HABITAT IS THE PLACE WHERE WE LIVE. FOR MUCH OF HUMAN existence, habitat and home were pretty much the same thing. The farmer lived on the land or within walking distance to the cultivated fields. The home of the tradesman was above the workshop, which was also the store. The professor lived at the college. Technology changed the workplace, as well as what we consider home. Traditional roles of men and women related to home and workplace have also changed.

"House" is at the root meaning of ecology, and the design of dwellings and workplaces is fundamental to architecture. From Vitruvius to Frank Lloyd Wright, architects have addressed how to fit buildings to a given site. In the first century B.C., the Roman architect and engineer Marcus Vitruvius Pollio devoted much of his ten books on architecture to the understanding of the site and of the primordial elements of air, earth, fire, and water. In the planning of a city, he noted the need to "regard and attend to the natures of birds and fishes and land animals. . . ."[1] According to Vitruvius, the designs of houses should conform to the nature of the region and to diversities of climate, observing, "Different things are found in different places. . . ."[2] The American architect Frank Lloyd Wright advocated an "organic" approach to architecture. Wright sought to blur the distinctions between the inside and the outside of buildings. Such wisdom should be used in the planning of groups of houses that form communities as well as communities that comprise cities and their regions.

Urban morphologists provide a good explanation of "the smallest cell of the city," which can be used to understand the physical elements of habitats.[3] They observe that this "smallest cell . . . is recognized as the combination of two elements: the individual parcel of land, together with its building or buildings and open spaces."[4]

In the unfortunately underrecognized classic-in-waiting *Reading the Landscape: An Adventure in Ecology* (1957), May Theilgaard Watts observed that fashion plays an ecological role in the transitions of vegetation surrounding a house: "There has been a definite succession of these plants; and the major ecological force in determining this succession has been *style.*"[5] We create ecologies inside and around our houses that reflect the fashions of our time. We need place-specific styles, fashions that provide "adventures in ecology."

Although we engage in ecological relationships, we have difficulty seeing the places where we live as ecological spaces. Physical habitats are necessary because we need places to interact with each other—to live our lives, to do our work. Our natural environments set certain conditions for the places we live and work: it rains and we need a roof over our head; it freezes and we need heat. The structures that keep us dry and warm establish boundaries for the spaces we inhabit. These physical boundaries mediate our relationships with natural processes as they set frameworks for our interactions with other people.

THE NATURAL HOME OF AN ORGANISM

Habitat, as Nabhan points out, is "etymologically related to *habit, inhabit,* and *habitable*; it suggests a place worth dwelling in, one that has *abiding* qualities."[6] Ecologists define habitat as follows:

> that part of the environment at which exchanges actually occur between the organisms and the resources which they utilize; e.g., a forest tree's habitat is that part of the forest in whose air and soil it obtains water, oxygen, carbon dioxide, nitrates, and other nutrients; in which its flowers are fertilized by suitable insects, and its seed is dispersed by suitable agents.[7]

Or, as more succinctly stated by Noss and his colleagues, a habitat is the "multidimensional place where an organism . . . lives."[8] Each species possesses its own habitat. I am addressing the human species here. Our habitat is closely associated with where we live, our home. The standard definition of habitat, the "natural home of an organism," supports this observation.[9]

A difference between the natural habitats of plants and animals and those of people is the greater mobility in human societies. Other animals need to move, too—defending a territory, foraging in a home range, finding a mate, dispersing to a new home range, and migrating seasonally—but humans can more easily relocate from Madrid to Antarctica. While we possess greater mobility to move from place to place, we also have the technology to alter places to suit our needs. Of course, we should ask: At what cost—to ourselves, to our environments, and to other living things?

Home is the principal human habitat, but what is home? It is the place where you live, your residence or dwelling. But you do not live only in your house. Traditionally, home was both residence and workplace. Although these two functions have been divided in most contemporary, industrialized cultures, they now appear to be coming together again. As a result, for this discussion, I consider home and workplace, separate or together, as human habitat. Then how do these habitats vary in function and structure, what are their edges and boundaries, how do they interact, how do they accommodate diversity, and can they be adapted?

Habitat and home are closely related to the concept of niche. We seek appropriate places to function, and niches provide suitable locations for our activities. The ecologist Paul Sears wrote:

> Any species survives by virtue of its niche, the opportunity afforded to it by environment. By occupying this niche, it also assumes a role in relation to its surroundings. For further survival it is necessary that its role at least be not a disruptive one. Thus, one generally finds in nature that each component of a highly organized community serves a constructive, or, at any rate, stabilizing role. The habitat furnishes the niche, and if any species breaks up the habitat, the niche goes with it.[10]

The niche includes "the complete set of habitat requirements of a species."[11] Eugene Odum distinguishes habitat and niche as follows: "The habitat is the organism's 'address,' . . . (where it lives), and the niche is its 'profession' (how it lives, including how it interacts with and is constrained by other species)."[12]

Various professions differ in their niche requirements. A surgeon needs an operating table; a veterinarian with large thoroughbred patients requires an even larger surface. Both need an elaborate support system to monitor the patient's vital signs and to supply nutrients, painkillers, and liquids. The contemporary studio of the architect or the artist differs from the work space of even two decades ago. Computer monitors have replaced drawing boards; digital media have taken the place of paintbrushes and thinner. Activities define an individual's niche. We inhabit a physical niche that relates to how our profession, our work, occupies a niche in our society and our communities.

People have lived through agriculture for centuries. Farming requires interaction with other species, which constrain the activity. Sontag and Bubolz explore small-scale agricultural enterprises through their integrated family ↔ farm ecosystem model.[13] They explain that "considered from a spatial dimension, the farm land, plants, buildings, and other constructions constitute the real physical environment of the family. The family, together with this primary resource environment, is an ecosystem."[14] The family and the farm are "mutually interdependent" and comprise "a life system of interconnected parts."[15]

Farm families have been able to exist in relative spatial isolation. Productivity, of course, is enhanced by cooperative actions, such as harnessing water or sharing breeding secrets. Other resource-dependent livelihoods cannot exist without shared labor. Mining and forestry, for example, require workforces of some size to transform rock or trees into useful products. The homes of the miners and loggers are usually close to the exploited resources and clustered in towns. The homes of wheat or dairy farmers are also located near the natural resources upon which they depend, but their farms will be more dispersed from one another.

The stockbroker depends on another type of resource, information. Traditionally, the stockbroker left home, sometimes commuting long distances, to gather with other stockbrokers to transform information into profits. Now, a day trader can remain in pajamas in a mountaintop retreat in the Rockies, connected to a modem and performing stock transactions at will. However, we continue to be social animals, so sooner or later the day trader will need to dress in something other than pajamas, leave home, and interact with other people. We should also ask: Who requires more resources? Is the ecological footprint of the commuting stockbroker in a three-piece suit larger or smaller than that of the mountaintop day trader in pajamas? What would be the cumulative impact on nature of hermits and their mountaintop modems?

THE LEGIBILITY OF DOMICILES

According to French philosopher Gaston Bachelard, "A house constitutes a body of images that give mankind proofs or illusions of stability."[16] The wall between the bedroom and the bathroom exists as proof of a certain reality. At night, in a dream, the wall may drift away, an illusion of separation. Or a tornado or hurricane may blow the wall away, evidence of yet another reality.

Walk around a house and ask: What does it say about its inhabitants? Are there books? Computers? Where is the kitchen? How big is the garage? The house plan and its contents offer legibility about a people and their time and place. Likewise, one can read a workplace, its layout and elements. How does the office of a stockbroker differ in 2009 from 1929? How does Frank Gehry's studio differ from Leonardo's? Step inside the cab of a combine—how has the workplace for harvesting wheat or corn changed since it was done by hand?

The spatial organization of homes and workplaces varies with culture. In the Mediterranean, courtyard housing is common. Rooms are organized around an open garden. The fronts of houses align with the street. In contrast, in much of North America houses have front and back yards. Traditional Korean homes were organized around an interior space and were heated by an elaborate steam-heating system under the floors. Islamic houses reflect specific sex distinctions.

In the United Arab Emirates, the traditional Dubai-style house has the main living area on the second floor, facing out to the Persian Gulf. It is located in an outdoor porch-like space, wrapped around a wind tower, used to keep air in constant movement. In summer, this outdoor living area is where cooking is done, food is consumed, and people sleep. Slats in the walls around the area can be removed to allow sea breezes to flow across the space. Rooms facing onto the outdoor area have low doors and windows. The low, slatted windows permit warm air to enter, and then rise to the ceiling. The hot air can escape through various openings. This keeps the air cool at the floor level. For this reason, much of the daily activity of the household members occurs while seated on the floor, on elaborate rugs. People sitting on the floor can also easily look outdoors through the low windows. The outdoor spaces direct stormwater toward drainage outlets, including holes in the center of thresholds.

The technologies of the Dubai house are elegant, with construction materials drawn from the locale—coral from the sea as well as mud and straw from the land. Traditionally, builders of the Dubai region pull these materials together in ways that maximize human comfort. In the United States, we use technology to alter environmental conditions so that our homes and workplaces are comfortable. Heat allows people to live and work in Minneapolis winters, while air conditioning enables people to survive Phoenix summers. Heating and air conditioning improve indoor livability but separate humans from their outdoor environments.

PATTERN LANGUAGES

Our homes possess multiple functions: we gather there with family and friends, we eat and sleep, we recreate, we learn, we make love, we quarrel, and we may even do some work. At our workplace, we do our job, but we also interact with others in ways beyond work-related activities. Home and workplace help establish our identity, our status, our place.

Houses, offices, schools, factories, barns, and other workplaces are comprised of rooms. They form cells of the building structure. In fact, the root of the word "cell" is *cella*, Italian for "small room," especially one in isolation, such as a monk's or nun's room in a monastery or a prisoner's room. Camera means "room" in Italian, too, and rooms can be viewed as storages for our memories. As a camera records impressions, rooms catalog many of the events in our lives. We display images from our past in rooms, often "taken" with cameras we can hold in our hands. We decorate our walls with mementos passed down from previous generations, or objects from our travels, or art we like and may keep to enjoy or as an investment.

We design a room for specific and/or multiple functions. With the rise of industry, rooms have become as specialized as land uses. This cell for cooking, that one for eating, another for "living," others for toilet, bathing, laundry, sleeping, or keeping the cars (and assorted junk). The uses of rooms vary with culture. For example, the European water closet has a specific function. This use is the same in the American bathroom, but the bathroom serves other functions as well.

The structures of home and workplace also vary considerably from culture to culture. The relationship between function and structure has also changed through time. Traditionally, buildings reflected their functions—form indeed followed function and was adapted to the regional climate. The Chicago architect Dankmar Adler observed that "function and environment determine form."[17] Gabled roofs were necessary, and are still rather handy, for locales with snow. Interior courtyards provided refuges, and still are pleasant, in desert climates. Moreover, building materials were drawn from the region: stone, brick, adobe, mud, wood, straw, stucco.

For much of the twentieth century, the international style prevailed in building design. Modernist architects advocated a universal style that was at once functional and fair. This notion was first criticized by the writer and architectural critic Lewis Mumford, who was soon joined by the planner-sociologist Herbert Gans, the landscape theorists J. B. Jackson and Ian McHarg, the architects Robert Venturi and Denise Scott Brown, the writer Tom Wolfe, and, eventually, scores of others.[18] This chorus of critics argued that one size—one style—does not fit all.

These voices contribute to a rising tide of approaches for "timeless ways of buildings." For instance, Christopher Alexander advocated a "pattern language" for building.[19] Type and context reemerged as important (timeless) principles for designing buildings. In praise of Venturi, the Yale architectural historian Vincent Scully observed, "contextuality, not a jealous style, is literally the determinant of [Venturi's design], which is, however, enlivened by human wit. . . ."[20]

Building type is related to function. Location, or context, relates structure to environment. A barn, for instance, clearly functions for agricultural use. As regional contexts for barns vary, so do their structural forms. The classic Pennsylvania Dutch barn with its pitched roof and protective overhang for cattle fits its use and its context. The several-stories-high Pennsylvania Dutch barn is much higher than the ranch barn in the Southwest. The desert climate of the Southwest encourages lower buildings, with roofs closer to the ground.

Architectural theorist Kenneth Frampton calls for design and planning based on "critical regionalism." As Steven Moore explains, critical regionalism means "that architecture should evoke meaning and thought rather than emotion and excitement—that architecture should evoke critical consideration of cultural and ecological origins of construction practices. . . ."[21]

Such environmental understanding may be gained through a critical dialogue between what is and what was, as well as between what is proposed and what is possible. I sit in a Best Western motel room next to a freeway in Tempe, Arizona. The motel walls are decorated with historical photographs. The images show Tempe before automobiles, before air conditioners. Not long ago, this was a small farm town surrounded by orchards. Now, its limits merge with other jurisdictions to form a metropolis with a couple million people. Many images record the Salt River and its floods, before the river was first pumped dry and later converted into a lake filled with water from another river—the Colorado. Was what was better than what is? Or, is what was simply different?

The Best Western is near the Tempe Town Lake, and I can look across to new downtown development and to where more is proposed. How sensitive is this new development to the Arizona climate? This question is rhetorical, because an Israeli graduate student answered it a few years back in her master's thesis: the buildings aren't responsive to the desert temperature and will create heat islands.[22] Since we know this, we can propose different building forms better suited to this place. We resist because the technology—in this case, air conditioning—is available to situate the buildings as we please. But at what cost?

Technology will continue to change how we design our habitats, but how will it do so? Will the computer, the Internet, the fax machine, and mobile telephones reconnect home and workplace? Or, will these technologies enable us to sprawl farther apart? What about the electric car—will it too permit us to use private transport even more to commute farther distances? Current structures are not necessarily an indication of future forms, or, as Lewis Mumford, drawing on the American architect and planner Albert Mayer and the French poet Paul Valéry, observed, "Trend is not destiny."[23]

Humans need to interact with each other. Our natural environments do set certain conditions, and we should follow nature's lead. Change may be a given, but some constants seem necessary to optimize our interactions and to live within the natural constraints of our planet. Perhaps there are no constraints to human imagination; even so, shelter from some natural elements and access to others appear helpful to fuel that ability to dream.

THE FENCE AND THE BOUNDARY LINE

Each individual possesses a territory or a field. The psychologist Kurt Lewin "conceived of all behavior as a change of state of a field in a prescribed period of time," according to Young, who noted that Lewin "used this conception to refine the totality of the <u>life-space</u> of an individual or a group as a field."[24] Lewin asserted that a person cannot be isolated from his or her environment. He used "topological diagrams" to map the relevant environments, or life-spaces, of individuals. The life-space of the person was mapped with an outer boundary that distinguishes the psychologically relevant space of the individual from the psychologically irrelevant space.

The theologian Reinhold Niebuhr observed, "The fence and the boundary line are symbols of the spirit of justice. They set the limits upon each man's interest to prevent one from taking advantage of the other."[25] Governments record such boundaries on maps or in deeds, indicating ownership. We may own property, but can we retain title to land, water, or air? Notions of property change. In North America, Europeans replaced one property regime with another as they colonized a New World already inhabited by another people. American concepts of land once extended from the earth to the heavens, but changed with the advent of radio and air travel. The creation of the Internet spawned many new property, as well as copyright, issues. Still, we seem to need to hold some proprietorship over not only our personal spaces but also our ideas, which can become our intellectual property.

Houses have clear edges, and property has distinct, and legal, boundaries. Fence lines frame farmsteads. Still, the edges and boundaries of habitats blur. We occupy spaces beyond the boundaries of our homes and our work spaces. Walk into an office, a classroom, or a factory. Territories are marked—some personal, some official: a photograph of a loved one here, a postcard from a friend there, a college diploma above the desk or on the ceiling over the dentist's chair. We wear uniforms and display licenses that underscore our roles, our legitimacy to be in the rooms we occupy.

In the past, and today in many places, several generations of a family co-inhabited a space, or a series of interconnected spaces. Edges and boundaries possessed fewer markers of distinction. Even so, it seems we need some boundaries for the spaces we inhabit. The sizes and shapes of these spaces vary with culture and with climate. Some climates encourage outdoor living; in other places, weather forces people to conduct most activities indoors.

We can learn something about a home and its occupants by studying the trees and other plants that surround it. Which plants are native and which are imported? Do the plants form boundaries? Do they block views from neighbors? A lemon tree is possible, with a little irrigation, in Arizona, but is unlikely outdoors in Ohio. Pear trees and oaks flourish in Ohio, whereas a saguaro is impossible. Conversely, oaks and pears do not thrive in the Arizona deserts. Trees, cacti, and shrubs remind us of the other habitats that overlap with our own.

Our habitats are distinct but intersect with those of our neighbors and our coworkers. Our ecotones form public, or at least semipublic, spaces. We can invite a friend into our private habitat, but we more commonly interact with friends, colleagues, and acquaintances in the ecotones of our habitats unless we mutually desire more intimate companionship.

OVERLAP AND SIMULTANEITY

Ecotones are spatial areas of interaction, but what types of intercourse occur there and in our habitats? Interactions are sometimes explained by the mix of uses that occurs in a space. Planners and geographers link "land uses" to specific spaces. Most spaces, however, contain multiple uses—and sometimes a startling array and juxtaposition of uses. For example, Via Appia Antica (the Appian Way) in Rome is among the world's oldest highways. Along the Appian Way, practitioners of the world's oldest profession attempt to attract today's Romans and tourists amid the ruins of ancient tombs and the spectacular villa estates of the contemporary wealthy.

Habitats possess a myriad of activity but may be almost vacant of humans temporally. In large American cities, executives abandon downtown office buildings for the bedrooms of the suburbs at dusk, only to reverse themselves the following dawn. But even in this extreme case, life continues downtown and in the suburbs with and without the executives.

Christopher Alexander and his colleagues observed that "[a] building cannot be a human building unless it is a complex of still smaller buildings or small parts which manifest its own internal social facts."[26] "Habitat" could be substituted for "building" to explain the importance of interaction within our homes and workplaces.

Traditionally, families ate together within their homeplace, and this remains a common practice in many places today. Eating is only one of many important activities that occur within the habitat. Activities present opportunities for interaction. Shopping, recreation, learning, and working bring people together, as do civic and religious places, which I address in chapter 3. Even activities that may appear to pull people apart, such as watching television or studying, can provide opportunities for interaction.

As people colonize their homes, they bring along with them other living things. Gardens, lawns, and trees are planted. Dogs, cats, parakeets, goldfish, and hamsters are raised. At home, we interact with pets. Humans share their homes with a wide range of animals—cockatiels and fire-bellied toads, hamsters and canaries, pythons and box turtles, as well as those old-favorite domesticates, the cats and the dogs.

Architect and zoo director David Hancocks observes:

A fundamental shift in our relationships with wild animals . . . unfolded within the flickering light of the Paleolithic fire circle, when the first wolf ancestor of the dog scavenged food scraps and started an association that led to its becoming the first domesticated animal. Humans quickly learned the benefits of owning animals. The dog, for example, provided many benefits: security, amusement, and play, greater hunting success and devoted companionship that invited the sharing of affection. Humans also learned something about themselves from this new partnership: those who had canine companions were distinguished from those who did not.[27]

Our pets connect us to the wild, but they are no more (or less) wild than we are. Pets and people have domesticated each other through their interactions. We open the door to let pets out in the middle of the night. They jump onto our lap, often right when we need to touch a furry creature. They annoy us, as we no doubt annoy them.

We also share our habitats with species that have not been domesticated. Cats sometimes carry indoors some of these creatures, such as rodents and birds, toads and beetles. Our interactions are seldom as direct as those of a cat. Still, our spaces overlap with many other living things.

Take a stroll around the house. If the walk breaches the territory of a bird, then it attacks. Our steps may disrupt the mating of squirrels or a column of ants marching across a sidewalk. If a dog accompanies us on our journey, other behavioral changes occur. Sparrows scatter as they become aware of the dog's presence, squirrels rush to nearby trees as the dog barks, and robins take flight as the dog bounds toward them.

We consider some species to be pests. They bite or otherwise bother us and our pets. Some chew away at the foundations of our homes; others destroy our gardens. Our pets become prey and predator in the pathways and gardens of our homes.

We interact with our habitats with all our senses. Úrsula Iguarán, a central character in Gabriel García Márquez's *One Hundred Years of Solitude*, found her way around her home by feeling changes in the sun's angles as well as by noise and smell after she went blind and before she started to shrink.[28] Úrsula knew the rhythms of her house and its inhabitants.

Our senses are on high alert in our homes. We listen to the rain and wind at night. An odd light across a wall in the middle of the night can cause a sudden fright. Why is the neighbor's dog barking at this hour? We seek to protect our families at home.

Family provides a basic component of who inhabits a home. What constitutes a family is a matter of considerable anthropological inquiry. The simple, or nuclear, family consists of a father, a mother, and children. Various forms of complex or extended families are perhaps more common. Anthropologists identify two types of complex families: the stem family and the joint family. A stem family consists of two or more conjugal units united by filial ties. The joint family contains at least three units, two of which are of the same generation and descendant from the third. A "grand joint family" consists of a single conjugal unit in the eldest generation and multiple units in the second generation. A "*frèrèche* joint family" is comprised of multiple units in the eldest generation.[29]

Clifford Geertz contends that "some form of family" is universal to all societies. He notes that families are necessary for people to persist and to reproduce.[30] A family, according to Sontag and Bubolz, "consists of a group of interacting and interdependent persons who share common values, goals, resources, and a commitment to each other over time."[31] Blood relationships constitute part of what can make a family, but *commitment to each other over time* is equally or more important. "[I]t's time that makes a family," the novelist Fae Myenne Ng has noticed, "not just blood."[32]

Family is one type of habitat interaction; work is another. Integration of family activities occurs within the home and associated places. Work activities occur in the office, at the shop, in the factory, at school, or on the farm. Each activity requires the integration of spaces.

The integration of habitats involves how interactions coalesce in space and time. A building relates to the parcel on which it is located as well as to adjacent buildings. The more complex these relationships, usually the richer the integration. A high wall, for example, provides a clear barrier between spaces that can inhibit interaction and result in the segregation of habitats. Courtyards, on the other hand, can create a common space among several dwellings and encourage interaction.

THE DIVERSITY OF POSSIBILITIES

Highly complex sets of interaction contribute to diverse habitats. Internal and external interactions occur. A home shelters its inhabitants from harsh weather conditions. We need shade when it's hot outdoors and heat when it's cold. We need to stay dry. Interiors are differentiated for various uses— eating, sleeping, working, and relaxing—yet infinite combinations exist for the arrangement of these uses. Likewise, outside spaces present many uses and endless possibilities for combinations. These external spaces reconnect us with nature, as do windows, which open to views of the outdoors, until we shut the blinds or close the curtains.

My colleague Michael Benedikt, an architectural theorist, once told me that east and west sunlight from the windows "has a certain loveliness, in color and in its depth of penetration into the building." He added, "a building that is largely illuminated by east and west sunlight changes more in its internal brightness and light/shadow patterns as the day goes by, making it livelier to live in."

Conversely, north and south windows can be designed to maximize solar gain and/or shade depending on the latitude. East-west windows connect us to daily rhythms, north-south orientations to annual cycles.

In constructing habitats, adapting to environmental conditions enables us to inhabit diverse places. When taken to extremes, as air conditioning and heating systems permit, more homogeneous habitats result. Such artificially cooled and/or warmed structures require significant energy. Alternatively, structures can be designed to respond more harmoniously to natural processes. In such cases, less imported energy is required and greater variation in structure design results from place to place: the pitched roofs for snow removal in northern climes, the interior courtyards of the Mediterranean region for shade.

Elements of our habitats vary with climate and from culture to culture. Toilets are an example. Americans go to the bathroom, even when they are at work (and clearly not bathing). Europeans use the water closet. Americans fill their toilet bowls with water; in the wet Low Countries, the Dutch conserve during flushing. In some cultures, one is confronted by a simple, smelly hole in the floor; in others, the range of possibilities available to relieve and to refresh oneself can be baffling.

We fill our places of bathing with a variety of objects. Some people use thick, fluffy towels; others dry themselves with paper-thin cloths. The Dutch and the Scandinavians have long washed their hair and bodies with environmentally friendly soap. Americans often obsessively focus on hygiene, but now seem to be shifting to more "green" products. In Italy and France, the emphasis falls on making oneself pretty.

The choices of such products shape our habitats, their fragrance and color. The selection can also influence the shape of cities and the global economy. Once Cincinnati was called Porkopolis because of the concentration of hog slaughterhouses. Soaps can be produced from pig fat. Procter & Gamble originated from this practice and remains both an important employer of Cincinnatians and a major force in the global marketplace. Procter & Gamble's marketing strategies have been so effective that its products can likely be found around the bathtubs and showers (and the washing machines) of the environmentally conscious Swedes, the hygiene-fixated Americans, and even the beautiful French.

FINGERPRINTS OF OUR VALUES

Winston Churchill once observed that "We shape our buildings, and afterwards our buildings shape us."[33] Our buildings and our homes leave fingerprints of our values, of our ability to adapt. Humans are an amazingly resourceful species when it comes to adaptation. We can travel from Albuquerque to Bologna on vacation and (after jet lag and a few Italian lessons) adapt to a radically different environment. Living there for a longer time would of course require more than a few language lessons. We constantly adapt ourselves and our habitats.

The shower leaks, and we replace the bathroom. A frost kills a tree, and we plant a new sapling. The challenge is finding appropriate forms of adaptation. An American who talks loudly and wears an equally loud shirt as well as tennis shoes and a baseball cap will stand out in a crowd in Bologna. If the new tree dies after the next frost, perhaps a different species should be selected.

Habitats are adapted every day by everyone. Vernacular habitats are those that reflect local culture, local conditions. Habitats can also be designed by architects, interior designers, and landscape architects. Design can elevate the meaning of habitats. Architects have developed a sophisticated understanding of buildings.

Vitruvius and Palladio, in particular, connected building to place. "Men, in the old way, were born like animals in forests and caves and woods, and passed their life feeding on the food of the field," Vitruvius wrote in his second book on architecture twenty centuries ago.[34] He noted that fire brought people together: "because of the discovery of fire, there arose at the beginning, concourse among men, deliberation and a life in common."[35] Assembly led to the need to construct shelters. These early shelters were close to nature, people began "to make shelters of leaves, some to dig caves under the hills, some to make of mud and wattles places of shelter, imitating the nests of swallows and their methods of building."[36] The primordial substances of the Greeks—fire, water, earth, and air—played a central role in how Vitruvius suggested building be linked to site.

Fifteen centuries later, Andrea Palladio suggested that ideal sites for country estates be

> in elevated and healthy locations, that is, where the air is moved by the continuous blowing of the wind and the land, because of its incline, is cleansed of its damp and noxious vapors so that the inhabitants remain healthy, happy, and of good complexion and are not annoyed by mosquitoes and other small insects that are produced by the decomposition of stagnant and marshy water.[37]

Unfortunately, architects do not design most habitats. People adapt their surroundings in less inventive ways. Still, we invest time, energy, and money in adjusting our homes and workplaces to fit our needs and desires as well as those of our family and coworkers. We Americans move around a lot, so we are constantly tampering with our habitats. We purchase an old house and remodel it. We see a vacant lot and imagine a place to sell burgers or gas.

In many other cultures, people tend to stay put. They may be forced to move because of war or natural disaster, but generally they prefer to grow in place. But even in cultures where moving is not the norm, people adapt their habitats constantly. The traditional Korean courtyard house has been replaced by the high-rise apartment in the new towns that circle Seoul. These thin high-rises differ from their bulkier counterparts on the peripheries of Madrid and Paris. The Seoul apartment buildings are relatively narrow with, usually, two families sharing one elevator. However, each floor can have two, four, or even more elevator cores. This corridor scheme can result in six or more apartments on each floor. Inside each apartment, the furnishings recall the elements of a traditional house, albeit several stories above the ground.

HOME IMPROVEMENTS

Even the "homeless" construct habitats. A park bench or a cot presents an opportunity to sleep. The dumpster or the soup line provides meals. A clearing in the brush or the woods becomes a place for toilet or for sex. Impulses transcend the confines of four walls and a ceiling.

Through the process of improving our habitats, we seek to better ourselves. Households provide sites for constant flows and interactions of people and pets, of family and friends, of essentials and wastes. We tinker with those engagements through the arrangement of indoor and outdoor spaces.

We plant gardens, we construct new rooms, we paint walls, we install new ceiling fans, we rotate mattresses, and we upgrade our hard drives.

A habitat forms the context for our most intimate interactions. We interact with our family and our closest friends in our home. When we move, we bring pieces of our former homes along. A child goes to college, but her parents keep her room intact. She now calls her dorm room "home," but she resists any alterations to the bedroom where she grew up.

When we move into a new place, we begin to make it over to reflect our tastes, our values. We redo the kitchen, the bathrooms, the garden. We take down wallpaper and put up photographs of our children and our parents. We try to find a patch of sunlight where our cacti from the Sonoran Desert can adapt to a place of greater rainfall.

Humans possess this ability to move from place to place, to alter their surroundings to fit their needs and desires. The challenge becomes to understand and to respect these new places. In making changes to suit our own needs, we should recognize the others—human and nonhuman—who lived in this habitat before us. While we adapt, we interact with the past and plant the seeds for possible futures.

The terms "habitat" and "ecology" are interwoven, yet we have difficulty seeing the places where we live, the rooms we inhabit, as ecological spaces. "One learned to build the rooms one wanted to visit," the novelist Richard Powers writes in *Plowing the Dark*. "And ecology was a room that wanted visiting."[38]

Our habitat consists of the physical features and biological characteristics necessary for our lives. We eat there (usually), and it provides shelter. Our habitats fulfill many functions in our lives, and they come in many structural arrangements. Some structures fit their environments better than others; some structures are more comfortable to inhabit than others; some structures change with time and with different needs. Habitats have edges and boundaries but frequently overlap with other habitats. Interaction among individuals and between individuals and their surroundings occurs in habitats. Such places integrate activities and can display great diversity. We adapt habitats, then we adapt to them. Habitats are an element of community.

COMMUNITY

Plans, policies, technologies, institutions, and the built form of settlements literally and figuratively crumble in our hands if there is no community to attend to them.

—SEYMOUR MANDELBAUM

COMMUNITY IS DERIVED FROM THE MEDIEVAL LATIN *COMMUNITAS*. The author James Howard Kunstler notes that it shares the same root as communicate, *comunicare*, "to put in common."[1] Seymour Mandelbaum of the University of Pennsylvania planning department defines community "as a group of people who [communicate] with one another."[2] Moura Quayle and Tilo C. Driessen van der Lieck of the University of British Columbia also acknowledge this common root between community and communication, but they observe that "the Latin word *communis . . .* means common in the sense of sharing equally or together with others."[3] "The very stuff of life," is how journalist Alex Marshall defines community, "our relationships with our family and friends and neighbors, and how and whether those relationships come about."[4]

In ecology, a community is "an association of interacting populations, usually delimited by their interactions or by their spatial occurrence."[5] As a result, communities are both places and processes. Ecologists name and classify communities according to their "(1) major structural features such as dominant species, life forms or indicators, (2) the physical habitat of the community, or (3) functional attributes such as the type of community metabolism."[6]

These definitions raise numerous questions about the ecology of human communities. What is an association of interacting people? How do people interact spatially? Humans are certainly the dominant life-form of cities, but what exactly are the major structural features? Do human communities exhibit metabolism? What about other functional attributes? We can seek to answer these questions by viewing community as both a physical phenomenon and a social process.

THE IDEA OF COMMUNITY

Community provides a central concept in the social sciences as it does in architecture and planning. According to the planner Elizabeth Morris, "implicit notions of community are deeply embedded in contemporary urban conflicts and planning dilemmas."[7] Designers and planners approach their work with "deeply embedded" notions about the organization and function of communities. Architecture and planning, although related disciplines, can have different views of community. Many architects believe their work can "create community." Conversely, some planners—especially those who see themselves as applied social scientists—believe the physical arrangement of space has little or no impact on "community."[8] I argue that we do indeed live in a physical world, and as a result, interventions in that world have implications that range from the subtle to the quite direct. For example, a social planner who advocates for educational reform could set in motion renovations to school buildings. An architect's design for renovating an elementary school will influence the well-being of the students as well as their teachers and parents.

Morris writes that community is "a creation of human choice, not a de facto object of the social world."[9] Her assertion echoes Evernden's that nature is also a social creation.[10] Both community and nature are certainly compelling and enduring results of human culture. In general, Morris's thoughtful review of the idea of community takes a rather traditional path from its modern foundations in the Western intellectual tradition through the infusion of urban ecology in the early twentieth century (e.g., Robert Park and Ernest Burgess)[11] on to structural-Marxist-postmodern analysis. Along the way, physical "environmental deterministic" views of community are shed in favor of structuralist interpretations (that are also very much "social creations").

A flaw in Morris's analysis is the implicit equalization of "environment" and "ecology." She suggests that "the concept of social networks developed by anthropologists has made a strong contribution to community research and practice."[12] "Social network" is an ecological concept, not in the old Park and Burgess notion of urban ecology, but in its focus on interactions.

Furthermore, in spite of the dismissal of physical geography as a defining force, we do inhabit a material world, a social creation or not. And so, we need theories of community that address our surroundings (our environments) as well as our interactions (our ecologies).

The debate about which form of settlement contributes most to democracy accompanied the establishment of the United States. Jefferson's dispersed agrarianism emerged in immediate competition with the Boston of the Adamses, Franklin's Philadelphia, and Hamilton's New York City. Actually, the contrast began earlier: for example, the contained native mesa villages of the Hopi as compared with the dispersed Navajo settlements of the American Southwest, or the organized Spanish *pueblos* as opposed to the dispersed French voyageur camps. More recently, Lewis Mumford's decentralist regionalism conflicted with Jane Jacobs's urban village.[13] Unfortunately, Mumford's vision could not counter the more deleterious consequences of American suburban sprawl, and Jacobs tended to gloss over the ugly ramifications of racism in the dense, U.S. urban context (as did Jefferson in his agrarian vision). Design manifestations of this debate include Frank Lloyd Wright's Broadacre City and his protégé Paolo Soleri's radically different "organic" manifestation of Arcosanti. Perhaps the most troubling aspect of this debate is that it is always presented as an either-or situation. Either dispersion exemplifies the most democratic and ecological form of human community, or the compact city does. If unity in diversity is a valuable lesson from ecology, then perhaps we should advocate both dispersion and density.

COMMUNITIES IN BITS

Community represents "a framework of shared beliefs, interests, and commitments [that] unites a set of *varied* groups and activities," according to Philip Selznick, an emeritus professor of law and sociology at the University of California at Berkeley.[14] Selznick also identifies the "complex set of interacting variables" that constitutes communities: historicity, identity, mutuality, plurality, autonomy, participation, and integration.[15] These seven elements interact in ways that provide a community with its culture. That culture is communicated through language and modified through technology.

Neighborhood forms a specific type of human community, defined by vicinity. People live near one another in a particular locality. My former neighborhood in Tempe, Arizona, in cooperation with several others, learned to speak in the dialect of traffic engineers: established roadway, high-occupancy vehicles, continuous straight passing lanes, connector ramp, noise abatement, geographic balance in the region, grade separation, infrastructure impact, unrecoverable congestion, flyover, auxiliary lanes, half diamond interchanges, and so on. Retired schoolteachers and ministers, truck drivers and computer programmers, small business owners and dentists can actually carry on conversations with such terms. The community's learning resulted from self-preservation, a response to ongoing highway widening proposals by the Arizona Department of Transportation.

Technology does change community. *Wired* carried a piece on the creation of a new virtual, digital community. A "kingdom," well at least an Internet Web community of lonely computer geeks, has been created in a Madison, Wisconsin, bedroom. Its founders dub their nation Talossa, from a Finnish word meaning "inside the house."[16] As of September 2002, Talossa had 102 "cybercits," of which approximately eighteen were women. These cybercits created their own history, symbols, laws, and (online) culture largely through Internet technology (although they claim their kingdom "is far older than the Internet").

Publications such as *Wired* and *Artbytes* document cultural changes resulting from new technologies. Innovations can lead to new forms of community, such as the Internet kingdom of Talossa. Technological changes also alter existing communities. Old neighborhoods in Rome and other ancient cities have adapted to railroads, subways, automobiles, telephones, and the like.

Layers of interwoven urban fabric can result, with a community formed through contemporary technologies overlaying older communities of earlier technologies and even languages. On a stroll through Rome, Japanese, German, and Italian speakers gaze at buildings with Latin inscriptions. Communities of cell-phone-speaking Italians overlay the ancient neighborhoods of the Roman Empire and the Papal States.

On a walk in the French Quarter of New Orleans, Japanese, German, and Italian speakers encounter signs in English selling rum-based Hurricanes to go and transvestite sex shows. Among buildings with gaslights and second-story balconies, contemporary communities of gay artists and young professionals overlay earlier Spanish and French ones.

TISSUES

Both urban morphologists and landscape ecologists provide useful vocabularies for describing the function, structure, and change of communities. According to the approach of the British geographer Conzen, analyses should be undertaken of building form, land use, and the town plan.[17] Conzen's town plan refers to the existing layout rather than a planned or projected arrangement. The main elements include buildings, plots, and streets. The American geographer Michael Schmandt notes that building form concerns the "physical characteristics of the structure—features such as color, height, and architectural style."[18] Schmandt defines land use as "the activity or function of a parcel or parcel section."[19]

Conzen's plan unit parallels the Italian use of *tessuto* to describe urban connectors. According to Moudon, "Plan units or 'tissues' are groups of buildings, open spaces, lots, and streets, which form a cohesive whole either because they were all built at the same time or within the same constraints, or because they underwent a common process of transformation."[20] The Taylors, several generations of pioneers in international and community development, advocate the concept of "tensegrity" when considering community structure.[21] Their concept echoes the use of the term by the consciousness movement pioneer Carlos Casteneda, the sculptor Kenneth Snelson, and the architect-engineer-inventor R. Buckminster Fuller. Fuller created the term by contracting the words "tensional" and "integrity":

> Tensegrity describes a structural-relationship principle in which the structural shape is guaranteed by the finely closed, comprehensively continuous, tensional behaviors of the system and not the discontinuous and local compressional member behaviors. Tensegrity provides the ability to yield increasingly without breaking or coming asunder.[22]

Whereas Fuller used this principle to construct his dome structures, Daniel Taylor-Ide and Carl E. Taylor apply it in their community development work. Drawing on their medical training, they observe that healthy communities possess tensegrity structures. Tensional (pulling) and compressional (pushing) components combine to produce a dynamic structure. For example, the shops in a neighborhood center attempt to pull in customers. To do so, benches might be provided along the streets. But the same benches can attract vagrants. The shopkeepers, in turn, seek help from the local police to push out the homeless.

The function, and resulting arrangement, of buildings, open spaces, lots, and streets at the community scale varies. Pedestrians fill the 20-foot-wide (6.1 meters) Bourbon Street in New Orleans each night. Most pedestrian activity in my former Tempe neighborhood, with its 30-foot-wide (9.2 meters) streets, involves solitary daily trips to the common mailbox structure.

People create streets, parks, zoos, and buildings through design, planning, engineering, and construction. The architect Roberto Behar observes that "communities result from both memory and desire."[23] In America, the forces of memory and desire are especially apparent. Little Italy contains remnants of the Old World, as remembered by those who shaped it. But the memory has been transformed by the desire to create a new community. The pattern repeats itself in various Chinatowns across North America, the Over-the-Rhine neighborhood in Cincinnati, Little Havana in Miami, and so on.[24] Disneyland and Walt Disney World attempt to capture memory, but without the desire of communities living in place through time, it is not a very accurate memory.

Community structure changes also through erasure. Functions or styles change, and structures are replaced. But community structures are the depository of both memory and desire, so as parts are erased, sections may be conserved or preserved. Technology alters the function and structure of communities. Automobiles, airplanes, telephones, central heating, fax machines, e-mail, refrigeration, central heating, and air conditioning influence the structure of communities, often dramatically.

Once imprinted on the land, the physical structure of a community may remain intact for generations. The core of the old Polish capital, Kraków, is its Wawel hill and castle. As the city grew, a wall and a moat were constructed around the enlarged city. This wall encompassed the scenic main market square with its Sukiennice or Cloth Hall, churches, and town hall. Outside the wall was the main Jewish neighborhood, Kazimierz. Although Jewish people lived in other parts of Kraków, their community life focused on a square with six nearby synagogues and a market a few blocks away.

Kraków continued to grow into areas beyond the wall and moat, which included the Jewish neighborhood. The Austrians, who controlled the city during Poland's nineteenth-century partition, tore down the wall, filled in the moat, and built a park, as they had done in Vienna. As fortifications with medieval origins had become obsolete, new parks circled the city.

"Ghettos," as such, did not exist in twentieth-century Kraków or other Polish cities prior to the 1939 Nazi invasion. As Primo Levi describes the situation in Łódź, "As in all cities of a certain importance in occupied Eastern Europe, the Nazis hastened to set up a ghetto in it, reinstating, aggravated by their modern ferocity, the regime of medieval and Counter-Reformation Ghettos."[25] Ghetto is an Italian word, first used in Venice to indicate where the Jews lived and the place used by Venetians as a dump. The word derives from *getto* (*gettare*—"to throw," in Italian).

The German-created ghettos in Poland and elsewhere in Eastern Europe appropriated, perverted, and ultimately destroyed Jewish communities such as Kazimierz. The ghettos became places to concentrate the Jewish population before removing them to concentration camps. These ghettos were located in existing Jewish communities to facilitate the control and the collection process.

The Germans used Kraków as a headquarters. It was the only major Polish city not physically destroyed during the Second World War. The Jewish people were removed from the ghetto and murdered, but much of the physical community remained. In addition to the genocide of the Polish Jews, the Nazi invaders sought to eliminate other elements of the Polish nation, especially leaders, intellectuals, and "troublemakers." For example, soon after the 1939 invasion, the Germans rounded up most of the professors of Jagiellonian University—one of the oldest in Europe—and shot them.

The German plan was to eliminate the Jews and other "undesirables," level the Polish cities, replace them with German new towns, and enslave the surviving non-Aryan populations. Unfortunately, much of the plan was executed. But Kraków, as well as the physical form of the Jewish community, survived. The synagogues, markets, and houses degraded during the Communist era. Since 1990, the Kraków ghetto, the Kazimierz neighborhood, has experienced a renaissance. A Jewish cultural center has been built, many buildings restored, and the neighborhood resettled. A community founded centuries ago, which suffered considerable assault and injury, is healing.

If home and workplace are central to habitat, then it is the civic places and the spaces that connect them that provide the essential elements of community. Civic places include the landmarks that have been preserved and maintained through time. Schools; universities; government buildings, from the city hall to the post offices; and churches, synagogues, and mosques are significant civic places. Bars, restaurants, downtown business districts, and shopping malls comprise important elements of community. Although bars or restaurants may not be public, civic places, they may be connected by civic spaces—parks, streets, sidewalks, and even parking lots.

DO FENCES MAKE GOOD NEIGHBORS?

When does one community end and another begin? The city of Phoenix has been divided into "urban villages" that are neither urban nor villages. Banners and entry markers announce when one is leaving one "village," or neighborhood, and entering the next, from Encanto-Palmcroft to Willow, for example. One cynic observed about the Phoenix system of banners and "welcome-to" signs that everything and everybody was so new that they had to be told where they were.

American communities have been spatially divided by ethnicity, prejudice, and economics. Communities of interest—religion, occupation, and hobbies—tend to be nonspatial in North America and Europe. In eastern and midwestern American cities, ethnicity is still evident in many communities; in western cities, ethnic conclaves are often less obvious, except perhaps in the Hispanic and Asian neighborhoods.

Chicago once boasted of having the second largest Polish population outside of Warsaw. Italian, black, Irish, and white Anglo-Saxon Protestant immigrants settled distinct Chicago neighborhoods. In the late twentieth century, Phoenix emerged as one of the most rapidly growing cities in the United States. Many new residents of the Phoenix metropolitan region arrived from the Chicago region of northern Illinois, northwestern Indiana, and southeastern Wisconsin. Like Chicago with the Poles, Phoenix perhaps now has the largest Chicagoan population outside of Chicago. Former Italian Americans, Polish Americans, African Americans, Irish Americans, and WASPs are Chicagoans in Phoenix, where the Chicago Bears football team regularly attracts more fans than the Arizona Cardinals when playing in Phoenix. Communities can be mobile, but as they move, some elements of what's been left behind are often retained.

Once boundaries are established, they can persist for a long time. For instance, as with other medieval towns, Genoa was defined by its walls. In the eleventh century, the Knights of Malta built a hospital for those wounded in the Crusades outside the walls of Genoa. Between the walls and the hospital, a *borgo* developed, populated by many poor people. In the *borgo*, many illicit activities occurred. Now in the middle of Genoa, the old *borgo* remains inhabited by the poor, and after nine centuries, it continues to be a rough neighborhood.

Around the globe from Genoa, a sewer replaced the main river through Guadalajara, Mexico, from north to south. In colonial times the

Río San Juan del Dios separated the Spanish and the Indians, west and east. The colonial imprint lingers, and, today, classes remain divided in communities roughly in the same way with the wealthier in the west and the poorer to the east.

Economic segregation, an element of all settlements throughout history, became arguably even more pronounced in late-twentieth-century American cities. In ancient Rome, the patricians lived in *villas*, the proletarians in *insulae*. In Renaissance Rome, wealthy nobles and cardinals constructed villas outside the city, in part to avoid the plague. Amsterdam was planned so that the wealthiest gentlemen had houses on the most grand canal, the Herengracht. Rich Londoners as well as their country gentry cousins were able to convene at Bath. In the late nineteenth century, wealthy Philadelphians settled the Main Line—so named because it was the main line of the Pennsylvania Railroad. Streetcars facilitated the development of new suburban communities, including Frederick Law Olmsted's innovative Riverside, Illinois, outside of Chicago.

This trend toward living in suburbs continued into the early twentieth century and was made accessible to a broader economic spectrum by the automobile. As the sociologist-planner Herbert Gans pointed out in 1967, much of the hostility generated against these new suburbs by the intelligentsia resulted because of their new access to less affluent individuals.[26] The widening gap between the rich and the poor, which became especially pronounced during the 1980s in the United States, found physical form with exclusive communities redefining the suburban edge of many metropolitan regions. Gated "communities" present one strategy that the more affluent have employed to separate themselves from the riffraff.

Gated communities seek to protect their inhabitants from crime. Gates and walls form physical boundaries. Of course, safety has been a motivating factor in urban design since the early civilizations of Mesopotamia. As Don Luymes, a member of the University of British Columbia landscape architecture faculty, notes, "while gated communities are not new—Victorian London was fragmented by more than 250 closed streets . . . and St. Louis has a long history of private, gated streets . . .—they represent a burgeoning form of territorial control."[27] Luymes indicates that one reason for this "burgeoning form" is the fear of crime. He found that "the fear of an increase in crime has become rampant in the suburbs."[28] Although design for safety has been a constant, the areas considered "civilized" have changed.

J. B. Jackson observed:

In the traditional medieval concept of the universe the whole world was . . . divided into three spaces: one was where men lived and where they created their own defined spaces—gardens and plowed fields. A second was the open space where cattle grazed and where there were no fences, and a third space was everything beyond. In Latin, these were called, respectively, *ager, saltus,* and *silva*: "horrida silva," according to Tacitus.[29]

The University of Pennsylvania landscape historian John Dixon Hunt has called these the "three natures," and, beginning with Jefferson, Americans have been drawn to the middle landscape, the middle nature.[30] Meanwhile, beginning with Thoreau, Emerson, and Whitman, *horrida silva* grew to a more elevated status in the New World. Our communities now occupy all three natures, and the boundaries between them have become less distinct. What is an urban community? What is a rural community? What is a suburban community?

Definitions and examples can be provided for each, which may be as much a reflection of character or aspiration as size or form. Increasingly, we inhabit ecotones that combine elements of rural and urban and suburban. Simultaneously, the boundaries and edges between what is natural and what is cultural have become fuzzy. We live in a tangled web of nature and culture, but a danger looms that the cultural will obliterate the natural. "Land is community," Leopold observed, and so communities should fit the land. We should seek out the ecotones between the cultural and the natural.

PUBLIC DISCOURSE

Such seeking out of ecotones implies interaction. Communities, practically by definition, are interactive. Sounds can be a form of interaction, such as the church bells chiming out the time in Catholic communities or the muezzin, the *mu'adhdhin*, calling the devoted to prayer at the Moslem mosque. The piazzas of Italy were traditionally a space for community interaction. People gathered there, exchanged information, shopped, heard political proclamations. Piazzas were, and many still are, forums for public discourse. The private life of one's home, one's habitat, was put aside for the public space of the community.

Many argue that such interaction has declined, or has become considerably more difficult in modern societies. For example, Robert Putnam, the former dean of Harvard's Kennedy School of Government, employs the metaphor of "bowling alone" to illustrate how a decline in civic engagement has resulted in diminished "social capital" in American communities.[31] As the landscape architect Douglas Paterson suggested, "without social interaction to guide us in our thinking, the caring (or even an understanding of the need for caring), essential to the making of community quickly evaporates."[32] Interaction prompts us to care about those we contact as well as about the environments where those interactions occur.

Interaction with nature is as vital for community as social intercourse. Again Paterson makes a keen observation, "Few definitions of community exist that do not contain nature as central to the idea of community; the very spiritual existence of a stable, psychologically secure community rests on its sense of dwelling in an Arcadian world."[33] When we lose contact with nature, our existential spirit becomes thwarted. Since the nineteenth century, communities of a certain size and stature have constructed public zoos and botanic gardens, in part to provide connections with animals and plants.

Interactions among people and between people and nature can be segregated or integrated activities. Although there may be some reasons for segregating activities in a community (who, after all, wants to live next to a rendering plant or a fireworks factory?), overall, integrated communities seem more healthy than ones where there are unnecessary divisions.

Communities change as a result of interactions. Gentrification can be viewed as a form of ecological invasion as one group replaces another. As middle- and upper-income professionals purchase and renovate houses in deteriorated urban neighborhoods, property values and community appearance improve. The existing lower-income residents, if they own homes, can profit from such a transformation. Renters do not accrue similar benefits. Low-income families can be replaced by gentrification and forced to relocate in less desirable places. Community cohesion may falter and institutions may crumble as a result of such transitions.

Institutions can stimulate or stymie gentrification and other processes of community change. A city can designate a neighborhood as an "historic district." Property owners in such districts will be eligible for tax benefits, low-interest loans, and even direct grants from city, state, and national governments. To be eligible for such benefits, however, properties will be subject to specific restrictions concerning property maintenance. Higher-income individuals may be more capable of fulfilling such requirements, forcing out families with less means.

In other cases, public and private institutions may favor individuals and families with more limited resources. For example, a government can pro-

vide incentives to banks if they provide loans to lower-income people in depressed urban neighborhoods. Such a policy may help improve the quality
of the neighborhood while strengthening its existing community cohesion.

THE CHALLENGES OF DIVERSITY

Integrated communities result in diverse, pluralistic places. Arguably, diverse communities are more interesting than homogeneous ones, but pluralism can provide many challenges. Many individuals and a variety of
physical elements compose communities. People can be cooperative, conflicting, gregarious, jealous, withdrawn,. . . the list is long. Tolerance then
becomes an essential element for diversity to thrive in a community.

In obvious homage to Aldo Leopold, William Vitek and Wes Jackson
collected a series of essays to illustrate that communities are "rooted in the
land."[34] Because lands vary widely, communities reflect the diversity of
those roots. Some community origins clearly can be found in the soils;
other backgrounds emerge from other impulses to interact. An academic
community's roots differ from those whose members literally work the land
or, for that matter, from those who make products. At the same time, members of these different communities may share the same roots and even
form larger communities, like, for instance, the Islamic scholar who interacts with others of the same faith, including farmers and factory workers.

Diversity exists within and among communities. As the theologian
John B. Cobb Jr. notes, "a healthy community must call for responsibility to
others beyond its own membership. It must call for cooperation with other
communities."[35] Cobb advocates networks as follows: "A community of
local communities would be a grouping of communities that took responsibility for one another, that provided an important part of the self-identifi-
cation of the local communities (and thus their members), and that made its
decisions in ways in which all the member communities participated."[36]

From a distance, Toledo appears to be part of the granite prominence it
occupies in central Spain. Even closer, its faded ocher structures melt into
the rock to form an urban mass on the steep bluffs above the Tajo River. In
medieval times, Christian, Arab, and Jewish communities blended to produce a center for classical learning that laid the seeds for the Renaissance.
Before the Inquisition, Toledo provided an example of Cobb's "community
of local communities" (at least among Christians and Jews). Today, medieval
mosques and synagogues remain in the dense maze of streets that form the

neighborhoods of the city. The physical form remains a blend of Moorish, Jewish, and Christian urbanism, although the Moors departed more than five hundred years ago and the Jews were banished during the Inquisition. This urban artifact lingers as a testimony to the possibilities and the challenges of pluralism—of a community of diverse communities.

ECOLOGICAL FOOTPRINTS

Some communities adapt better than others. Once again, Rome offers a good example. A walk through the streets of Rome reveals layers upon layers of time at every corner. On the other hand, a walk through Newark, St. Louis, and Detroit can cross empty quarters where little from the past remains. Still, Detroit, St. Louis, and Newark once prospered. It should be remembered that Rome had long periods of decline. The renaissance of fading communities in the Rust Belt of the United States is possible, just as decline is probable for many Sun Belt communities.

Still, as one wanders around the vacant streets of downtown St. Louis, one ponders what went wrong on this southwest corner of the Rust Belt. This place must have seemed as strategically located at the juncture of the continent's great rivers, near the Vandalia, Illinois, terminus of the National Road. Major east-west roadways, including U.S. 40 and Interstate 70, as well as great railroads intersected the rivers at St. Louis. Canyon walls of once magnificent buildings line empty streets with uninhabited rooms, monuments to a community whose aspirations could not be sustained.

Adaptation requires adjusting to change. According to Wallace Stegner,

> . . . a place is not a place until people have been born in it, have grown up in it, lived in it, known it, died in it—have experienced and shaped it, as individuals, families, neighborhoods, and communities, over more than one generation. Some are born in their place, some find it, some realize after long searching that the place they left is the one they have been searching for. But whatever their relation to it, it is made a place only by slow accrual, like coral reef.[37]

The creation of community is an ancient theme. The New Testament in Revelation describes the layout of a future holy city, the New Jerusalem. Plato and Aristotle posed theories for ideal societies and ideal community design. Vitruvius devoted significant portions of his treatise on architecture

to the understanding of site and the design of community. Alberti rediscovered, criticized, and expanded Vitruvius in the Renaissance.

In the Veneto region of northern Italy, the villas of Palladio were more
communities than estates. At villa Emo, for example, the complex included a system of *borgo*, farm fields, irrigation canals, mills, and farm buildings
in addition to the striking main house. Theater designer and geometer
Rachel Fletcher notes,

> Emo is an expression of Palladio's desire to harmonize buildings organically
> with their physical surroundings. The villa was built originally to support a
> farming economy—the [Emo] family was the first, in fact, to bring maize, or
> corn, to the region. The orientation is south, actually 10° east of south, the
> correct adjustment for a winter season solar gain. The villa also aligns with a
> series of irrigation canals that water Emo's surrounding fields. The design
> marries building form and natural function. A massive stone ramp on the
> south side of the building, for example, also serves a threshing floor.[38]

The ideas and designs of Vitruvius, Alberti, and Palladio were especially
influential as the Western Hemisphere—the New World—was being settled by Europeans. Philip II's Laws of the Indies of 1573 were tested first
in his hometown, Valladolid, in northern Spain. The laws were based on
Renaissance principles of design. The urban historian John Reps illustrates
how the laws possess similarities to the ideas of both Vitruvius and Alberti. As Reps explained, the laws begin "with the selection of a suitable site.
One on an elevation surrounded by good farming land and with a good
water supply and available fuel and timber was favored. The plan was to be
decided upon before any construction, and it was to be ample in scope."[39]

William Penn and Thomas Holme's plan for a "greene countrie
towne"—Philadelphia—also placed much emphasis on site selection. John
Reps quotes Penn's instructions for locating a suitable site and the required
amount of land:

> . . . let the rivers and creeks be sounded on my side of Delaware River,
> . . . and be sure to make your choice where it is most navigable, high, dry,
> and healthy; that is, where most ships may best ride, of deepest draught of
> water, if possible to load and unload at the bank or key side, without boat-
> ing or lightening of it. It would do well if the river coming into that creek be
> navigable, at least for boats, up into the country, and that situation be high,
> at least dry and sound, and not swampy, which is best known by digging up
> two or three earths, and seeing the bottom.

> Such a place being found out, for navigation, healthy situation, and good soil for provision, lay out ten thousand acres contiguous to it in the best manner you can, as the bounds and extent of the liberties of said town.[40]

With the site selected, the planning of the city proceeded. Penn appointed Captain Thomas Holme Surveyor General of Pennsylvania. Holme, an Irish settler under Oliver Cromwell and resident of Waterford in 1682, had already some twenty-two years of colonial experience as soldier, surveyor, Quaker writer, and landowner in Ireland.[41] He arrived in Philadelphia in June 1682, followed in October by Penn. Holme's Philadelphia plan extended only halfway from the broad Delaware River to the muddy Schuylkill. Penn extended the city of the peninsula to give it frontage to both rivers. The combined Holme-Penn plan was drawn up in 1683, and maps of it were used for the basis of advertising in London.

Morris observed that the gridiron was "clearly being used as a means to an end. Both the drawing and Holme's [written] description refer to a closed urban programme which is in total contrast to the open-end uses of the gridiron as an end in itself, as generally employed across the American continent by later city 'planners'. . ."[42]

Morris traced the physical plan for Philadelphia back to two English precedents.[43] The first was incorporation of "open space" into the plan. Penn had apparently studied earlier English colonization experience in which open squares were located in the gridiron system. He was also familiar with Inigo Jones's design for Covent Garden in London and with nearby Lincoln's Inn Fields, where he had studied law at Lincoln's Inn in 1665.[44] The second influence was the planning that was done for London after its Great Fire. The plan developed by Richard Newcourt, with its main central square and four smaller corner ones, bears a close resemblance to that of Philadelphia.[45]

Penn and Holme believed their plan would create community. Their physical arrangement of space would facilitate the settlement of Philadelphia and its surroundings. The scheme applied a geometric structure intended to link people to nature.

According to James Coke, the pattern created for Philadelphia of the gridiron street system, open spaces, and uniform spacing and setbacks for buildings was important for its influence on other American cities.[46] "The gridiron," wrote Coke, "is a major type of street system and continues to dominate the American townscape. Perhaps because it was a principal port of entry, Philadelphia was widely copied as towns sprang up in the west."[47]

Like Philadelphia, Thomas Jefferson's imprint on community in the

United States is writ large. After writing the Declaration of Independence in Philadelphia, Jefferson served as governor of Virginia and on several diplomatic missions in Europe. While in Europe, he collected town plans of major cities. He witnessed the application of Renaissance principles in portions of cities formerly occupied by fortifications. As Count Emo brought corn from the New World to plant at his Veneto villa, Jefferson went searching for rice in northern Italy. He had stumbled on the northern Italian Palladio earlier in books. Look at Washington, D.C., and witness the synthesis of French Baroque garden design and the architecture of Palladio.

Early Americans were industrious planners, designers, financiers, and builders of new communities. They were pretty good at it, too. America was a new community for many, but it was also an already settled land. The Western Hemisphere had been settled from west to east, the reverse of how settlement is described in standard American history texts. North and South America were replete with diverse settlements—large and small, generally better adapted to nature then the European overlay.

This contact with nature changed European thinking as well. The new Americans were influenced by the first Americans in more ways than corn-on-the-cob and Marlboros. The Transcendentalists elevated nature and planted the seed for a new form of community design. Whereas the plazas of the pueblos and the streets of Philadelphia were laid out in rectilinear grids, Olmsted's design for the suburban community of Riverside had winding streets. Philadelphia had rows of street trees in front of its town houses; Riverside had clumps of trees in front of its single-family houses. In the United States, John Nolen, Clarence Stein, and Henry Wright, and many lesser talents followed Olmsted's lead. Then, Columbia, Maryland, and Reston, Virginia, attempted to infuse more diverse social values into new community design. Later, with the Woodlands in Texas, social plus ecological and economic imperatives were considered. Now, Andres Duany, Elizabeth Plater-Zyberk, Peter Calthorpe, Stefanos Polyzoidis, Elizabeth Moule, and others advocate a new urbanism, a return to the lessons of traditional community design and planning.

These architects assert, "Put simply, the New Urbanism sees physical design—regional design, urban design, architecture, landscape design, and environmental design [and presumably interior design, product design, and graphic design]—as critical to the future of our communities. . . . The belief is that design can play a critical role in resolving problems that government programs and money alone cannot."[48]

Andres Duany and his New Urbanist compatriots are effusive about the centrality of design in community and regional issues. They provide a stinging criticism of the planning profession for abandoning design as a policy and implementation tool. "Town planning," Andres Duany and his colleagues write, "until 1930 considered a humanistic discipline based on history, aesthetics, and culture, became a technical profession based upon numbers. As a result, the American city was reduced into simplistic categories and quantities of sprawl. Because these tenets still hold sway, sprawl continues largely unchecked."[49]

Planners, engineers, architects, and landscape architects attempt to construct contemporary communities. Architects and landscape architects tend to address more of the aesthetic aspects of community than planners who focus more on policy and engineers who address utility. Increasingly, all of these disciplines turn to ecology to inform their work. For example, the architect Peter Calthorpe has written,

> . . . ecology has come to represent, for me, a real counterpoint. Not the literal ecology which deals with natural systems and seems to stop just short of the human habitat—but a broader, more philosophic "ecology" which teaches diversity, interdependence, and whole systems are fundamental to health. It is this perspective and attempt to translate it into specific form for our buildings and communities which has directed my work.[50]

The "ecological footprint" concept can help planners and designers shape new communities and adapt existing ones. This concept was developed by William Rees at the University of British Columbia, who defines an ecological footprint as ". . .the *area of land and water ecosystems required, on a continuous basis, to produce the resources that the population consumes, and to assimilate the wastes that the population produces, wherever on Earth the relevant land/water is located.*"[51] Our shelter, energy, food, and other resource demands can be translated into estimates of the land and water areas necessary to support them.[52] Rees makes the point that communities have become ecologically disconnected from their geographic locations and that no place "*can be sustainable on its own.*"[53]

COMMUNITY DEVELOPMENT

Paterson notes that community is a "central building block to humanity as well as democracy" but that "North Americans have been in the process of escaping from community for over a hundred years."[54] As a result, he recommends, "Revisions to community must assume radical proportions wherein the interventions made return us to the root ideas and processes . . ." of community.[55] What are those root ideas and processes? Selznick's complex set of interacting variables—historicity, identity, mutuality, plurality, autonomy, participation, and integration—present the basic elements of community.[56] Selznick contends, "A fully realized community will have a rich and *balanced* mixture of these elements."[57]

A community then may be defined as people sharing space. Or, more ambitiously, as "human-scaled, civic-minded social order."[58] Sustainable communities "encourage people to work together to create healthy communities where natural and historic resources are preserved, jobs are available, sprawl is contained, neighborhoods are secure, education is lifelong, transportation and health care are accessible, and all citizens have opportunities to improve the quality of their lives."[59]

The call for more sustainable, more livable, communities continues an age-old tradition in the search for ideal human groupings. But, Cobb warns, "Community, like everything worthwhile in history, is ambiguous. There have never been ideal communities and there never will be. But without communities, however imperfect, society can only decay."[60]

We can move from one physical community to another and remain a part of a social network. I have worked at several universities. Each campus forms a distinct physical community, but as I have moved, I have remained a part of larger disciplinary communities. I inhabit the ecotone between at least two fields, both of which have national and international networks.

While each university has a similar social structure, a hierarchy of decision making and power, each has distinctions, too. An agriculturally based, land-grant institution has a different heritage than an entrepreneurial research university in a rapidly growing metropolis. An institution with a land-grant base differs from one that grew out of a normal school, and social structure lingers from these pasts.

As I sit at my computer and communicate with an editor in Colorado or a collaborator in Milan or my mom in Dayton, Ohio, it may not be obvious that I am engaged in ecological interactions with far-flung communities. An ecological view of contemporary human communities helps us fathom the overlapping nature of physical and social relationships.

A few mothers chat while hovering over a gaggle of elementary kids at a bus stop. Colleagues gather for a professional meeting from all parts of a nation. Italians stop by their neighborhood bar for a quick shot of espresso on their way to work. Communities take multiple forms across landscapes but always involve both sharing and communication.

LANDSCAPE

The landscapes we know and return to become places of solace. We are drawn to them because of the stories they tell, because of the memories they hold, or simply because of the sheer beauty that calls us back again and again.

—TERRY TEMPEST WILLIAMS

A LANDSCAPE IS COMPRISED OF ALL THE NATURAL AND CULTURAL features, including the fields, structures, neighborhoods, hills, deserts, forests, and water bodies, that distinguish one part of the surface of the earth from another part. A landscape is that portion of land that the eye can comprehend in a single view, including all its natural and cultural characteristics. The single view represents a larger space. In addition to the visible, physical aspects, landscapes possess significant symbolic content. They are imbued with meaning and identity.[1] "Landscape is, first of all, the unity we see, the impressions of our senses rather than the logic of the sciences," cultural geographer Donald Meinig reminds us.[2] Moreover, "the visual bias of *landscape* must be reconciled with the fact that experience involves all the senses."[3]

Landscape, like communities, form patterns, or as J. B. Jackson observed, "communities and landscapes have always been organized into patterns. . . ."[4] Landscapes are the sum of their parts, the culmination of many dynamic processes. They reveal human culture—the values of individuals and communities. "The landscape of any farm is the owner's portrait of himself," as Nina Leopold Bradley quoted her father, Aldo, as saying.[5] In the same way, the landscapes of neighborhoods and cities provide portraits of their inhabitants.

Flying from west to east across North America, you can see that the landscape below changes from brown to green much of the year. On occasion, white can provide a common surface, but mostly the view moves from earth tone to verdure. As the color changes, so does the settlement—from large ranch to farm; from sparsely populated, with several gigantic growing metropolises, to ever connected small towns and big, aging cities. We see color and nature and culture and perceive the combinations to be portraits of not only Leopold's farmer but all the dwellers of the landscapes outside our windows.

THE IDEA OF LANDSCAPE

Landschap (Dutch)–*landschaft* (German)–landscape (English) presents a powerful yet underappreciated concept in the Dutch–German–English–North American tradition. In its original Dutch, *landschap* designated "such commonplaces as 'a collection of farms or fenced fields, sometimes a small domain or administrative unit.'"[6] *Landschaft* means "the land shaped by men," based on its earlier meaning of "not a town exactly, or a manor or a village, but a collection of dwellings and other structures crowded together within a circle of pasture, meadow, and planting fields and surrounded by unimproved forest or marsh."[7] The English elevated the term to "shed its earthbound roots and acquire the precious meaning of art."[8] Eventually, Dutch and German scholars helped return the term to its earthy roots through the field of landscape ecology.

The southern, Latin equivalents *paesaggio* (Italian)–*paysage* (French)–*paisaje* (Spanish) also mean "scenery," but with a different underlying cultural subtext. Perhaps, the Italian *paesaggio* may not be a very good translation of "landscape," or at least what the latter term is becoming to mean. *Territorio* might be closer, but it too has limitations. Some Italians argue that "landscape" is a northern import, a term the English brought with their Grand Tours. This observation displays irony because many of these Englishmen were searching for the *campagna* of the Italian painters. In any case, language is dynamic, and, from wherever it originated, the idea of landscape is taking hold in southern Europe and elsewhere. The meaning is broadening everywhere beyond its aesthetic basis, but without abandoning its visual and cultural values.

Landscape ecologists introduced the idea of landscape as a scale. According to these ecologists, landscapes consist of repeated groupings of interacting ecosystems with similar climate, geomorphology, and disturbance regimes.[9] Joan Nassauer of the University of Michigan observes that land-scape ecology "directs our view of nature to a new scale."[10] This new view offers insights into the complexity of nature not afforded at more specific scales, such as the individual organism and the site.

THE LANGUAGES OF LANDSCAPES

Careful explorations of the languages of landscapes can reinforce the ef-forts of those who believe in the broader potential of the interacting natu-ral and cultural processes that we see. Language depends on grammar. In her insightful *The Language of Landscape*, landscape architect Anne Spirn probes all the rules of grammar—modification, agreement, correspon-dence, subordination, and coordination—for the worlds around us.[11]

The failure to understand and to respond thoughtfully to the grammar of landscapes results in deleterious consequences for people and nature. The Mill Creek neighborhood of West Philadelphia provides a touchstone for Spirn. She illustrates how by ignoring the grammar of this place, peo-ple have suffered and a landscape has become impoverished.

The Mill Creek neighborhood became a focus of Spirn's University of Pennsylvania and MIT classes as well as her own reflective practice. As Philadelphia expanded west across the Schuylkill River, William Penn's grid for his "greene countrie towne" continued as well. The expansion ig-nored the grammar of the terrain created by Mill Creek, a Schuylkill trib-utary. The deep structure of the place was violated; the free-flowing creek became a sewer. "Buried in a sewer," Spirn writes, "its floodplain filled in and built on, Mill Creek still carries all the stormwater as well as the wastes from half of West Philadelphia."[12]

As a result, Mill Creek's largely African American community has ex-perienced many problems, including sewer overflows, flooded basements, abandoned houses, vacant lots, and declining property values. Spirn's West Philadelphia Landscape Project offers strategies to reverse these trends. She seeks to help the residents of the Mill Creek neighborhood to under-stand their "deep context." With her students, she has created visions and places with the community to recover its grammar in order to heal and re-store the neighborhood.

Deep context presents a framework for critical regionalism. Spirn traces "context" from its Latin root, *contexere*, "to weave." She notes, "Con-text is a place where processes happen, a setting of dynamic relationships, *not* a collection of static features."[13] Furthermore, Spirn observes, "Deep context is enduring, its rate of change prolonged, but even deep context can be altered over time."[14] Spirn's deep context may be viewed as an extension of the deep structure concept. Deep structure may be thought of as Ian McHarg's "layer cake" of physical, biological, and social processes. (I return to the layer cake idea in chapter 5.) Deep context is Spirn's temporal and spatial weaving of their interactions through culture.

This framework offers landscape architects (and architects and planners) not only the opportunity to avoid making mistakes that can cause harm to people but also a palette from which to apply in their art. In addition to her own work, Spirn dissects the creations of other landscape authors, including Sven-Ingvar Andersson, Frank Lloyd Wright, Lawrence Halprin, and Rich Haag—poets all. Haag's work, in particular, assumes a mystic lyricism reminiscent of Walt Whitman or Theodore Roethke, especially his two masterworks—the Bloedel Reserve and Seattle's Gas Works Park. Photographs of the Bloedel Reserve capture the haunting allure of its misty Bainbridge Island location in Washington's Puget Sound. The essence of Gas Works Park is more difficult to capture with a camera. Both landscapes provide refuge and renewal but in divergent ways. In Bloedel, one retreats into nature and is renewed. Gas Works provides a refuge from the surrounding city while representing a recovery from the Industrial Revolution. Spirn calls them "two chapters in the same story."[15]

With Bloedel and Gas Works, Haag indeed transcends polemics. So does Spirn with *The Language of Landscape*. Nature, art, the past, and functionality inform the authorship of landscapes. When combined with the skill of a Rich Haag, a place of meaning results. Likewise, Anne Spirn, the author, weaves ecology with creativity, precedent with function. Furthermore, through her work in West Philadelphia, Spirn, the landscape architect, has helped a community reconnect with its natural history. Both Haag and Spirn provide optimistic stories for architects of landscapes.

While Anne Spirn writes persuasively of the "language of landscape," I contend that there are as many languages for landscape as there are cultures. Each culture regards its natural and social features differently. Still, some universality may exist. The ancient Chinese and Kevin Lynch in post–World War II Boston both offer approaches to analyze and design landscapes. The architect-turned-planner Lynch taught at MIT from 1948 into the early 1980s, although he formally retired in 1978. He authored the standard text on site planning. *Fêng shui* differs from Lynch's notions of site planning in many respects.[16] However, solar orientation, topography, and water flows play important roles in both approaches.

In addition to cultural differences, types of landscapes elicit varying vocabularies. One can differentiate between natural or rural landscapes, as well as between those modified relatively little by people and built landscapes. Furthermore, built environments can be public or private.

When I left home to attend the university, my father and mother moved from the small, manufacturing city of Dayton, Ohio, to the rural, vacation-orientated Jamestown, Kentucky. They bought a "lodge," a motel really. My father cased the area frequently for additional real estate. (His unrealized dream was to purchase a McDonald's or Kentucky Fried Chicken franchise.)

Catty-corner, across the street from the motel, he and my mother bought a twenty-acre site, which, unbeknown to them, came with a tobacco base. As a remnant of the New Deal, this base permitted the landowners to grow a certain amount of tobacco annually. This base could be (and was in my parents' case) transferred to a farmer. My parents' lot is not well suited for a fast-food franchise, but it has proven to be a great source of Christmas trees. Underlain by limestone, a ravine dominates the site. The gorge-like channel runs northeast to southwest, and its configuration poses difficult challenges for development. The best slopes for solar orientation are too steep for development; the more gradual slopes are too cool. A meadow above the ravine presents the best place to build, but it is difficult to access from the highway. Left undeveloped, oaks, chestnuts, cedars, and blackberry vines provide habitat for squirrels, raccoons, foxes, and various snakes.

People possess a rich vocabulary for describing such landscapes. The origins of this language derived from their desire to survive. They needed to know what they could eat, and what could eat them. The natural landscape presented the menu.

Built landscapes—public and private—produce different combinations of terms, often overlapping or derived from the prose of natural places. The Dutch, who have created much of their landscape and arguably even the concept of landscape, certainly understand the languages of built environments.

The great Dutch *landschapsarchitect* Nico de Jonge approached his most notable designs as a formalist. Inspired by the French garden design tradition as well as the agricultural expanses of the American Midwest, his geometric designs featured broad vistas framed by row after row of trees. De Jonge's designs reflect the underlying function and structure of the polders, that is, land reclaimed from lakes or the sea. The Dutch polders were created, through brilliant hydrological engineering, for farming. Nico de Jonge celebrated this framework of canal and field.

His own home and summer place stood in stark contrast to the well-ordered fields that he designed in East Flevoland and Walcheren. Among the well-ordered lawns of Renkum row houses, Nico de Jonge's jungle distinguished itself. His gigantic ferns and wild, twisting vines contrasted the neat rows of the neighbor's tulips.

His summer place in Walcheren provides a more dramatic contrast. Snuggled close to a dike and the dual rows of poplars that de Jonge planted, the small hut merged with the ground. Three tiny rooms and a water closet sited among tangled flora, the structure disappears from the road. A deeply religious man, de Jonge sought to touch the divine through the earth. A retreat designed as a ruin, his private space contrasted and contradicted the surrounding formal public landscape.

Private and public, natural and naturalistic landscapes: each with their own set of words, their rules of grammar.

THE STRAIGHT AND THE CURVED

The landscape structures we create can be rational or irrational, and sometimes both simultaneously. The structures can relate to function or be divorced from it and, again, sometimes both connected to and separated from function. Landscape structures can adapt to change or resist it, or adapt while resisting or resist while adapting.

Take the North American grid. The grid that dominates much of the North American landscape remains a legacy of Thomas Jefferson. The American landscape was parceled like a large chessboard as conceived by Jefferson. A child of the Enlightenment, he was influenced by René Descartes, Francis Bacon, and John Locke. Jefferson was also an idealist who viewed property ownership as the key to democracy. Ecologist Paul Shepard observed that Jefferson believed that "agriculture produced the only real wealth, that every man had a natural right to land, that cultivation earned the right of ownership, and that labor in the field dignified the farmer and purified him to nature."[17]

Jefferson's interest in Andrea Palladio of the Veneto is well known. Perhaps Jefferson was also swayed by a series of treatises on agriculture by the Venetian aristocracy that "extolled the virtues of country and farming life."[18] Jefferson studied Palladio before his single trip to Italy in 1787, but he did not come in search of Palladio. He came instead looking for information about the cultivation of rice.[19] Unlike the Italian villas around Rome and

Florence, which were used as retreats from the city for the rich, those near Venice were used for agriculture (also mostly by the wealthy). Much of the flat portions of the Veneto region were colonized according to the Roman *centuriatio* system of square plots of 710 meters × 710 meters (roughly 2,400 feet × 2,400 feet). In the mid–sixteenth century, the prominent Venetian landowner Alvise Cornaro published *Discorsi della vita sobria*, which "advocates the *vita sobria*, the ancient ideal of simple country life."[20] Cornaro considered the cultivation of the land to be "a divine occupation, comparable with the Creation. Agriculture equaled virtue, so it was difficult to conceive of anything more virtuous than money earned by tilling the land."[21]

This nexus with the land lies at the root of American democracy. However, there are many contradictory forces in Jeffersonian democracy, slavery being the most hideous but perhaps his views toward the land have yielded similar oppression. According to Shepard, "Jefferson admired sublime objects" in nature.[22] Jefferson acknowledged that not every acre of land could or should be farmed: "Whenever there are in any country un-cultivated lands and unemployed poor, it is clear that the laws of property have been so far extended as to violate natural rights." To put this statement in contemporary terms, Jefferson recognized that some lands were too environmentally sensitive to be farmed or settled.

In summation, Jefferson created the myth that "the small landholders are the most precious part of the state."[23] The small landholding, noble yeoman democrat was a creation by a landed gentleman whose slaves did the cultivation and were thus, at least theoretically, "purified" by nature. To facilitate the settlement of the nation by these noble yeomen, Jefferson wrote proposals that were incorporated into the Land Ordinance of 1785 and the Northwest Ordinance of 1787. The effect of these ordinances, when combined with the Homestead Act of 1862, was to divide the nation, and much of the continent, west of the Alleghenies into a giant, square-grid chessboard.[24] (Curt Meine notes that Canada's land survey followed a similar system.)[25] Some squares were set aside for schools; others were given eventually to railroad companies in return for their construction of rail lines. Even Jefferson, who placed private property on the highest pedestal, recognized that some lands were unsuited for settlement. So, Americans inherited a division of the land, rational in eighteenth-century views, that is incongruent with natural processes and, from an ecological point of view, irrational.

Other visions have also been advanced. John Wesley Powell was perhaps the keenest observer of the American West in the late nineteenth century. He provided a clear and practical vision for settling the arid and semi-arid regions and landscapes of the West by endorsing the use of drainage basins. Powell based his advocacy both on an understanding of natural processes and on his observations of native and Hispanic settlements. Drainage basins, which are also called catchment areas and watersheds, are relatively easy to delineate. They present a rather simple system to understand: a certain amount of water enters the watershed, a certain amount departs, and in the process, a certain amount of life can be sustained in between—a system not unlike the urinary system in humans. We can learn much about the body—or the watershed—by analyzing the water that leaves. Powell's rational proposal was not heeded. Instead, a different form of rationality was imposed on the American West, that of the Jeffersonian grid.

Is a watershed drainage basin a landscape or a region? The boundaries of all these terms are fuzzy, but smaller watersheds can be roughly analogous to landscapes. Certainly, the drainage basins of the Mississippi, the Nile, the Po, the Tiber, and the like are regional in scope. Watersheds and drainage basins help us understand landscapes and regions as parts of the nested hierarchy of nature from the cell to the globe. I return to the topic of river basins in chapter 5.

The structures within which landscapes function are both natural, like watersheds, and political-cultural, like Jefferson's grid. As a result, landscape structures are barometers, pee in the cup, of change.

LEAPING FENCES

In a literal sense, landscapes end at the limits of our vision. However, what we view symbolizes something larger. At one time, the notion of landscape was bounded by the garden wall. As the Englishman Horace Walpole observed of William Kent, one of the innovators in his nation's landscape design tradition, "He leaped the fence, and saw that all nature was a garden."[26] Walpole referred to the fence around the traditional garden. The garden wall constrained and contained previous landscape designs as well as ideas about landscapes. The English landscape gardeners invented not only a new approach for design—one based on natural processes and patterns—but also a new way of seeing landscapes.

The Harvard landscape ecologist Richard Forman suggests that a landscape is what is seen looking out an airplane window, in an aerial photograph, or from a high point of land. "How sharp is the boundary of a landscape?" Forman asked.[27] In response, he observes that in "mountainous regions where landscape mosaics are usually relatively small, contrasts are great due to sharp differences."[28] Meanwhile, where "natural geomorphic and disturbance processes predominate in flatter terrain, boundaries of landscapes also tend to be rather sharp."[29] But, Forman notes, "where human activities and land uses are more independent of the distribution of natural resources, boundaries of landscapes tend to be less distinct."[30]

The boundaries of landscapes are constrained only by our imaginations, and many forces conspire to constrain those imaginations. After all, our imaginations may be dangerous. New visions force us to think about other possibilities, about other options. Landscapes, like imaginations, stretch boundaries.

If landscapes are bounded by what we can see, then we need to peek around the corners of the edges of what is seen. What will we see then? What's possible, or what are our limits?

Of course, the most interesting landscapes are often those where boundaries overlap. Such places collect stuff in new combinations. Landscapes overlap to form never-ending ecotones of places upon places, nature upon cultures, cultures upon nature. We gaze out our windows and are amazed by what we see and ponder the possibilities outside our vision.

INTERACTION, INTEGRATION, AND INSTITUTION

Landscape is more process than place. The very essence of landscape involves interaction and integration. The landscape architect–geographer Ervin Zube of the University of Arizona and his colleagues identified seven defining characteristics of landscapes, illustrating how fundamental interaction and integration are:

(1) Landscapes surround. They permit movement and exploration of the situation and force the observer to become a participant.

(2) Landscapes are multimodal. They provide information that is received through multiple senses and that is processed simultaneously.

(3) Landscapes provide peripheral as well as central information. Information is received from behind the participant as well as in front, from outside the focus of attention as well as within.

(4) Landscapes provide more information than can be used. They can simultaneously provide redundant, inadequate, ambiguous, conflicting, and contradictory information.

(5) Landscape perception always involves action. Landscapes cannot be passively observed; they provide opportunities for action, control, and manipulation.

(6) Landscapes call forth actions. They provide symbolic meanings and motivational messages that can call forth purposeful actions.

(7) Landscapes always have ambiance. They are almost always encountered as part of a social activity, they have a definite aesthetic quality and they have a systemic quality (various components and events are related).[31]

Landscapes are dynamic entities defined by their interacting parts and their integrative whole. The parts of the landscape are both cultural and natural; the whole forms a visual synthesis. The visualness of landscapes is important because it represents the most fundamental way that people interact with their surroundings. People are "predominantly" visual animals, Tuan asserted, hastening to add the importance of the other senses in perceiving the environment, too.[32] Those other senses are arguably more important at the habitat and community scales, whereas interactions with landscapes are dominated by how we see them.

Looking west from Denver, we see the Front Range, which dramatically marks the terminus of the Great Plains. The landscapes of the Rocky Mountains differ from those in the flatlands to the east, but the landscapes interact. You can see the Front Range from the plains, and there are views from the mountains back to the wide expanses below. The frequent climate changes in Denver, Boulder, Fort Collins, and Colorado Springs result from this physiographic juxtaposition.

The mountains supply the source of water for the urban expanses along their base. The Denver Water Board controls large expanses in the mountains. Denver citizens recreate at several of these areas, such as Winter Park. The water board collects, stores, and then diverts water from the higher ground, as it attracts skiers and summer picnickers to the slopes above the flatlands. People move up the slopes to recreate, with water flowing downhill to sustain homes, businesses, and ranches.

THE MIX OF LIFE

The same basic landscape elements—weather, rocks, terrain, water, soils, plants, animals, people, buildings, and time—come together in endless landscape combinations. A volcano causes a small mountain to be formed with a different geologic structure and terrain than the basins around it. The climate, soils, and vegetation differ, too—the weather daily, the plants by season. One can simultaneously see both places—the volcano top and the basins—and their variability. Add a river and its floodplain, and, again, different soils and vegetation and, probably, animals appear as well. People plant crops along the river, let animals graze in the expansive basins, and grow grapes on the slopes. The grapes differ with elevation and result in distinctive wines. Grapes produce wine, but with many possible variations. Of course, the same grape will result in a different wine from year to year.

Landscapes can be adapted by people to maximize or minimize diversity. Our actions can increase or decrease the productivity and beauty of the landscape. People make these changes differently through time, so in each landscape there are traces of the past, exhibiting temporal diversity. Landscapes also house diverse possibilities for the future. Such potential has sometimes been put in place by law or design, resulting in a latent landscape, a landscape in wait. New settlements may exist on paper, but have not yet been realized on the ground.

We humans add diversity to landscapes by our very presence, and we are present almost everywhere. The Sonoran Desert of the American Southwest and Mexico's northwest contains a variety of challenges for habitation. During the summers, most animals spend the daytime underground and emerge at night. Humans adapt to the environmental challenges differently.

As early as 300 B.C., the Hohokam began diverting the waters of the Salt and Gila Rivers. Their irrigated fields depended on an elaborate system of canals and ditches. The Hohokam created a landscape of agricultural villages spread across vast desert valleys. Around A.D. 1450, they abandoned their villages, canals, fields, and temple mounds for unknown, but much speculated on, reasons.

In the nineteenth century, American settlers discovered the Hohokam canal system, rebuilt it, and created a new agricultural landscape. These settlers plotted small towns from midwestern models within Jefferson's grid. Cotton and citrus plantations resulted in rectangular landscapes of white spots alternating with the shiny deep green of citrus foliage and the powerful fragrance of orange blossoms. Subsequent settlers of Japanese and Dutch ancestry expanded the horticultural operations, adding flowers to their square fields. As the small towns grew into small cities, dairy operations expanded. This mixture of orchard and field, town and dairy cows, transformed rapidly after the Second World War with the spread of air conditioning and refrigeration technology. Between 1975 and 1995 alone, some 40 percent of the agriculture in the Phoenix metropolitan area was converted to a new suburban landscape, which continues to diversify and grow denser.

Other environments pose similar challenges for human settlement, and the resulting landscapes reflect the human capacity to mold nature to fit human needs. The winters of Minnesota provide challenges as extreme as the Arizona summers. Minneapolis and Saint Paul were established at the end point of navigation on the Mississippi River. With the coming of the railroad, a transportation nexus resulted. Surrounded by fertile lands, landscapes of industry, commerce, and agriculture were created in the river valleys. Businesses in downtown Minneapolis are connected by a system of second-story walkways to protect businesspeople and shoppers from the elements. Large malls fulfill similar functions around the periphery. In fact, the first enclosed shopping mall was built in Edina, a suburb of Minneapolis. Although the landscapes outside the malls of Minneapolis and Phoenix differ, the experience inside can be quite similar and equally discounted from nature.

RECONSTRUCTING NATURE

Landscapes adapt to technological change. Clever engineers convert wetlands into farm fields. After a while, a highway is built, connecting the area to faraway markets. A town is constructed. Then the soils become too salty; fertilizers compensate for a while; but then some farmlands need to be abandoned, and wetlands reappear. As Schama noted, "Landscapes are culture before they are nature; constructs of the imagination projected onto wood and water and rock."[33] Landscapes are nature as adapted by culture. Nature translates many processes. Culture may be viewed as human nature as modified by technology. Culture transforms a multitude of patterns.

Design and planning are instruments of culture that can be used to modify landscapes. Ecological planning has been defined by Ian McHarg as the approach "whereby a region [or landscape] is understood as a biophysical and social process comprehensible through the operation of laws and time. This can be reinterpreted as having explicit opportunities and constraints for any particular human use."[34] McHarg described ecological design as building on planning and introducing the subject of form: "There should be an intrinsically suitable location, processes with appropriate materials, and forms. Design requires an informed designer with a visual imagination, as well as graphic and creative skills. It selects for creative fitting revealed in intrinsic and expressive form."[35]

Health should be a central consideration in landscape design and planning, as several individuals have noted.[36] Landscape architect Bruce Ferguson of the University of Georgia asserts that the concept of homeostasis can be applied to the health of landscapes: "Disease is a departure of a homeostatic system from its 'home state.'"[37] Furthermore, Ferguson suggests using, like human medicine, the Hippocratic injunction, "Above all, do no harm," for landscape interventions.

What is the current status of landscape ecological design and planning? Overall, environmental science has advanced, but the environmental design arts (architecture, landscape architecture, planning, and other associated design fields) are underachieving and are not living up to their potential. Three main factors contribute to a potentially positive future, and three major drawbacks present obstacles. The positive trends in science and design include

- the widespread interest in sustainability,
- the rise of the science of landscape ecology, and
- the significant contributions made by environmental artists and writers.

These are the drawbacks:

- "Landscape" is confused with "landscaping" by the general public in North America.
- Landscape architects, the primary innovators in the field, tend to be somewhat shy practitioners who, until relatively recently, published little and were not deeply engaged in scholarly research. Thus, many landscape architects have tended to follow the whims of fashion rather than the rigors imposed by science as it interacts with art.
- Too few designers or planners have serious ecology in their palette, because sustainable design has not been viewed as economically feasible to pursue by private firms or public agencies.

Sustainability and sustainable development have become popular topics in North America, as they have elsewhere in the world. Most planners and policy makers, and certainly a large segment of the public, believe that we should indeed learn to live within our means, that we should use resources more wisely, and that we should leave the Earth in good shape for our children. There is also widespread agreement that we need to seek optimum balances among the often competing concerns for environment, economics, and equity.

But how do we achieve such a balance?

Landscape-level planning and design are imperative. Beatley and Manning, in fact, assert that "McHargian-style" landscape ecological analysis has "become a commonplace methodological step in undertaking almost any form of local planning."[38] Understanding the landscape is thus an essential first step toward sustainability.

Landscape ecology enhances the science of such understanding. The ecology of landscapes involves the study of the structure, function, and change in a heterogeneous land area composed of interacting ecosystems. Landscape ecologists study the reciprocal effects of patterns on processes, across varied terrains, at a variety of temporal and spatial scales. Among several others, Richard Forman has been central to importing this essentially European concept to North America.[39] Landscape ecology has helped North American ecologists recognize the obvious—that is, people are living beings and thus engaged in ecological interactions with their environments.

Increasingly, landscape ecology is influencing community and regional planning, land evaluation systems, environmental impact assessment, wetlands and habitat protection, geographic information systems, soil conservation, forestry, and greenway development. Designers also turn to landscape ecology for principles to guide their more site-specific projects. Forman and his colleagues note, "If society decides, for example, to add a road, a nature reserve, or a housing tract, . . . [landscape ecological] principles will help accomplish the goal by maximizing ecological integrity, and minimizing land degradation."[40]

Art—both the visual arts and literature—contributes to the influence of landscape. Earth, or environmental, art in particular has been influenced by European trends, especially the work of artists Robert Smithson and Nancy Holt. For example, these words exemplify Smithson's philosophy:

One's mind and the earth are in a constant state of erosion, mental rivers wear abstract banks, brain waves undermine cliffs of thought, ideas decompose into stones of unknowing.[41]

Environmental literature has emerged as a more "homegrown" American phenomenon. From the Transcendentalists on, writers remind us of the centrality of landscape in North American culture. Here, I mean all of North America—Canada, Mexico, the United States, and the various Indian nations. Landscape plays a role in American culture similar to the city in Europe.

Henry David Thoreau wrote:

> The earth was the most glorious instrument,
> and I was audience to its strains.

The poets lay this challenge before us: Listen to the earth, understand the genius of the place, before altering the landscape. Landscape architecture and landscape planning are thus poised to be among the most important disciplines of the twenty-first century, but challenges remain.

The first challenge in North America is the bastardization of "landscape" into "landscaping." Many Americans view landscape architecture as little more than exterior decoration. Frequently, plants are added cosmetically to hide ugly buildings, roadways, or other eyesores.

American landscape architects are at least partly responsible for this problem. The discipline commenced gloriously with Frederick Law Olmsted, who then bequeathed it to his son (Frederick Jr.) and his nephew (John C.), as well as Charles Eliot and John Nolen. The senior Olmsted designed Central Park in New York City with the English-born architect Calvert Vaux in 1857. The immediate popular success of Central Park created a demand for a new profession with a broad range of projects. City and national parks, new communities, college campuses, and regional greenway systems formed the landscape architecture repertoire. A new vision for a greener urban America was established. Beginning in the latter part of the nineteenth century, landscape architecture was taught at state land-grant, agricultural colleges, then at Harvard University in 1900, and since at many universities in North America and around the world.

For much of the middle of the twentieth century, however, landscape architects retreated behind the garden wall. Landscape architects had been instrumental in establishing the city planning profession in North America, but a schism developed between the designers and the planners. The designers increasingly focused on the estate gardens of the affluent, drifting away from the pressing social and environmental issues of the time.

Landscape architecture enjoyed an equally glorious renaissance with the environmental movement of the 1960s and 1970s. Led by Ian McHarg, but involving others such as Phil Lewis, Carl Steinitz, Lawrence Halprin, Rich Haag, Carol Franklin, Leslie Sauer, Anne Spirn, John Lyle,

Laurie Olin, and Grant Jones, landscape architects became reengaged in a
wide variety of environmental and social projects—waterfronts were re-
designed, roads rerouted, wetlands protected, new communities designed,
and parks and greenways laid out.

But again the profession retreated. This time, many landscape architects
were consumed by the corporate greed of the 1980s. Several became involved
in large-scale, frequently destructive, development projects. Others became
engaged in superficial, glitzy "art" projects that were pale versions of the earlier, more profound work of the likes of Smithson, Holt, and others. Yet,
there is hope. Certainly, the three influences noted earlier—sustainability,
landscape ecology, and earth art—present hope. So, too, does the rise of a
stronger theoretical base in landscape architecture.[42] Nothing is as practical as a good theory, or so the saying goes. Ian McHarg's call to arms, "Design with nature," provides a wonderfully practical theory.

LANDSCAPE MOSAICS

Moving from a landscape of sunlight to a landscape of rain prompts numerous observations. You cannot see as far in the rain. During a storm, the
rain obstructs the view. In between precipitation events, denser vegetation
encloses space. Overhead, a canopy of leaves limits the line of sight upward,
where often a layer of clouds reduces or even eliminates the blue in the sky.

In 2001, I moved from Tempe, Arizona, to Austin, Texas. From a
landscape of wild cacti and cultivated citrus, I entered a landscape where
oaks form green umbrellas around stone houses. In central Texas, creeks
and rivers actually flow with water, which was seldom the case in the desert
landscape of Arizona. As I watch the purl of a central Texas stream, I ponder past landscapes and how they inform my reading of this new one. I
stand on the Balcones Fault, where the Cretaceous limestone of the Hill
Country to the west begins to give way to the lowland Black Prairie to the
east. The karst topography efficiently collects water in the vast Edwards
Aquifer below my feet.

From my past experiences, I look for ecological disturbances in the
landscape, heeding the insight of Aldo Leopold who warned, "One of the
penalties of an ecological education is that one lives alone in a world of
wounds."[43] Landscape ecologists developed a vocabulary to assess the ecology of landscapes.[44] This vocabulary seeks to make wounds visible by accounting for space and time. Landscape ecologists describe places in terms

of patches, edges and boundaries, and corridors and connectivity. Forman uses "land mosaics" to explain how these elements fit together and interrelate in specific places.[45]

Landscape mosaics have diverse structures and functions, and they adapt to change in various ways. Diversity results from both natural and cultural forces. Adaptation of landscapes is largely a cultural undertaking. We adapt landscapes through planning and design, but also through farming, mining, engineering, recreation, and legislation. Perhaps two of the strongest cultural architects of landscape are writing and the visual arts. Poets and prose writers help us envision landscape interactions that would be difficult to unravel by looking alone.

For example, Theodore Roethke wrote:

> It was beginning winter,
> An in-between time,
> The landscape still partly brown;
> The bones of weeds kept swinging in the wind,
> Above the blue snow.[46]

In looking at landscapes, Wallace Stegner suggested we expand our color spectrum and our horizons: "You have to get over the color green; you have to quit associating beauty with gardens and lawns; you have to get used to an inhuman scale."[47] Stegner imaged a future for the western United States that was "both prosperous and environmentally healthy, with a civilization to match its scenery."[48] Images of landscapes by painters and photographers help capture the ephemeral complexity that is a place. The works of Georgia O'Keefe and Ansel Adams in particular remind us of the grandeur of a specific region—the American West. But other landscapes have their poets and painters, too, and we should learn from their insights about how to create civilizations worthy of the natural landscapes we inhabit.

THE ECOLOGICAL REGION

One's sense of the scale of the place expands as one learns the region. The young hear further stories and go for explorations which are also subsistence forays—firewood gathering, fishing, to fairs or to the market. The outlines of the larger region become part of their awareness.

—GARY SNYDER

IN SPITE OF ITS WIDE USAGE, REGION REMAINS A CHALLENGING word to apply. A variety of communities and landscapes with some common characteristics form a region. Governmental agencies and others use the region to delineate multijurisdictional areas, such as those comprised of more than one town, city, county, state, or nation. Environmental scientists identify regions in reference to parts of the surface of Earth, such as drainage basins, physiographic provinces, climatic zones, or faunal areas. Geographers define a region as an uninterrupted area possessing some kind of homogeneity in its core, but lacking clearly defined limits.[1] Even the standard dictionary definition is ambiguous—"any more or less extensive, contiguous part of a surface of space." Still, the idea of regions, especially bioregions or ecoregions, presents an important concept. The words bioregions and ecoregions have been used interchangeably, although the latter clearly implies interacting biological and physical systems. The biogeographer Robert Bailey of the U.S. Forest Service explains an ecoregion as "[a]ny large portion of the Earth's surface over which the ecosystems have characteristics in common."[2]

Benton MacKaye defined regional planning as "a comprehensive ordering or visualization of the possible or potential movement, activity or flow (from sources onward) of water, commodities or population, within a defined area or sphere, for the purpose of laying therein the physical basis for the 'good life' or optimum human living."[3]

According to MacKaye, a comprehensive ordering referred to "a visualization of nature's permanent comprehensive 'ordering' as distinguished from the interim makeshift orderings of man." MacKaye quoted Plato to emphasize this thought—"To command nature we must first obey her."[4] MacKaye found the purpose of the "good life" or optimum human living incorporated in what the U.S. Congress has called the "general welfare," and what Thomas Jefferson (and Aristotle) called the "pursuit of happiness." MacKaye concluded that regional planning is ecology.

MacKaye provided the following definition:

> *Human ecology*; its concern is the relation of the human organism to its environment. The region is the unit of environment. Planning is the charting of activity therein affecting the good of the human organism; its object is the application or putting into practice of the optimum relation between the human and the region. Regional planning in short is applied human ecology.[5]

This chapter begins with a discussion of region from an ecological perspective. Then the topics of language, culture, and technology as well as function, structure, and change from a regional perspective are addressed. Edges, boundaries, and ecotones are viewed as fields for interaction and integration and as institutions. Regions possess diverse manifestations, which make them a challenging and interesting topic. Planning acts as a means for human adaptation to regional processes.

THE IDEA OF REGION

One cannot address the concept of region, especially that of the *ecological region*, without mentioning Patrick Geddes and Lewis Mumford. Mark Luccarelli, a senior lecturer in American studies at the University of Oslo in Norway, and Robert Wojtowicz, a professor of art history at Old Dominion University in Virginia, have probed the intellectual sources for Mumford's ideas.[6] Wojtowicz illustrates the especially strong influence of Geddes, the Scottish biologist, sociologist, and town planner. Luccarelli links Mumford to the "green" American literary and intellectual tradition of Ralph Waldo Emerson, Henry David Thoreau, and Walt Whitman (which continues with the likes of Terry Tempest Williams and Russell Scott Sanders).[7]

Mumford merged his American Emerson et alia literary base, with the sociopolitical heritage of Frederick Law Olmsted and Thomas Jefferson, to a European perspective that, via Geddes, was connected to the French geographer Frédéric Le Play and the Russian Petr Kropotkin. Geddes developed a method of "regional surveys," the purpose of which was to identify a region's positive and negative attributes.

> Every region, he [Geddes] says, has its heritage of good and its burden of evil. Every inhabitant should strive to know what his [her] region contains, not only its wealth of natural resources, scenic beauty, and heritage of culture but the opposite picture as well: the evils of ugliness, poverty, crime, and injustice. The citizen must first study all of these things with the utmost realism, and then seek to preserve the good and abate the evil with the utmost idealism.[8]

Geddes posited that the regional survey was essential to understand the human settlement of places. According to Geddes:

> The whole topography of the town and its extensions must be taken into account, and this more fully than in the past, by the utilization not only of maps and plans of the usual kind, but of contour maps, and, if possible, even relief models. Of soil and geology, climate, rainfall, winds, etc., maps are also easily obtained, or compiled from existing sources.[9]

The basic concept put forth by Geddes and seized upon by Mumford (and later by McHarg) contends that a region represents an entity that can be understood by an examination of its parts. The components include physical, biological, social, and cultural phenomena, Leopold's "land pyramid." The structural and functional organization of these components varies from place to place, from region to region. McHarg suggested that such examinations, or chorographies as geographers call them, should be undertaken through the systematic, chronological collection of information organized like a "layer cake," as mentioned earlier. In this way, the older and more fixed components of the environment, such as rocks, can be used to understand the development of more recent phenomena, such as soils. The interaction of these phenomena over time establishes the natural character of the region.

NAVIGATING LANGUAGE AND WATER

People in New Orleans speak differently than Bostonians, as Sicilians speak differently than Venetians. Patterns of speech derive, in part, from features of the region. Within the United States, two "Miami" regions exist, each having starkly different features. The Great Miami River Valley in Ohio is named for the Miami native people, horticulturalists who called themselves the "Twatwa." In 1791, Twatwa warriors under Little Turtle handed the U.S. Army the worst defeat it would ever suffer at Indian hands. The Great Miami Valley falls at the southern limits of the Wisconsin glaciers. The Great Miami runs roughly parallel to the Little Miami. Both drain into the Ohio River. (A third Ohio river, now called the Maumee, was once also named Miami, Miami of the Lake, which flowed north into Lake Erie.) Terminal moraines and small stream and river valleys dominate the landscape. The Adena and Hopewell built mounds mimicking the moraines, the most spectacular in the shape of a serpent. The mound builders also constructed a system of forts along the rivers for defense. Euro-Americans—first French explorers, then English, and later mostly Germans—settled the river valleys, establishing agriculture and constructing canals. Many places and institutions in Ohio are called "Miami," including Miami University in Oxford (a clear aspirational reference to another university town, in a region far away).

The second Miami region covers much of southern Florida. After separating from their traditional homeland in Georgia as part of the Creek people, the Seminole Indians developed a complex culture in the Everglades. Spanish colonists vied with English pirates for control. Early American settlement included black slaves. The Seminoles provided safe refuge for runaway slaves in a landscape dominated by wetlands and coasts. More recent settlers include transplanted New Yorkers—mostly from central and eastern European roots—and Cuban refugees. Many places and institutions in south Florida are called "Miami," including the University of Miami in Coral Gables.

The cultures of many places reflect the natural environment of the region. Much of Europe comes to mind—France, Italy, and Spain, for example. In France or Italy or Spain, one can sit in a village and drink the distinct wine and eat from the distinct cuisine of the region, in a structure of distinct architecture or on a terrace with a distinct garden design of native plants.

Italy has been unified as a nation only since 1861. Before that, it was split up in many small principalities, merchant fiefs, duchies, and religious and city states. This division made it vulnerable to frequent foreign invasions. Each wave of invaders introduced new elements to the culture (while being seduced by the charms of the rich existing cultures). The rugged mountain terrain of the Italian peninsula and nearby islands made the flow of goods and information difficult. As a result, regional dialects, wines, and cuisines evolved. Marcella Hazan observed:

> Take, for example, the cuisines of Venice and Naples, two cultures in whose culinary history seafood has had such a major role. Just as Venetians and Neapolitans cannot speak to each other in their native idiom and be understood, there is not a single dish from the light-handed, understated Venetian repertory that would be recognizable on a Neapolitan table, nor any of Naple's vibrant, ebulliently savory specialties that do not seem exotic in Venice.[10]

Several Italian regions derived great wealth through the mastery of water management technologies, Venice and its region, the Veneto, being the most obvious. In Lombardy, Milan also owes its prominence to water. The city lies roughly halfway between the Ticino (to the west) and the Adda (to the east) Rivers, tributaries of the expansive Po to the south. The Ticino and the Adda feed water from the Alps to the Po, the major transportation corridor across northern Italy even before the times of the Etruscans and Romans.

Milan is connected to the Ticino and the Adda, and hence to the Po and the sea, by an elaborate canal system, called *navigli* because boats can travel on them. The Naviglio Grande, the Naviglio di Bereguardo, and the Naviglio di Pavia are the canals linked to Ticino, while the Naviglio Martesana and Naviglio di Paderno connect with the Adda. These canals were constructed beginning around A.D. 1000 by Milan in fierce, bitter, and sometimes violent, competition with rival city-states and other regions, notably, Lodi and Pavia.

The *navigli* raised Milan to dominance in northern Italy. The Lombardy canal system provided not only an excellent transportation opportunity but also irrigation for farmers and hydraulic energy for manufacturing. "This network lent itself to early industrial development in the towns, in the villages and in the countryside: grain mills, presses for vegetable oil, basins for husking rice, paper and felt mills, presses for working metals, tanneries for leather. In short, all economic activities revolved around the waterways. . . . "[11]

The *navigli* system in Lombardy developed over centuries. Many architects, engineers, and political leaders contributed to its design and construction, including Leonardo da Vinci, who arrived in Milan in 1482 to work for Duke Lodovico Sforza. Leonardo, who maintained a lifelong interest in water flow and water power, helped improve the *navigli*, designing locks and contributing to the theory of hydrology. His ferry still crosses the Adda at Imbersago close to Lecco, a reminder of Leonardo's fascination with water.

Other regions, including the Miami Valley of Ohio and metropolitan Miami, Florida, grew as a result of water management. The Ohio-Erie and Erie-Miami canals opened up central Ohio to trade, manufacturing, and agriculture much as the *navigli* did for Lombardy. Dayton, the principal city of the Great Miami Valley, was prone to flooding and was destroyed by floods in 1913. The region owes its recovery to the Miami Conservancy District, which built a series of earthen dams around the city. The land behind the dams fills during heavy rainfalls. At other times, these rich lands are farmed. Dayton has been spared from the negative consequences of flooding ever since the system of earthen dams was completed.

In Florida, the Miami metropolitan region splayed out as the Everglades were drained. The U.S. Army Corps of Engineers built the complex system of canals and dikes so that the rich lands could be farmed. As water flows fell, seawater entered the aquifer and fertilizer runoff encouraged the growth of algae and invasive species. These negative ecological consequences prompted conservation and restoration efforts in the Everglades.

Regions can be defined by several natural phenomena, from physiographic features to flora and fauna. How human cultures manipulate water through technology arguably is at the root of how we conceive the region. However, regions have been conjured up from many perspectives.

THE PURSUIT OF HAPPINESS

Prior to the sixteenth century, when Europeans began invading the Americas in large numbers, the native people lived in a variety of cultural regions. The Hopi of the Southwest inhabited a clearly different region than the Miami—the Twatwa—in what is now Ohio or the Lenni-Lenape of the Middle Atlantic region. The American explorer John Wesley Powell recognized the way various native peoples settled the West and used that observation for his plan for settling the American West based on its ecology. According to Carl Frederick Kraenzel, a former University of Texas at El Paso sociology professor, Powell's 1878 report to the U.S. Congress about the American West "stressed the need for new land and water use policies, an adapted land-settlement pattern, and an adapted institutional organization and way of living that was intimately suited to the conditions of the arid and semi-arid lands."[12]

The idea of connecting regional structure and function prompted a small group of mostly New York intellectuals, including Benton MacKaye and Lewis Mumford, to organize the Regional Planning Association of America (RPAA) in 1923. The backgrounds of the RPAA group ranged from architecture to accounting. Although their interests diverged, the notion of a "regional city" pulled them together.

At about the same time, beginning in 1922, a small band of writers founded the literary magazine *The Fugitive* at Vanderbilt University, for the southern United States. Allen Tate, Robert Penn Warren, and John Crowe Ransom attempted to rescue the more positive elements of their culture that had been lost in the Civil War and its aftermath. These "agrarians" especially emphasized ties to the land. They influenced other southern scholars, notably, Howard W. Odum, who explored the concept of regionalism as a sociological theory "inherent in the larger application of ecology to human society."[13] According to Odum, "The story of a nation or of a region or of any human society begins with Nature's endowment of resources and their influence upon the culture of the people."[14] The Southern regionalists advocated regional reconstruction, institutional capacity building, and education.

A group similar to the RPAA was founded a few years later (1939) in the San Francisco Bay area. Known as "Telesis" and associated with the University of California–Berkeley, the group sought to preserve and enhance the environmental and cultural qualities of the Bay region. The broad-based Telesis explored the interdependence of the design and planning fields. Members of the group were originally employed at New Deal agencies such as the Farm Security Administration and the National Resources Planning Board and later were active in city and regional planning agencies and design firms. Telesis had considerable influence in the Bay region and contributed to the beauty of its built environment. Group members included leading scholars, artists, architects, lawyers, and conservationists. Of those involved in these groups, especially Benton MacKaye explicitly linked regional planning to ecology.

A regional view can enable cities to cope with change. Imagine living in New York City in the mid–nineteenth century, or Chicago early in the twentieth, or Los Angeles in the middle of the twentieth. What was Rome like in the first century or again in the sixteenth and seventeenth? Or Amsterdam in its Golden Age? These cities with their surrounding lands became exciting, creative places to live in the midst of periods of dramatic population growth. These were times when science, art, and commerce advanced, the course of history altered. Each of these cities prospered through regionalism. New York emerged with the construction of the Erie Canal and through the control of the Hudson River drainage basin for drinking water. Similarly, Rome and Los Angeles thrived through the importation of water from distant sources. Conversely, water needed to be removed from swampy Amsterdam and Chicago in order for urban areas to be constructed. Chicago and Amsterdam also benefited from regional connections to agricultural hinterlands.

Such regional cities also experienced considerable social and environmental disruption. Consider the polluted Thames and the deadly thick fogs of London, the great fire of Chicago, or the plagues of tuberculosis and cholera that killed scores in Paris and other great cities. Epidemics, war, and pulmonary disease occurred frequently in the rapidly growing cities of the past. In many cases, important cultural innovations resulted from such catastrophes—for example, building codes to avert overcrowding and unsafe construction, as well as sanitary sewer systems that acknowledged the relationship between disease and water quality. New York City launched the urban park movement; Chicago initiated the large-scale, civic improvement movement during periods of considerable change.

None of these great cities stood alone; each depended on a larger region for water, food, and other vital supplies. These regional cities prospered when that connection was reinforced. They floundered during times when those essential ties weakened.

WATERSHEDS

We often undertake regional planning, such as that advocated by MacKaye and his RPAA colleagues, with the presumption that an inherent understanding exists of the meaning of the word region. The interpretation of this term varies. Regions may have political, biophysical, sociocultural, and/or economic boundaries depending on who is defining them; as a result, maps representing such boundaries differ among various academic disciplines and government agencies. Political-regulatory regions are the quickest and easiest to identify. Most maps designate governmental jurisdictions. Political regions are simply civil divisions such as state, county, and township boundaries in the United States. Other nations contain similar civil divisions, but jurisdictional names vary from country to country. In Italy and Spain, regions form a level of government with some similarities to American states and French provinces. Although civil divisions bound a number of basic regulatory functions (zoning, subdivision ordinances, and building codes are U.S. examples), impingement or overlap of other regulatory agencies may be present and need to be considered in regional planning.

Some metropolitan regions organize effective political bodies for planning transportation, water, and/or open space systems. The Portland, Oregon, Metro is a good example of an agency that guides regional growth through the coordination of land use and transportation plans. Harkening back to the RPAA's advocacy of regional cities, Peter Calthorpe and William Fulton have renewed the position that metropolitan regions need to "be viewed as a cohesive unit—economically, ecologically, and socially—made up of coherent neighborhoods and communities. . . ."[15] As an elected regional government entity, Metro provides such a platform for the Portland metropolitan region of three counties, twenty-four cities, and 1.3 million people. Metro's ability to guide growth derives from Oregon's strong statewide planning law that requires comprehensive plans with housing and land-use goals as well as urban growth boundaries.

Planners and natural resource managers frequently employ biophysical regions. For example, since the 1930s the U.S. Department of Agriculture has used watersheds for conservation and flood-control planning. Likewise, the U.S. Environmental Protection Agency promotes watersheds for regional planning and maintains a "Surf Your Watershed" Web site. This type of biophysical region—the watershed—is popular with state and provincial natural resource managers in many parts of the world.

Biophysical regions may be described as the pattern of interacting biological and physical phenomena present in a given area, such as a watershed. Purely physical and more complex ecological regions have both been mapped.[16] For example, watersheds are mapped by following drainage patterns, which are relatively easy to trace on a topographic map. Ecological regions are delineated through the mapping of physical information, such as elevation, slope aspect, and climate, plus the distribution of plant and animal species. Bailey contends that climate plays a primary role in defining ecoregions: "Climate, as a source of energy and water, acts as the primary control for ecosystems distribution. As climate changes, so do ecosystems. . . ."[17] As a result, weather patterns play an important role in ecosystem mapping as well as natural resource management. For example, watersheds can be used for flood-control management as well as water-quality planning. For both purposes, charting the amount of precipitation falling in a watershed, where it falls, and how it flows assists in the understanding of flooding patterns and water pollution levels.

Sociocultural regions represent an elusive type to delineate and to map. Unlike many phenomena that constitute biophysical regions, people with widely varying social characteristics can occupy a single settlement space. Groups of people can coexist relatively independently, but some level of interdependence is more common. Both independence and interdependence can be useful in defining a sociocultural region. Human movement in response to seasons means also that different populations may occupy the same space at different times of the year. For example, an Idaho rancher will move livestock out of the high country in the autumn to lower elevations with warmer temperatures. In winter, the same Idaho mountains attract skiers from settlements located at lower elevations.

Wilbur Zelinsky, a Pennsylvania State University geographer, promoted a wider use of vernacular regions to describe social and cultural components of regions.[18] Basically, a vernacular, or a commonly known, region represents the spatial perception of indigenous people. Since vernacular regions are commonly known and evolved locally through time, they can be viewed as popular regions. Zelinsky advises that regional, ethnic, and historical questions may be answered by exploring vernacular regions. While popular regions are well known in Europe (again, those in Italy, France, and Spain provide good examples), popular regions are not as widely recognized in North America. A few American writers have suggested popular regions, such as Ernest Callenbach's "ecotopia"[19] from the San Francisco Bay area north to Alaska and Joel Garreau's "nine nations of North America."[20]

Functionally, economic regions overlap sociocultural regions. Often economic processes dominate our view of social processes in metropolitan regions. For example, metropolitan regions may be defined by such factors as daily trips to work, the circulation of newspapers, housing markets, and/or sports teams. Regions may be branded because of their economic health, such as the Rust Belt in industrial decline in the northeastern United States and the robust Sun Belt in the South and the West.

Agricultural regions emerge as a common delineation of this type, and are often taken as a synthesis of all regional types. The basic resources of agriculture encompass the biophysical factors of soil, water, and plants and the sociocultural factor of people, with climate providing a linkage, a measure of coincidence for the production of food and fiber. Frequently, labels from agriculture substitute as synonyms for more incorporative regional types: for example, Cotton Belt for the southeastern United States and Corn Belt for the Midwest, or, even more specific, the Napa Valley of California and the Kentucky Bluegrass.

Photographers and poets often appreciate and explore regions at a finer grain than the rest of us. They use images and language that enable us to see our surroundings in greater depth. In photography, light varies with latitude and longitude. Light meters help the photographer adjust the opening of the lens to the place and to the time of the day. A picture taken in early morning in Arizona will differ from one taken at the same time in Holland. Photographers can manipulate those differences to reveal more about the desert Southwest and the lowlands of Holland.

Likewise, poets have long recognized the importance of regionalism. T. S. Eliot, for example, in his attempt to define "culture," found region to be a particularly useful idea by which to examine unity and diversity: "we have not given enough attention to the ecology of culture," a "regional problem" that can best be addressed by giving "our attention to the question of unity and diversity within the limited areas that we know best" though the "regional problem has to be seen in [a] larger context."[21] The Kentucky poet, Wendell Berry, defines region in the following way:

> The regionalism that I adhere to could be defined simply as local life aware of itself. It would tend to substitute for the myths and stereotypes of a region a particular knowledge of the life of the place one lives in and intends to live in.[22]

Similarly, Gary Snyder, a poet who strongly identifies with the biomes of northern California, especially the Sierra forests, has long urged a return to regionalism for at least a partial cure of the ills that beset humankind: "people have to learn a sense of region, and what is possible within a region ... we are extremely deficient in regional knowledge ... it takes a long time to get to know how to live in a region gently and easily and with a maximal annual efficiency."[23]

William Carlos Williams was perhaps the first American poet-bioregionalist, or at least Lawrence Buell suggests that is the case.[24] Buell links Williams's New Jersey–based bioregionalism to Walt Whitman before him and to Berry, Snyder, and other contemporary poets. Buell quotes Snyder mixing images from traditional ecology with the new: "place will have been grasslands, then conifers, then beech and elm. . . . And then it will be cultivated, paved, sprayed, dammed, graded, built up."[25]

Gary Snyder advocates bioregions as a context for reinhabiting the earth.[26] Such regions are defined through their flora and fauna. As the Santa Fe landscape architect Clair Reiniger explains, bioregions are "life territories, from the Greek *bio* for 'life' and Latin *regio* for 'territory.'"[27]

The writer Kirkpatrick Sale elaborates bioregions further as "part of the earth's surface whose rough boundaries are determined by natural characteristics rather than human dictates, distinguishable from other areas by particular attributes of flora, fauna, water, climate, soils, landforms, and by human settlements and cultures those attributes have given rise to."[28] Extending bioregions to explicitly consider interactions, including human exchanges, returns us once again to the ecoregion concept. Bioregions then are defined by their life-forms, ecoregions by system interactions.

A region forges a complex entity that involves many phenomena and processes. To be useful, information about these phenomena and processes must be ordered. This involves establishing cores and boundaries, hierarchical classifications, and interrelationships.

On a map, regional boundary lines—be they watersheds, jurisdictions, or newspaper circulation—can be carefully rendered. Such boundaries can tend to appear more real than the zones they symbolize and to divert attention from actual connections and separations. Boundaries are most often determined for planning purposes through the political process. Goals can be established for planning in a variety of ways, and these goals result in irregular boundaries, a well-recognized problem of regional (and other levels of) planning. A significant difficulty in preparing, and especially in effecting, regional plans is that most "real" units rarely coincide with governmental jurisdictions. The boundaries of metropolitan New York, Los Angeles, London, Tokyo, and Paris enclose other municipalities and overlap with additional authorities. River basins seldom occur entirely within a single state or province, and many of them (such as the Rhine, the Rio Grande, the Yukon, and the Congo) cross international borders.

Although challenging jurisdictionally, river basins (or watersheds as they are frequently called) are often advocated as an ideal unit for regional planning. For example, one of Howard W. Odum's well-known ecologist sons, Eugene, promotes the use of river basins because they encompass a variety of ecosystems and landscapes. Furthermore, the National Research Council of the National Academy of Sciences notes:

Managing water resources at the watershed scale, while difficult, offers the
potential of balancing the many, sometimes competing, demands we place on
water resources. The watershed approach acknowledges linkages between
uplands and down-stream areas, and between surface and ground water, and
reduces the chances that attempts to solve problems in one realm will cause
problems in others. Watershed management is an integrative way of thinking about all the various human activities that occur on a given area of land
(the watershed) that have effects on, or [are] affected by, water.[29]

Watersheds indicate the direction of drainage. Water purls this way or that.
Forces, geologic or vegetational, influence that direction. People confront
similar watersheds with their lives. Do they live here or there? In the United States, the South or the North, the Northwest or the Southwest pose
different choices, different ways of life. But, then such choices are influenced by deep forces. Does a Jersey Girl ever leave the Garden State? How
many generations does it take for a community of people to leave the flow
of their native drainage basin, be it the Po or the Vistula or the Raritan?

INSTITUTIONAL MEMORIES

Region provides both a discriminatory device and an integrative concept.
Factionalism presents a challenge for contemporary human relations, as it
always has. A realistic conception of region can be an integrative factor, can
help leaders resolve conflicts. Identity, likewise, has always been a human
problem, but especially so in the mass societies of the modern world, so
that a popular or even a mythical formulation of region can be a factor in
group discrimination, thus helping to distinguish and to establish identity.[30] "I am a citizen of the United States" exemplifies a regional proclamation to separate the speaker from others in the world, but also to integrate
the speaker with other citizens of that country, to establish identity
through both separation and integration. On another level, the claim "I am
a Yankee Doodle Dandy" or "Don't Mess with Texas" accomplishes the
same purpose in the same way, though even more "regionally" defined.
Such pronouncements provoke distinction in one direction and provide
identity in the other.[31]

  Human ecology—as a study of the relationships between parts and
wholes—may present a key to the integration of regional types, structure,

and complexity. A region can be viewed as a frame for multidisciplinary research to work toward the synthesis needed to think and to plan ecologically. Human ecology addresses how humans interact with each other and with all components of their environments. Regional interaction then can be approached as both a basic concept and an explanatory device. As Gerald Young explains human interactions:

> In human ecology, the way people interact with each other and with the environment is definitive of a number of basic relationships. Interaction provides a measure of belonging [to a region]; it affects identity versus alienation, including alienation from the environment. The system of obligation, responsibility and liability is defined through interaction. The process has become definitive of the public interest as opposed to private interests that prosper in the spirit of independence.[32]

Historical interactions help explain regional identity. The past illustrates how Italy and Spain became comprised of units of government called regions. Take, for example, the Lombardy region of Italy, named for the Lombards, the invaders of Rome, who stayed put in the river valleys of northern Italy. Lombardia, as it is called in Italian, is a tapestry of past allegiances and controls that contribute to the present-day composition of the region. Adjacent towns once were part of the Republic of Venice or the Duchy of Milan or the Vatican, sometimes reversing and re-reversing jurisdiction. On the larger stage, various parts of the region were controlled by France, Spain, and the Austrians. As rule was imposed from outside and became fragmented from within, the region emerged as an economic powerhouse. Lombardia, in general, and its capital, Milan, has become an innovator in commerce and industry.

The Spanish region, Castilla y León, provides an example with a split identity due to its history. After the departure of the Moors, the region Castilla y León has remained a solid part of Spain but not a unified region. The ancient Roman city León was the capital of a kingdom during the Middle Ages. León played a significant role in the conquest of the Christians over Islam in the Iberian peninsula. The current capital city of the region, Valladolid, is much less well known than León, whose citizens do not enjoy playing second fiddle politically to their more industrial neighbor. There are calls for León to separate from Castilla. The regional differences between the Basques and the Catalonians within Spain are more well known, but even within the bedrock region of Castilla y León, fault lines exist.

In spite of the rifts among regions in Spain and in Italy, regions exist as official institutions. Regions interact internally and with other regions. They form integrating devices, forging historical circumstances into a contemporary identity.

Regions institutionalize memory, formally and informally. In his quest to capture Philadelphia, the English General William Howe outflanked George Washington's troops in the Brandywine Valley. The valley forms the western portion of the Philadelphia region, providing a home for many of its elite as well as those of Wilmington to the south. The bucolic rusticity of the valley has been captured by the various Wyeths, whose works are displayed in an institution devoted to their art.

Several voluntary associations attempt to maintain the environmental quality of the Brandywine Valley. These groups cooperate with, and challenge, governmental agencies. The Brandywine battlefield reminds visitors and residents of the regional role in the birth of the nation. Longwood Gardens, created by Pierre S. du Pont and his family in the Pennsylvania portion of the Brandywine, provides a link to a French past that is as checkered as the layout of plants. Institutions maintain memories of the past as well as create new myths and legends for the future.

BLENDING PLACES

Tuscany and Sicily, Vermont and New Mexico, or Quebec and British Columbia—the very names of these regions, these jurisdictional entities, illustrate differences. The Tuscans trace their heritage to the Etruscans, Sicilians to the Phoenicians. Vermont is in New England; New Mexico was once part of New Spain. Quebec celebrates its Frenchness; British Columbia, well, its orientation is obvious, albeit with a recent Chinese overlay.

Regions exhibit diversity within larger nations through dialects. Regions have clear cores but blurry edges. Language diversity may be more apparent at the edge than in the core. Diversity in language and dialects can be especially apparent in the ecotones between regions. The Mexico–U.S. border possesses such ecotones where, on either side of the national border, one hears both *cerveza* and beer being ordered, followed by either a thanks or a *gracias*. Similarly, in the islands of the Wadden Sea off the coast of the Netherlands, *brood* becomes bread while *kas* is cheese as the Dutch language morphs into English. Whole new combinations can be created, too, like Spanglish, again along the U.S.–Mexico border.

Kevin Lynch advanced diversity as one of the crucial elements of regional metropolitan form. He characterized regional diversity as "a wide
range of variation of facilities and activities, these varieties being rather finely mixed in space."[33] A region needs its open fields to contrast its crowded
streets. Homogeneous regions exude a brittle dullness that cannot be sustained because, if for no other reason, there is no point to maintain it.

The New York City metropolitan region certainly typifies Lynch's definition. The region covers parts of three states and provides homes for some
20 million people. The landscapes vary from the highlands of New Jersey
to the beaches of Long Island and the city streets of Manhattan. The approximately 1,500 cities, towns, and villages include many leafy suburbs in
Connecticut and New Jersey as well as small towns clinging to an agricultural heritage. The region possesses rich valleys: the Hudson, the smaller
rivers of New Jersey, and the canyons created by Wall Street.

The people who live in the New York metropolitan region can trace
their heritage to every corner of the planet. Languages and cuisines intermingle in this finely mixed space. Some of the richest and some of the
poorest Americans live there. Some of the trendiest dressers walk the city
streets as do individuals whose religion-dictated garb appears medieval. If
America is a melting pot, then the New York region is a lumpy stew. Ethnic diversity has not assimilated into the greater broth. Distinctions remain
and result in a lively mix of people and place. In contrast to Gertrude
Stein's Oakland, with its no there there, in the New York region, there is
here, here.

REGIONAL PLANNING

Artists, writers, designers, and architects can express forms of adaptation.
Their expressions can provide an identity for a region, shaping future adaptations. Antoni Gaudí's dramatic imprint is evident on Barcelona. A Catalan nationalist, Gaudí's work manages to reflect the region's landscape and,
at the same time, create a new expression that influences all subsequent
adaptations. Nature and mysticism merge in the towers of El Templo de la
Sagrada Familia and along the ceramic benches of Park Güell. One cannot
imagine Barcelona or Catalonia without picturing the brilliant regionalism
of Gaudí.

Kevin Lynch also considered adaptability as a crucial element for regional metropolitan form. He described vibrant regions as those with a "low

cost of adaptation to new functions, and the ability to absorb sudden shock."[34] Dull regions tend toward atrophy; clever ones challenge all others.

A common definition of planning is one that outlines as objectives the attainment of balance and equilibrium between competing forces, which can again be defined as a problem of conflict between unit and whole. In this sense, region is a particularly appropriate scale because, as Howard W. Odum describes it, "always, regionalism is a two-way concept. The region, yes, but primarily the region as a composite unit of the whole,"[35] a way of saying that regions, once acknowledged, are reminders of the part-whole problem: "we have to distinguish between that which concerns the area primarily and that which pertains to the area in relations to other areas, or to the place of the area in some total structure."[36]

EARLY-TWENTIETH-CENTURY REGIONAL PLANNING IN THE UNITED STATES AND THE NETHERLANDS

Regionalism has influenced planning in the United States and elsewhere at various times in different ways. The ideas about regionalism developed by Mumford, MacKaye, and others were embraced on a broad scale during Franklin D. Roosevelt's New Deal of the 1930s. The regional planning programs of the New Deal were enacted in response to the human suffering of the Great Depression. These efforts marked the first of two major flourishings of regional planning during the twentieth century. Examples of such programs include the Tennessee Valley Authority, the Columbia Basin Irrigation Project, and the Greenbelt new towns. Other nations embarked on similar projects that involved the harnessing of human and natural resources for social purposes. Throughout Europe, road building, electricity and telephone extension, and water and sewer construction received considerable attention. The Zuiderzee reclamation works in the Netherlands is a notable example of ambitious, large-scale planning. Dutch planners and engineers transformed an inland sea (the Zuiderzee) and flood-prone coastlines into new lands with productive farmlands and planned new communities.

The Tennessee Valley Authority (TVA) stands as one of the more successful examples of regional planning in the United States or internationally. The TVA stresses cooperation between levels of government and the provision of multiple benefits for citizens. The jurisdiction of the TVA is generally limited to the drainage basin of the Tennessee River, but some of its activities extend beyond this. As a result, the TVA provides a model for

Eugene Odum's ideal of the use of river basins as the optimum unit of planning. The Tennessee River drainage basin, an area of almost 41,000 square miles (106,149 square kilometers), covers parts of seven states: Alabama, Georgia, Kentucky, Mississippi, North Carolina, Tennessee, and Virginia.

Before proceeding with a discussion of the TVA, it is appropriate to take note of its first chairman, Arthur E. Morgan, and his influence on this project.[37] Morgan, a humanist engineer, was born in Cincinnati and had served as the chief engineer and organizer of the Miami Conservancy District and later as the president of Antioch College. As noted earlier, the Miami Conservancy District came into being after the disastrous 1913 floods destroyed Dayton. The city's business leaders, including John H. Patterson, Edward Deeds, and Charles Kettering, banded together during the disaster to institute many municipal reforms. These leaders retained Morgan to develop a scheme to protect the city from future flooding. He designed a system of five earthen dams; behind each dam, large open spaces would act as catch basins during times of flooding. The Miami Conservancy District purchased easements on this land, where farming and recreation are permitted but no structures are allowed.[38] Today, this system provides an open space network for Dayton, and flooding has not caused major damage for nearly a century. Morgan brought this practical experience and the philosophy of regionalism with him to the TVA, but perhaps he was a bit too idealistic, because disagreements over principles resulted in his removal from office by President Roosevelt in 1938.

The U.S. Congress established the TVA in 1933 as a part of Roosevelt's New Deal to lift the nation out of the depths of the Great Depression. President Roosevelt asked Congress to create "a corporation clothed with the power of government but possessed of flexibility and initiative of a private enterprise."[39] Under this innovative legislation, a broad plan was proposed for the Tennessee River drainage basin. Congress established the semi-independent authority to promote the economic and social well-being of the people of the entire region. The rich timber and petroleum resources of the region had been ruthlessly exploited, leaving a derelict landscape and an economically depressed population. The people of the region ranked among the poorest in the United States at the height of the Great Depression.

The 1933 act recognized the potential of water as a basic resource that could be used to revitalize the region. The three broad, basic powers granted the TVA were the control of flooding, the development of navigation, and the production of hydroelectric power. As a result, the authority was conceived as having multiple purposes. The multiple-use plan extended beyond the three basic purposes to include reforestation, soil conservation, outdoor recreation, new community building, the retirement of marginal farmland, and the manufacture of fertilizer.

A second regional effort, also a product of New Deal legislation, was the Columbia Basin Irrigation Project, located in east-central Washington State. Like TVA, the project involved the harnessing of water resources for social purposes through comprehensive planning. The general authorization for the project came from the National Industrial Recovery Act of 1933, with specific project authorization from the Rivers and Harbors Act of 1937 and the Columbia Basin Act of 1943. The project, like the TVA, incorporated several purposes: irrigation, power generation, navigation, regulation of stream flow, flood control, and recreation.

Before the project, the Columbia Basin was a sparsely populated desert region. Attempts to homestead the area from the late nineteenth century on had been thwarted because of the lack of water and the lack of appropriate irrigation technology, although lands close to streams were successfully settled. Irrigation became feasible with the construction of the Grand Coulee Dam (another New Deal project begun in 1934). From the 1930s on, much effort was devoted to the planning of the Columbia Basin Project, covering some 1.1 million acres (445,500 hectares).

The planning activities encompassed extensive resource inventories of the Columbia Basin, land classification, suitability analysis, the establishment of optimum farm sizes, and economic and transportation studies. The U.S. Bureau of Reclamation coordinated the planning efforts under the leadership of Secretary of Interior Harold Ickes, a strong supporter of the project. The combined venture of federal, state, regional, and local agencies was called the Columbia Basin Joint Investigations.

The Columbia Basin Joint Investigations began in 1939 and was completed in 1942, generating various reports that were published between 1941 and 1946. Three hundred people, representing forty federal, state, local, and private agencies, participated in the studies, which all together focused on twenty-eight separate problems in sixteen divisions.[40] These endeavors generated a general, comprehensive plan for development and settlement and provided the basis for the Columbia Basin Act of 1943. Following completion of the Grand Coulee Dam in 1941, the Columbia Basin received its first water in 1948, and development continued into the 1980s.

In the early 1990s, further irrigation development ended as a result of environmental concerns. Since then, more emphasis has been placed on other purposes, such as fish and wildlife, recreation, and power generation.

Still, farmers continue to irrigate some 671,000 acres (271,755 hectares) of land. Water for these lands is supplied by the 300 miles (483 kilometers) of main canals, about 2,000 miles (3,218 kilometers) of laterals, and 3,500 miles (5,632 kilometers) of drains and wasteways of the Columbia Basin Project.

A third example of regional planning during the New Deal era was the Greenbelt new towns. The intellectual impetus came from those involved in the RPAA, in this case the architect Clarence Stein and the architect who became a landscape architect Henry Wright. Their influences included the British garden cities of Ebenezer Howard, idealized in America by those involved in the RPAA. They advanced a straightforward idea: A regional approach could alleviate urban squalor. The establishment of new communities, buffered by gardens or green space, formed a key element in this approach.

The New Deal economist, Rexford Guy Tugwell, provided leadership for the Greenbelt new towns. Tugwell taught at Columbia University and had been educated at the University of Pennsylvania. As the undersecretary of the Department of Agriculture, he proposed the Resettlement Administration. This administration was established to develop a comprehensive approach to alleviate the socioeconomic problems of rural regions. In less than two years, from 1935 to 1936, Tugwell's agency planned and constructed three new communities and started a fourth.[41]

The three built new communities were Greenbelt, Maryland; Greenhills, Ohio; and Greendale, Wisconsin. (A fourth, Greenbrook, New Jersey, was planned but never constructed.) Tugwell's ideas for these new communities dovetailed those of the RPAA in his unbiased acceptance of the automobile as an element to be affirmatively considered in the planning process. For example, Lewis Mumford believed cars were essential for the fourth migration, that is, a "backflow" of people into rural regions that were largely bypassed by earlier American migrations.[42] The design of the new communities consisted of low-rise, single- and multi-family housing units, with a traditional design, clustered commercial and public facilities, a surrounding greenbelt, and a road network linking the communities to their metropolitan region. Each town had its own interdisciplinary design team consisting of architects, planners, and civil engineers. John Nolen, who was a leading early-twentieth-century town planner, advocated that each team be led by a landscape architect to ensure "the proper placing of the plan upon the ground. . . ."[43] Through time, these communities remain quite popular with their residents and exemplify new town planning in America.[44]

America's New Deal planning programs had, and continue to have, an international influence. The Zuiderzee reclamation works was actually begun earlier than the projects of the New Deal, but even so, its planning was influenced by the TVA and Greenbelt new towns. Like the American undertakings, this Dutch example involved a comprehensive regional approach to harness natural resources in order to solve social problems.

The Dutch landscape resulted largely from human intervention in natural processes, and it maintains an eloquent equilibrium between people and their environment. The Zuiderzee reclamation works is a long-term, large-scale planning effort. The Zuiderzee (Southern Sea) was an inlet of the North Sea that extended into the heart of the Netherlands. As early as 1667, the Dutch speculated on damming the Zuiderzee and reclaiming it, but lacked the appropriate technology. However, it was not until the late nineteenth century that the engineer Cornelis Lely developed serious plans for reclamation.[45]

In 1918, the Dutch parliament passed the Zuiderzee Act. That legislation established goals for flood protection, water control, the formation of a freshwater reservoir, transportation, and the creation of farmland. Engineers realized these goals by damming the Zuiderzee and creating a large lake, the IJsselmeer. New land, called polders, displaced this lake under the direction of a government agency, the IJsselmeerpolders Development Authority. The planning for several of these polders coincided with the American New Deal programs and was influenced by New Deal regional planning. New farmland was created; new villages and cities were built. Dutch planner-architect Coen van der Wal calls this herculean effort "planning the ordinary."[46] An extraordinary, national commitment resulted in "normal" places for people to live and to work.

REGIONAL PLANNING IN THE UNITED STATES DURING THE LATE TWENTIETH CENTURY

Following the noteworthy beginnings of the early twentieth century, regional planning languished, and for years it was considered an oddity in American academic circles.[47] Regional planning was rebounded in the 1960s, but its rebirth came in the form of fraternal twins. For the sake of simplicity, the writings of John Friedmann epitomize one twin, while those of Ian McHarg illustrate the other.[48]

Friedmann defined regional planning as "concerned with the ordering of human activities in supra-urban space—that is, in any area which is larger than a single city."[49] McHarg would have no doubt accepted this definition, for he described a metropolitan region in the following way: "A city occupies an area of land and operates a form of government. The metropolitan area also occupies an area of land but constitutes the sum of many levels of government."[50]

From here, however, each offers widely different perspectives. According to Friedmann, "regional planning theory has evolved out of special theories in economics (location) and geography (central places); [while] city planning theory is based on human ecology, land economics and the aesthetics of urban form."[51] This view of regional planning, based on economics and social science, may be contrasted to McHarg's natural-science approach. McHarg stated repeatedly that "the world, the city and man as responsive to physical and biological processes—in a word to ecology—are entirely absent from the operative body of planning knowledge. If the planner is part social scientist, part physical planner, he is in no part natural scientist or ecologist."[52]

John Friedmann studied in the Program of Education and Research in Planning at the University of Chicago and then taught for many years at the University of California–Los Angeles before retiring in Australia. The Chicago school has pioneered the social sciences since the early twentieth century. For a brief spell, this school provided the leadership in changing the planning profession in the United States by introducing techniques of sociology and economics. As a result, many planners abandoned the environmental design arts and came to think of themselves as applied social scientists. Meanwhile, McHarg revolutionized planning in a different direction. He and his University of Pennsylvania colleagues initiated new ways to apply the biophysical sciences in the planning process.

The sociologist Carl F. Kraenzel proposed an approach to regional planning somewhere between Friedmann and McHarg. According to Kraenzel: "Regionalism, and regional planning, are a recognition that geographic and natural environment forces still set the broad limits within which culture can function. Culture, in cooperating with nature rather than fighting it, can also, within limits, use natural and geographic forces to its own ends. Regionalism and regional planning assist in defining the natural and physical limits within which culture can operate, and aid in pointing the way for a dynamic coordination between culture and natural forces."[53]

The ideas about economic fairness and ecological relationships discussed in academic circles during the 1960s started to influence legislation for new regional planning programs in the late 1960s and early 1970s. These programs reflected social and environmental concerns. A few examples of such programs include the Appalachian Regional Commission, New York's Adirondack Park Agency, the Tahoe Regional Planning Agency, and the New Jersey Pinelands Commission.[54] During the 1990s interest in sustainability, smarter growth management, and livability prompted renewed interest in regional planning. The Regional Plan Association can trace its efforts from the early twentieth century through the environmental decades to sustainability. Its third regional plan for the New York–New Jersey–Connecticut metropolitan area helps illustrate an approach grounded in concerns about sustainability.

John F. Kennedy was deeply moved by the poverty that he encountered in the West Virginia mountains during his presidential campaign. As a result, he formed a presidential panel and directed it to draft "a comprehensive program for the economic development of the Appalachian Region." President Lyndon B. Johnson used the commission's report for the basis of legislation that became the Appalachian Regional Development Act of 1965. Its provisions included the establishment of the Appalachian Regional Commission.

The Appalachian Regional Commission covers some 200,000 square miles (517,800 square kilometers)—all of West Virginia and parts of twelve other states with a population of about 22 million people. The commission is comprised of representatives from the federal and state governments. The president appoints a co-chairman, with another elected by the governors of the participating states. The Appalachian Regional Commission affects local government, too, through its multi-county development districts comprised of city and county officials.

The Appalachian Regional Commission concentrates on economic development, and thus illustrates the Friedmann orientation to regionalism. The commission's activities encompass highway building and community development. Programs have included a regional development highway system, vocational education projects, health projects, child development, community infrastructure development (roads, solid waste disposal, housing, and water and sewer systems), and environmental and natural resource projects.

In 1982, Robert Estall, a British critic of the Appalachian Regional Commission, concluded that the impact of these programs on the eco-

nomic health of the region had been "in the main positive and beneficial."[55] He noted that the regional commission has assisted local governments by helping to fund projects, and that local confidence has grown
along with the availability of this funding for projects and risk-taking. He
concluded that the Appalachian Regional Commission demonstrates that
"state governments can cooperate with each other, and jointly with the federal government, in a single forum of the kind represented by the regional
commissions, and such cooperative endeavor can aim at goals that could be
overlooked or ignored in an approach based solely on state or federal perspectives."[56] He also observed that this regional commission shows that
local areas can be involved effectively in plan production and implementation, especially when they are organized on a multi-county approach.

Although Estall made his observations in the early 1980s, they continue to ring true. The Appalachian Regional Commission continues to
undertake projects that address the five goals of its strategic plan: developing a knowledgeable and skilled population; strengthening the region's
physical infrastructure; building local and regional leadership capacity; creating a dynamic economic base; and fostering healthy people.

New York's Adirondack Park Agency offers an example of a multi-
county region within one state. The agency focuses on natural resource
management and economic development. The Adirondack Park encom-
passes some 6 million acres (2,430,000 hectares) and was created by the
New York legislature in 1892, having been set aside as a forest preserve in
1885. The park includes 107 towns and villages in twelve counties, and
consists of a patchwork of private and state lands. The Adirondack Park
Agency was established in 1971, after growing land-use conflicts in the region and discussion about the area being converted to a national park. The
legislature directed the agency to accomplish two tasks: write a master plan
for the state-owned lands, and propose legislation for land use on private
lands within the park. The public owns approximately 2.5 million acres of
the park, with the rest in private ownership.

The plan for state lands was adopted in 1972 with little controversy, but
the plan for private lands resulted in considerable debate and court action.
The private lands plan provides for control by the Adirondack Park Agency
over projects with regional impacts. Projects with less regional impact are
subject to local government review, but local plans must be approved by the
Adirondack Park Agency.[57] Currently, the Adirondack Park Land Use and
Development Plan regulates land-use and development activities on the 3.5
million acres (1,417,500 hectares) of privately owned land.

Like the Adirondack region, in parts of the United States, many city, county, and state governments and federal agencies overlap jurisdictionally—often with conflicting policies and programs. During the 1960s, the Lake Tahoe Basin region grew at a rapid rate. The area's natural beauty and recreational opportunities attracted many visitors and new residents. In 1969, the legislatures of Nevada and California created the bi-state Tahoe Regional Planning Agency. This agency attracted heated controversy and debate between environmental groups and development interests throughout the 1970s.[58]

To help resolve these conflicts, the U.S. Congress passed, and President Carter signed into law, the Tahoe Regional Planning Compact in 1980. This compact gave federal recognition to the regional agency and empowered it to establish environmental threshold carrying capacities. This approach illustrates a more McHargian orientation to regional planning. The Congress defined the threshold carrying capacities as "an environmental standard necessary to maintain a significant scenic, recreational, educational, scientific or natural value of the region or to maintain public health and safety within the region."[59] The Congress further directed that these thresholds be incorporated into the basin's regional plan and its implementing ordinances.

The agency adopted this plan in 1987, and it continues to evolve. The implementing ordinances of the plan regulate, among other things, land use, density, growth rates, land coverage, excavation, and scenic impacts. The Tahoe Regional Planning Agency's regulations attempt to bring the region into conformance with the threshold standards for water and air quality, soil conservation, wildlife habitat, vegetation, noise, recreation, and scenic resources.

The million-acre (405,000-hectare) New Jersey Pinelands, a United Nations–designated Biosphere Reserve, is situated in the midst of the most densely populated region of the United States. The plan for the area—known locally as the Pine Barrens—derives from the designation by the U.S. Congress, in 1978, of the Pinelands as the country's first national reserve, and the passage, in 1979, of the Pinelands Protection Act by the New Jersey legislature. To comply with these laws, the Pinelands Planning Commission was established by New Jersey Governor Brendan T. Byrne. This commission attempts to coordinate the planning activities of local, state, and national governments.

The Comprehensive Management Plan developed by this commission broadcasts a number of strategies for the region and also reflects a

McHarg-influenced approach. The components of this plan include a natural resource assessment; an assessment of scenic, aesthetic, cultural, open
space, and outdoor recreational resources; a land-use capability map; a comprehensive statement of land-use and management policies; a financial
analysis, a program to ensure local government and public participation in
the planning process; and a program to put the plan into effect.[60] The plan
culminated an intensive research and planning effort. Governor Byrne approved it on behalf of the state government, while Secretary of the Interior
Cecil D. Andrus, of the Carter administration, provided its federal blessing.

The Pinelands Comprehensive Management Plan evolved during the
same time as the Lake Tahoe process, and although the regions differ, their
plans and implementing regulations possess similarities. The Pinelands
plan attempts to balance preservation and development. The plan sets aside
some areas for protection and targets others for growth. Land use and development are regulated through environmental standards for wetlands,
vegetation, wildlife, water resources, air quality, scenic resources, fire, and
history. In addition to its regulatory and economic development programs,
the Pinelands Commission maintains ongoing educational efforts about
the ecology and the cultures of the region.

The regional planning undertakings for the Appalachians, the Adirondack Park, Lake Tahoe, and the Pinelands reflect the social and environmental awareness of the 1960s and 1970s, especially the interest in protecting our surroundings. The Pinelands plan, in particular, influenced the
American greenway planning of the 1980s. With the withdrawal of a federal commitment to social and environmental programs by the Reagan administration, planners adapted new strategies. Funds that had once been
available to purchase important landscapes through U.S. Department of
Interior programs evaporated during the 1980s.

As a result of the Wild and Scenic Rivers Act, the Interior Department is obligated to provide conservation assistance to those local communities that request it. Planners of the National Park Service's Rivers, Trails,
and Conservation Program (part of Interior) saw this as an opportunity to
create a funding source to replace those lost through budget cuts and to
promote greenway parks. Greenways exhibit more similarities to European
national parks than to American ones. Conversely, Jack Ahern illustrates
how American greenways have influenced European efforts to promote the
protection and enhancement of ecological networks.[61] Instead of blanket
public ownership, both public and private entities own lands within green-
lines. For greenways to be successful, regional cooperation must occur

among government agencies, environmental organizations, businesses, and individual citizens. Many successful examples exist.

In its third regional plan for the New York–New Jersey–Connecticut metropolitan area, the Regional Plan Association built on the greenway movement as well as its heritage and experience. An emphasis on sustainability was incorporated as well. By the early 1990s, the Brundtland Commission's call for sustainable development began to influence policy makers around the world. This impact becomes evident in the Regional Plan Association's third regional plan, published in 1996.[62]

The Regional Plan Association (RPA) incorporated in 1929 and produced its first plan that year. The RPA should not be confused with the Regional Planning Association of America (RPAA). In fact, Lewis Mumford of the latter group criticized the 1929 plan for not being strong enough in its efforts "to restrain development and deconcentrate the urban core."[63] Thomas Adams, the planning director of the RPA and the principal author of its first plan, opted for strategies to accommodate growth instead. The Adams-Mumford dichotomy echoes four decades later with the reemergence of regionalism under the banners of Friedmann and McHarg (who, after all, was a protégé of Mumford).

The RPA completed its second metropolitanwide plan in 1968. This plan attempted to address the issues of suburban sprawl, urban decline, and transportation. It "helped to protect hundreds of thousands of acres of open space and guided the rebuilding of regional commuter rail systems."[64]

Building on the three foundations of sustainability—equity, environment, and economy—the most recent plan seeks to optimize the intersections of these (too often viewed as competing) interests. The ultimate goal is to improve the quality of life in the region. The third RPA plan presents bold visions, including, among other things, the creation of "11 regional open space reserves, linked by a greenway network, and 11 downtown centers, supported by transit-oriented development."[65]

To implement this vision, architects, landscape architects, and planners from the RPA work with diverse civic and business groups as well as government agencies. The New York regional planners also cooperate with counterparts in other large metropolitan regions, including Milan, Shanghai, and Tokyo, to refine and to advance their vision. For example, with colleagues from Milan, a triptych of sites in both metropolitan regions was selected to explore the theme of "transforming the places of production."[66] Both the New York and Milan regions are bustling industrial and manufacturing centers facing decline and renewal, especially the emergence of the new information-based economy. In both regions, planners conducted on-location workshops for all six sites. In each region, three sites were selected representing the metropolitan core, a regional center, and a historic landscape. These cross-cultural, binational exchanges sought to strengthen and transfer expertise in regional planning research and expertise.[67]

GREENWAYS

In Austin, road signs welcome drivers to watersheds. As one enters the land above the Edwards Aquifer, signs remind the public of the area's environmental sensitivity. Along each roadway, these signs connect the traveler to the massive groundwater system below and the drainage and networks of Central Texas.

Frederick Law Olmsted observed, "Austin has a fine situation upon the left bank of the Colorado. Had it not been the capital of the state, and a sort of bourne to which we had looked forward for a temporary rest, it would still have struck us as the pleasantest place we had seen in Texas. It reminds one somewhat of Washington; Washington, *en petit*, seen through a reversed glass."[68] He continued, "The country around the town is rolling and picturesque, with many agreeable views of distant hills and a pleasant sprinkling of wood over prairie slopes."[69]

Olmsted came to Texas in 1854 seeking contact with the large, well-established German population, who, like his Northern sponsors, were opposed to slavery. The Germans had been recruited by the Spanish, before the Republic of Mexico was established and before Southern white Americans came with their black slaves. Indian settlements predated all these pioneers. Later, Czech and Polish towns were founded, many of which still retain their ethnic character.

The architecture and cuisine of the Central Texas region reflect this diverse cultural heritage. One of the best North American beers, Shiner Bock, carries the name of the town with Czech roots where it is brewed. Texas barbeque combines central European butchery with African cooking techniques and Hispanic spices. The wealth of this region represents a confluence of its natural capital with its social capital. This conjunction has produced a self-conscious culture.

While regions have been, and will be, viewed in terms of their economies and physiographies, ecology helps reveal how processes interrelate to form patterns. Along the Rio Grande from Las Cruces, New Mexico, into El Paso, Texas, a clear structure is evident (that extends both north and west into New Mexico as well as south and east into Texas and Mexico). The flat alluvial valleys are farmed, urban and rural settlements hug the terraces overlooking the farmlands, and the mountain slopes and prairies beyond remain open except for an occasional steer or rattlesnake.

We tend to know the region in which we live and identify with it. Television, radio, newspapers, sometimes magazines, and, increasingly, Web pages help define a region. Sports teams do, too. The Cincinnati Reds are followed by fans in Dayton, Lexington, Louisville, Indianapolis, and Columbus. As its peak, the Big Red Machine even humbled a class act from Boston. Leave Amsterdam by train, and loyalty to the beloved football team Ajax dissipates, disappearing by the time the train arrives in Rotterdam. The train route between Warsaw and Łódź is riddled with graffiti concerning the respective soccer teams. It's AC Milan versus AS Roma, Real Madrid versus Barcelona, the 76ers versus the Celtics, and so on and so on.

A more profound identity is also possible, one connected to the deep green structure of the region, its seasons, rocks, and rivers as well as its plants and animals. Ecoregions provide manifestations of this deep structure. Living things indicate what is possible in a place, what is best adapted and best suited to the climate and soils. The bright skies of Rome and Phoenix differ from the overcast ones of Utrecht and Seattle. The aridity of the Australian outback and the northern Mexican deserts contrast the lush forests of Costa Rica as well as those along the southwestern coasts of Alaska. A frigid November afternoon in Seoul differs on the same day in a warmer Dubai. Such differences should not be viewed as better or worse, but merely as elements that help define the region. Regional differences converge to form nations, and sometimes states (when people are persistently well organized), and then nation-states (when people transcend organization to think wisely about their futures).

NATION, STATE, AND NATION-STATE

There was nothing but land: not a country at all, but the material out of which countries are made. No, there was nothing but land.

—WILLA CATHER

A NATION IS A BODY OF PEOPLE ASSOCIATED WITH A PARTICULAR territory. Such a group of people needs to be sufficiently conscious of its unity to seek or to possess a government. A state is the body of people *occupying* a definite territory and organized under one government. Both involve the relationship of people to territory. In the United States, states comprise a legal subdivision of the nation. In other countries, Israel for instance, the nation and the state are one. In still other situations, nations of people have been separated from their state or have immigrated to other countries. As the American poet Walt Whitman observed about the United States, "Here is not merely a nation but a teeming nation of nations."[1]

Nations and states differ, although they usually are related. According to cultural anthropologist Yehudi Cohen, "'nation' is the territorial representation of the society, and 'state' is its political representation."[2] Nations may be teeming nations of nations, like Whitman's United States and increasingly many other countries, or relatively more homogeneous, or at least seeking to be homogeneous, such as present-day Iran. The nations of the United States and the Islamic Republic of Iran differ not only in cultural composition but also in state organization. The organization of nation-states varies widely. Even among nations that call themselves "republics," there are many forms of organization.

125

The notion of nation design and planning has been integral to the American project from Jefferson's proposals for subdividing the continent, through Abraham Lincoln's advocacy of homesteading and the transcontinental railway system; to Franklin Roosevelt's New Deal, Dwight Eisenhower's interstate highway system, and former U.S. Secretary of the Interior Bruce Babbitt's advocacy of a national biological survey. Marking and mapping provide ongoing exercises for the nation-building enterprise. Boundaries and identities are established in the process of everything from a street sign to a postage stamp.

Interaction underlies the concepts of both nation and state, as it does ecology. The interactions in nations and states involve humans. The challenge and the opportunity are to view those relationships as ecological. This chapter takes on that theme, but first explores the concepts of nation, state, and nation-state more fully.

THE IDEA OF NATION

A nation is a *community* of people from mainly a common descent, history, or language. Such a people may form a unified government or inhabit a specific territory. Nation seems especially bound to language. Italian and German united territories before Garibaldi or Bismarck achieved national unity. However, languages also transcend national boundaries, as English and Spanish illustrate.

Nations are interacting associations of people, ecological representations of collective human interactions. They can be relatively small, like the Netherlands, or quite large, like Canada and Russia. Nations come in all shapes and sizes, stretching across several time zones, encompassing many ecosystems and regions, or, conversely, as small as a medium-sized city. They can be very densely settled or sprawled across vast territories. Many of these concepts—interacting associations of communities, ecological representation, size and shape—apply to regionalism, too. When does a region end and a nation begin? Past regions, the city-states of ancient Greece and the Hohokam settlements in the American Southwest, contain many similarities to contemporary nations. Geography provides one distinguishing feature. Region, by definition, possesses some territorial limit, although the actual boundary may be fuzzy. Nations transcend geography. Regions may persist through time; nations are defined by history. Nations involve more willful human action.

Nations can be homogeneous or heterogeneous, open or exclusive. Japan is a relatively homogeneous nation; India is more diverse. Nations, previously more homogeneous, such as Germany, have become more heterogeneous through immigration. Some nations, such as the United States, more or less encourage immigration and are open to new citizens (albeit with periods of xenophobia and with a rather cumbersome bureaucratic process). By contrast, Switzerland maintains much more rigorous procedures for becoming a citizen.

THE IDEA OF STATE

Immigration matters are governed by the state. Nations may organize themselves into various state structures. A state is a political *community* under one government. Government structures vary as a result of legal traditions and politics. The nineteenth-century Swiss historian Jacob Burckhardt observed that the state may be viewed as a work of art.[3] We have many ideas about how to organize ourselves. Many states are closely linked with national identity, especially a specific ethnicity and/or religion. State organizations range from democratic to totalitarian. The power to manage the state can be broad based or concentrated among an elite or even in a single individual, as in a dictatorship. States embody conscious adaptations to the need to regulate the actions and the interactions of people. Like a community or a region, a state concerns associations of people. Jurisdictional authority distinguishes state from community and region. State represents a higher level of human organization.

States can be fair or unfair, largely based on how they govern interactions among their citizens. The "qualifications for being a *civilized state* amount to," according to John Le Carré,[4] electoral suffrage; protection of life and property; justice, health, and education for all; the maintenance of a sound administration infrastructure; roads, transport, and drainage; and the equitable collection of taxes. An additional qualification for a civilized state is how these activities occur in relationship to the natural environment. Are roads being built, for example, that deplete the natural capital for future generations? Can we construct drainage systems that restore the health of watersheds?

THE IDEA OF NATION-STATE

Nation-states combine collections of people into a political community. Nation-states change through politics, which can be viewed organically.

The Dutch author Harry Mulisch observed, "politics isn't a branch of economics, as Marx thought, or of theology, as my father thought, or of sociology, as other people think, but of biology."[5]

Nation-states are an extension of the ancient Greek city-state. The Greek city-state was an organic entity with the *polis* linked to its territory. Morris explains that *polis* "is the Greek word which we translate as city state; it is a bad translation, because the polis was not much like a city and was very much more than a state."[6] Town and country formed a solitary unit. Again according to Morris, "the life of the Greek city state was founded upon agriculture and remained dependent on it; city state and city were not necessarily the same even though the former was most embodied in the latter."[7]

In his dialogues with Socrates, Plato probes the essential nature of our lives. In his *The Republic*, he articulates a vision for the ideal political community, including the nature of justice. For Plato, reason could enable us to provide orderly governance in a changing world. Order can be derived, according to Plato, by understanding the forms of the world.[8] Such forms possess structures that can be revealed through images.

Aristotle, one of Plato's students, delved deeper into the natural sciences. He provided the foundation for what became biology and later ecology. The relationship between the natural world and how we govern ourselves was not abstract to the Greeks. Aristotle viewed change as the fundamental phenomenon of nature. Change occurs in nature and in human affairs. Changes result from various causes. How living entities respond, through their structure and their behavior, contribute to their individual being and function. Human beings respond to life's changes through their pursuit of happiness. A good life then is defined as one comprised of virtuous actions.

For Aristotle, the aim of the state should be to provide the good life for its citizens. People form political associations to govern how such a good life can be ensured. The ideas of Plato and Aristotle function as the bedrock philosophies for a wide variety of structures used in nation-states, as well as in the natural sciences.

CULTURE RULES

According to the geographer William Norton, "Language is a cultural variable and the principal means by which a culture ensures continuity through time."[9] People speak a language before it is written. Many indigenous peoples of the Americas passed along their most important myths through song. For example, one song of the Sioux or Lakota people, recounted by Black Elk, goes as follows:

> Father, paint the earth on me.
> Father, paint the earth on me.
> Father, paint the earth on me.
> A nation I will make over.
> A two-legged nation I will make holy.
> Father, paint the earth on me.[10]

"Language is . . . intimately associated with ideas of nationalism." Norton observed. "In medieval Wales, the words for language and for nation were synonymous."[11] According to Plato, language holds the capacity to both articulate the intelligibility of the world and to belie the true meaning of the world.[12]

Nation-states evolved as the spoken word became the written word. A nation of people can exist without a formal system of writing, but a state cannot. Communities of people with common characteristics form nations. They need to communicate through speech and other symbols, which in the past did not necessarily require writing. Many American Indian nations, for example, did not possess a written language. People organize themselves in governing structures called states that require a written language to function. Nation-states control territory and the means of production through the written word. People establish nation-states only after they have taken care of the basics. Cohen maintains that "nation-states can only develop among people who have the potential for producing surpluses and for making the technological advances that state systems precipitate."[13]

Nation-states arbitrate language, culture, and technology. In early American history, the Pennsylvania legislature voted whether German or English would be the official language of the commonwealth. English won, barely, because of a tiebreaker cast by a prominent citizen of German heritage. In contemporary states, similar debates abound between Spanish and English. Canada has worked out an unresolved, and perhaps irresolvable, mix of English and French. Still, many Quebecois question if they should remain part of the nation.

Nations establish institutions to exhibit their control over nature and the authority of rulers over the population. Throughout history, kings and queens, emperors and empresses, and lesser potentates created menageries and gardens. In the nineteenth century, national societies to prevent cruelty to animals were created, first in England (1824) and then in France (1845) and the Netherlands (1864). These societies were founded with humanistic goals, according to Hancocks, "aimed as much at elevating humankind as protecting animals."[14]

As these societies came into being, zoological gardens moved beyond the private preserve of the rich and powerful. Throughout Europe, zoos were founded in the capitals and other major cities. In the late nineteenth century, the U.S. Congress established a national zoo in Washington, D.C., "for the advancement of science and the instruction and recreation of the people."[15] Hancocks observed that the national zoo was founded as a response "to concerns about the loss of wildlife" and, as a result, started "on a different ethic and for different purposes than European zoos."[16]

Nowadays, European nations lavish support on their cultural institutions, sometimes in self-defense against American intrusions. The French, for example, vigorously patrol their culture for American pollutants. The Dutch adopt a more chameleon-like approach. Attending the North Sea Jazz Festivals in June, one might believe jazz originated in the tulip fields of the polders.

The United States, meanwhile, skimps on its institutional reinforcement of culture, depending instead on the captains of industry and volunteers. Take, for example, the downward budget spirals of the National Endowment for the Arts as well as most state universities. Many art institutions in the United States depend on private donations and volunteer time for their existence. Public research universities are moving from a state-sponsored to a state-affiliated status, relying more and more on private gifts and rising tuition.

In spite of its obeisant devotion to the private sector, most of the United States' vaulted technological innovations have resulted from public interventions in the free market. Sometimes technologies help people to circumvent national structure, as with the preferred use of cell phones over an ineffective national telephone system. Technologies often transform national cultures and international markets. The Finns are notoriously quiet people who increasingly communicate via cell phones. The Finnish company with a Japanese-sounding name, Nokia, sells its products to clients in every continent.

National television networks can dominate (with the aid of scramblers) until entrepreneurs start importing satellite dishes. Meanwhile, the

BBC exports its programming around the world. BBC radio and television represent a specific national culture and language to a global audience.

NATIONAL IDENTITIES

A national character can be rooted in a nation's soil. The communal identity of the Netherlands, for example, derives from the struggles of its people to ward off floods and to reclaim lands from the sea and other water bodies. As explained by the Columbia University historian Simon Schama, "when the political identity of an independent Netherlands was being established, [it] was also a time of dramatic physical alteration of its landscape. In both the political and geographical senses, then, this was the formative era of a northern, Dutch, nationhood."[17]

A fundamental function of the nation is to provide identity for its peoples. A structure for national organization is the state. Political ideology and tradition help determine a state's structural organization. In ecological terms, politics may be viewed as the dominant group's wish to control resources or, alternatively, as a form of altruism where conflicts over resources are channeled and resolved.

By providing identity, nations contribute positively to a number of human needs. Nations help us feel that we belong to a larger human community. National identity can be determined through language, religion, race, or political ideology, or some combination of these factors. National identities can have deleterious consequences, too, as when one considers his or her own group a master race or the chosen people—an unfortunate tendency of our species.

The media contribute to national identities. When living abroad, we eagerly seek out news from home. A Dutch professor once traveled to Ireland, where his students were contributing to a rural plan for Sligo, in the northwest of the country. The Dutch professor knew his students had some "left-wing" tendencies. He brought them several presents from the Netherlands, including *Trouw* and *Het Financieel Dagblad*, the most "right-wing" newspapers that he could find. "They would never read this at home," he observed, "but they will devour them here." He was right.

The American Academy in Rome attracts American Italiophiles. Nevertheless, each morning there is an elaborate queuing for the two *Herald-Tribunes* available. American scholars anxiously sip cappuccinos while waiting their turn to read sports scores, reports of six-year-olds shooting their playmates, and proposals for removing dams to allow rivers to mean-der and fish to migrate.

If Americans are at least partially defined by an attraction to wilderness and nature-dominated landscapes (or landscapes that look natural), and the Italian identity is at least partially determined by their urbanity, then the Dutch nation can be explained by the desire of its people to make landscapes. As Schama noted about the Dutch, "The land was not merely reclaimed but in the process both [land and people] were morally transformed."[18]

A national structure can remain long after the actual nation has tran-spired, or a structure will remain in spite of functional or governmental changes. The structure of ancient Rome persists in both the Roman Catholic Church and the hierarchies of many nations in North Africa and the Middle East. Many elements of the dynasties of ancient China endure in the People's Republic. Internal national structures tend to be remarkably resilient.

The social structure of nation-states reflects the necessity of organiza-tion. Cohen observes:

> The organization of social relations in a nation-state is characterized by sys-tems of social stratification in which the members of each stratum partici-pate in different technological activities and thus live by a different life style; correspondingly, each of these strata is distinguishable by its own symbolic system, in religion, cognitive processes, political ideology, attitudes to work, language, and art. Nevertheless, members of all strata are bound to each other—often in ways that are not immediately apparent—by complicated technological and economic interdependence, overlapping life styles, and mutually shared cores of ideas and symbols.[19]

Nations record their spatial structures on maps. Images of past and present—the growth of a nation—can be depicted. Geographers portray the hierarchy of cities and nationwide transportation systems, among many other elements. Maps represent the extent of the state, but can also mask national identities, as the Armenians remind us. For example, when European nations invaded and colonized Africa, Asia, and the Americas, indigenous communities, re-gions, and states were ignored. These native territories often maintained strong ties to natural processes. New England appeared on maps where the Iroquois and other nations had prospered for centuries. Maps of settled lands reflected European ambitions and conflicts rather than local realities. In much of the world, ambition replaced reality. The longing for national iden-tity, swept aside by state ambition, underlies many contemporary conflicts.

Nation-states balance change and continuity. Without change, nations, like regions, can waste away and become weak through the lack of innovation and challenge. Too much change, too quickly, can result in stress, which is harmful to people. Democracies account for change through the system of voting. An election can bring about a change or reconfirm the status quo. In general, people are skeptical of change, as Niccolò Machiavelli noted in the sixteenth century:

> There is nothing more difficult to carry out, nor more doubtful of success, nor more dangerous to handle, than to initiate a new order of things. For the reformer has enemies in all who profit by the old order, and only luke-warm defenders in all those who would profit by the new order. This luke-warmness arises partly from fear of their adversaries, who have the law in their favour; and partly from the incredulity of mankind, who do not believe in anything new until they have had actual experience of it.[20]

The microchip and the personal computer have changed the organizational structure of nation-states. These technologies make possible dispersed systems of business, production, information gathering, and governance. Organizations as diverse as General Motors, IBM, the former Soviet Union, and many centrally directed Asian capitalist nations were forced to restructure from the late 1980s through the 1990s as a result of new technologies. Some of these organizations were more efficient than others. In comparing Russia and Indonesia, *New York Times* journalist Thomas Friedman used a computer analogy, "Russia first needed to get a whole new operating system—capitalism—plus the software system to go with it, i.e., the rule of law. Indonesia had the operating system—capitalism—but it stuck with an old, centrally directed version that was fine in the 1970s but unsuited for the high-speed '90s. And Indonesia had very little software."[21] Friedman also inferred that capitalism had to be tempered with strong, legitimate institutions to collect taxes, to regulate business, and to provide a social safety net.

FAULT LINES

The frontier marks the border between two countries and also typifies a district on each side of the boundary. One feels the dissimilarity crossing the border from one nation to another. The street signs differ, as do the buses, the fireplugs, the money, and perhaps the trains. In the United States, and increasingly in the European Union, a welcome sign, and perhaps a place with promotional tourism brochures, marks the transition from one state to another. Within much of Europe, one's passport is likely to receive more scrutiny in a hotel than when crossing from one nation to the next within the European Union. The movement of people and goods between European Union member countries is eased through an understanding known as the Schengen agreement, so named because it was signed on June 15, 1985, in the Luxembourg town of Schengen. The agreement allowed people to cross internal borders at any point without checks. The original agreement applied to only five states but was subsequently extended to all European Union member states. Meanwhile, in North America, walls, attack dogs, and barbed wire mark the borders between the United Mexican States and the United States of America.

Americans are accustomed to thinking in continental terms. Europeans increasingly view their continent as a whole. Asians, of course, have had such a perspective for centuries. Peninsulas and islands throw monkey wrenches into continental-nation thinking. Denmark and England drag their feet about joining the single Euro currency. The Korean and Indian peninsula–subcontinents are divided.

As the word "subculture" indicates, human communities can exist within more dominant communities. This is true from the local to the national levels. The nations within nations frequently have less clear boundaries, often because a dominant nation wishes it so. For a Native American nation located within, say, Arizona, how does one know when one is within the Navajo or the Hopi or the Apache nation? Canyon de Chelly is within the Navajo nation and was previously occupied by a more ancient people, thought to be from whom the Hopi, the archenemy of the Navajo, are descended. Simultaneously, one is in Arizona and the United States. One can visit a Veterans of Foreign Wars post in Window Rock, Arizona, and hear tales of the South Pacific similar to those one would hear in South Philadelphia or suburban Seattle.

As noted in chapter 5, the regions—the ecotones—between nations often assume a character and culture unique to both. Such regions can also become the source of international conflict—Alsace-Lorraine, Northern Ireland, the frontiers between Poland and Germany as well as between Poland and Russia, Jerusalem, the Golan Heights, the Gaza Strip, the Kuril Islands between Japan and Russia, islands of Quemoy and Matsu between Taiwan and China—and so on. Unfortunately, the examples of conflict are far too numerous.

International ecotones may also be places of hope. The 4-kilometer-wide (2.5 miles), 250-kilometer-long (155 miles) strip of land along the thirty-eighth parallel between the divided Koreas has been abandoned since 1953. While the overall biodiversity has decreased, the Demilitarized Zone has become rich habitat for some species. The zone possesses the potential to become an important preserve, a green healing salve. Many Koreans believe that the Demilitarized Zone should become a peace park. Similar healing took place along the Berlin Wall with the reunification of the Germanys.

The European Union has resulted in more permeable boundaries among nations that had been at war for centuries. The North American Free Trade Agreement has created greater cooperation among Canada, Mexico, and the United States. For example, the Southwest Center for Environmental Research and Policy (SCERP) was established by Congress, to be administered by the U.S. Environmental Protection Agency with a consortium of U.S. and Mexican universities.

SCERP funded twin studies of the drainage basins for the San Pedro and Tijuana Rivers. Researchers explored the potential for an international, watershed-level approach for environmental planning in an urban (Tijuana) region and a rural (San Pedro) region. Unlike land, water and air move between nations. The San Pedro and Tijuana Rivers begin in Mexico and flow north into the United States. In both basins, the airsheds straddle the national borders.

The San Pedro headwaters begin in the Sierra La Elenita and the Sierra La Mariguita near the historic mining town of Cananea, Sonora, and flow north into Arizona. As a transition area between the Sonoran and Chihuahuan Deserts, the upper San Pedro watershed is recognized internationally for its biodiversity. The landscape is a dramatic composition of broad valleys punctuated by mountain ranges. In the winter, dustings of snow cover these mountains while the majestic white trunks and the bare branches of the cottonwoods line the river. During the summer months, leafy galleries preside over a flow reduced to a trickle. The area supports the second-highest-known number of mammal species in the world, and provides habitat for more than 390 bird species.

In addition to the SCERP-supported studies, the San Pedro watershed has been the focus of considerable research because of this biodiversity. All the studies suggest that greater international cooperation would help maintain and improve the environmental qualities of the watershed.[22] Similarly, the much more urban Tijuana basin straddles the U.S.–Mexico border. San Diego State University produced the *San Diego–Tijuana International Border Area Planning Atlas* in both English and Spanish "to help planners, researchers, developers, decision makers, and community members better understand the binational region. . . ."[23]

The Rhine crosses the borders of several European nations. The Nile begins in Burundi; crosses Rwanda, Uganda, and Sudan; and empties into the Mediterranean Sea after defining Egypt. The Mekong originates in Tibet, China; flows southeastward, forming the borders of Burma and Laos and then Laos and Thailand, before entering Cambodia; then ends at the South China Sea in Vietnam. Other rivers form international borders—the Saint Lawrence, the Rio Grande, the Heilongjiang or Amur, the Prut, and the Putumayo.

FREEWAYS

To balance authority and freedom, people have devised many means to guide their interactions at the levels of nation and state: religion, customs, law, and government. Religions declare what types of interactions are permissible or "moral" and which are not. Laws determine the limits of socially tolerable interactions. Conformance to laws varies, of course, from nation to nation as well as within many nations.

Italy is a nation of noble laws and of law benders. In this nation of Catholic anarchists, vivid contrasts abound. Tim Parks, an English writer who lives in Italy, commented about such contrasts in the Italian character, noting that there is "anarchy without, ceremony within."[24] In contrast to Italy, the Netherlands epitomizes a nation of law abiders. However, much is legal or decriminalized in the Netherlands that is illegal in Italy, the United States, and most other nations—prostitution, marijuana use, and euthanasia. Hard drug use is treated as an illness in Holland, needles are recycled, and there is open discussion about AIDS. The Dutch, who eat cheese for breakfast, consume raw herring in midday on their city streets; Italians avoid mixing cheese with seafood; Americans eat tuna melts.

Americans are smug about their two-party system and often make disparaging remarks about governance in Italy. But the frequent change in governments in Italy is deceiving. In contrast to the United States, with declining participation in elections, 90 percent of eligible Italians regularly vote. Their multiparty system, like others in Europe, appears to stimulate political interaction.

A nation must also interact with its past. History poses difficult challenges for interaction. Americans must cope with Vietnam; Germans, Japanese, and Italians with the atrocities, including genocide, of the Second World War; many Europeans with their colonial past; Israelis with their relationships with the Palestinians and vice versa; and so on. The challenge is to learn from our interactions with history.

"Longing on a large scale is what makes history," the American author Don DeLillo contends.[25] We seek connections with our past. Nation-states are institutions of large-scale longing. Individual and community memories come and go, but our national histories provide a common, even if inaccurate or debatable, thread of our past.

War and peace provide the poles of possibilities for interactions between nations. National defense strategies can prepare peoples to protect themselves, as well as to mobilize for aggression. Most nations have standing armies, navies, and air forces as well as mechanisms for enlisting able bodies in times of conflict or in periods of possible conflict. War veterans construct monuments in memory of victories and defeats. Museums overflow with the memorabilia from the battlefield.

Nations also prepare for peace. Treaties govern interactions between nations. Diplomats negotiate and monitor these agreements. Institutions of government devote themselves to peaceful exchanges—cultural and commercial. For example, in 1961, President John Kennedy initiated an attempt to promote peace through establishment of the Peace Corps. Instead of using more formal diplomatic channels, the Peace Corps relies on a person-to-person approach. Through such interactions, peace may be achieved through better understanding.

STATES OF THE NATIONS

Diversity exists among nation-states and within them. States respond to their dissimilarities with other states, as well as diversity from within. Often nations and states seek to eradicate internal differences and respond belligerently to others with alternative religions or politics. Wars, including civil wars, are a negative response to the diversity of others outside and within the nation. Peace can also be a response to diversity. Peace involves learning how to accept differences.

All nations depend on symbols for identity. National symbols seem especially important in diverse nations. Flags, parades, holidays, images on money and stamps, capitals, and anthems provide an abundance of symbolic opportunities. Americans love to fly their flag and flaunt their dead presidents on their greenbacks. Italians' attachment to their flag differs, equally patriotic but less sacred than the American devotion to the red, white, and blue. The images on the Italian pre-Euro currency also contrasted with greenbacks, including Maria Montessori on 1,000 lire bills and the face of Michelangelo Merisida Caravaggio on 100,000 lire bills. Now, Euro coins provide remnants of national identities.

The presumed ringleader of the September 11 terrorists, Mohammed (al-Amir Awad al-Sayed) Atta, studied urban planning. Apparently, Mr. Atta earned his first degree in architecture from Cairo and then pursued his graduate planning studies at the Technical University of Hamburg-Harburg. The topic of his thesis was the preservation of Aleppo, one of the oldest continually inhabited cities in the world. Abraham is said to have milked his gray cow on the acropolis of Aleppo.

The point being: Mohammed Atta understood the symbolic power of buildings and was a careful planner to disastrous ends. The World Trade Center symbolized the economic prowess of the United States. The Pentagon clearly stands for the nation's military strength. The presumed third targets—the White House and/or the Capitol—are symbols of government.

Some nations blend with their neighbors, like the Dutch and French portions of Belgium. The results can be surprising. Belgium beer tastes even better than Heineken, Amstel, or Grolsch, and is preferred by many Dutch people. The Belgium wine, however . . . well, the French still prefer their own.

Within nation-states, groups of people, even nations of peoples can be spatially separated, as with the Indian reservations in the United States. Formerly in South Africa, blacks, "coloreds," and whites were divided through *apartheid* (the Afrikaans term for "separateness"). Economic segregation often accomplishes similar results.

Some nations pride themselves on their plurality; others are known for their dislike of foreigners. Some nations assume everyone crossing their borders is a potential immigrant. Others construct elaborate screens to exclude people from entering and/or staying. Nations add to their diversity through immigration, conquest, and annexation. Nation-states maintain pluralities by ensuring that all groups participate in the processes of governance and decision making.

REVOLUTIONS

Mao Zedong and Thomas Jefferson shared the view that nations were not stable entities. They believed that revolutions were necessary to revitalize and reinvent a nation. Revolution has come to mean violent change, as occurred in China's Cultural Revolution and America's Civil War. Violence often leaves scars for generations. Peaceful transformations can occur as well, such as the nonviolence advocated by Martin Luther King and the Peace Movement by the hippies against the war in Vietnam. Although South Africa had a violent history of repression, the eventual transition from apartheid was largely peaceful. When the Berlin Wall came down, East and West Germany, and much of Europe, experienced a transition without violence. Such transitions provide hope for our species.

Nations adapt to change in varying ways at different rates. They are subject to many external influences. The Navajo nation, for example, is known for its jewelry making and sheepherding—both borrowed from the Spanish. A trip through Navajo country today reveals a fondness for pickup trucks, a cultural adaptation from (originally) other Americans and (more recently) from Japan—although Fords and Chevys seem to outnumber Toyotas within the walls painted by nature and time of Canyon de Chelly, the canyon in northeast Arizona inhabited, in turn, by the Anasazi, the Hopi, and the Navajo.

How do we plan and design nations to adapt through time? Jefferson and the other so-called Founding Fathers of the United States provide a good example. Their strategy was to put in place a rather firm plan that was easy to adapt through time. They created a system of checks and balances, so that power was decentralized yet hierarchical.

As a nation planner and designer, Jefferson contributed to both the legal structure and the physical form of the United States. In addition to writing the Declaration of Independence and the proposals that led to the Land Ordinance of 1785 and the Northwest Ordinance of 1787, he was responsible for the purchase of the Louisiana Territory from Napoleon Bonaparte. The Northwest Ordinance subdivided the nation so it could be settled by Jefferson's noble yeoman democrats. Through his visions for Washington, D.C., Monticello, and the University of Virginia's Lawn, Jefferson created elements of a national aesthetic that continues to persist. His ideas guided the settlement of the nation.

For example, the "Plan for Government of the Western Territory," largely authored by Jefferson in 1784, provided the blueprint for western settlement. This plan became the Ordinance of 1784 and influenced both the Land Ordinance of 1785 and the Northwest Ordinance of 1787. Essentially, Jefferson created a framework for the lands west of the Alleghenies. As Julian Boyd and his collaborators recount, "He had long been interested in the region west of the Alleghenies, not as a speculator, but as a statesman, a scientist, and a believer in agrarian democracy."[26] In fact, Jefferson opposed speculative interests, preferring instead actual settlers.

Jefferson's plan for the West emphasized state governments, based on constitutions, subdivided into counties and townships. It also dealt with the boundaries of the new states, how they would be admitted to the United States, and the relations with Indians. Jefferson's report to Congress declared, "there shall be neither slavery nor involuntary servitude in any of the said states, . . ."[27] Jefferson's vision, of course, was modified and even undermined by others.

Soon after his plan was submitted to Congress, Jefferson departed for Europe to become minister to France. With Jefferson out of the country, Congress repealed the Ordinance of 1784, replacing it with the Northwest Ordinance of 1787. The 1787 Ordinance retained many of Jefferson's proposals, such as the abolition of slavery, but it also "provided for a greater measure of local autonomy."[28] Historians note that the reason for the new law was to give land speculators and their supporters more control of the West. The new law protected speculative interests "from the actions of the inhabitants."[29] Jefferson's plan was the first of many in the new nation to be compromised for land speculation interests.

The writer-turned-politician Václav Havel played a role similar to Jefferson's in the creation of the Czech Republic. After the end of Soviet domination, he brokered the peaceful split of Slovakia and, through his words, imprinted a literary aesthetic about new international relationships. Havel argues that we need a new political model "of coexistence among various cultures, peoples, races and religious spheres within a single interconnected civilization."[30]

GROSS NATIONAL PRODUCTS

Texans view Texas as a nation. Becoming Texan almost requires a change in nationality. The state gives newcomers thirty days to become a Texan. (I had thought the endeavor took a lifetime.) Although Texas was an independent nation only for about ten years, and a part of an independent Mexico for only a little more than a decade before that, Texan and Mexican identities remain strong. The iconographic eyes of Texas are constantly upon you. The Lone Star flag flies ubiquitously. Five-pointed stars and longhorns are embedded into stone, concrete, metal, and wood of public and private structures. Many male names in Texas echo the heroes of the Alamo and the state's war for independence.

Obviously, Texas is part of a larger nation-state. A nation comes together in times of crises and employs the state to mobilize the response. After the September 11 tragedy, American flags joined the Lone Star across the state. Mobilization during a crisis requires multilayered interactions among many individuals in diverse environments. From emergency response to mail delivery, the actions of nations and states represent complex human endeavors. We often do not view nations and states in ecological terms. By adopting an ecological perspective of these interactions, we could gain a better understanding of the structures and functions of nation-states.

Nationalism is a unifying force, which can also drive people apart. The Balkans are notorious for ethnic and national strife. Marshal Tito, whose original name was Josip Brož, was able to form a relatively prosperous union of these warring groups together in Yugoslavia from the end of the Second World War until his death in 1980. Orthodox and Roman Catholics lived in peace with Muslims. Croats, Serbs, and Macedonians worked together and even intermarried. After the collapse of the Yugoslavian state, nationalism fueled savage wars in Croatia, Bosnia, and Kosovo.

New myths arose to fuel ancient animosities. The Macedonian government promulgated the assertion that Alexander the Great is the forefather of the modern state—in spite of considerable historical evidence to the contrary. Macedonian was made the official language even though ethnic Albanians comprise a quarter of the country. The Albanians are Muslims, but the Macedonian Orthodox Church became dominant in the state. Albanians responded with their own nationalistic chauvinism.

In spite of its shortcomings, a nation-state can provide its residents with a certain level of certainty. Safety and predictability are possibilities in nation-states, and much less certain in stateless societies. In ecological terms, nation-states provide predictable structures for our interactions with each other and our territories. Commerce, transportation, and education can be conducted more effectively in nation-states. Nations can isolate themselves from other nations or open their borders to outside influences.

They can be friendly or hostile to their neighbors. Nations can encourage the growth and development of their communities and regions and seek good lives for their citizens. Conversely, nations can be oppressive and doctrinaire. Whatever their governing philosophy, nation-states need to adjust to changing global conditions.

THE GREEN CHAOS
OF THE PLANET

. . . there are no fixtures in nature.
The universe is fluid and volatile.
—RALPH WALDO EMERSON

"THINK GLOBALLY, ACT LOCALLY" HAS BECOME A RALLYING CRY FOR
environmentalists. Richard Forman has reformed this phrase and suggested that we "Think globally, plan regionally, and then act locally."[1] How to
plan regionally and act locally within the local or regional context is best
addressed by the people who live there. We are left then with the challenge
of how to "think globally" yet remain sensitive to local and regional places.
Or, put another way: How can the landscapes of the planet adjust to
changes, while retaining their fundamental characteristics?

I sat in an Atlanta airport café on September 11, 2001, en route to
Dulles in Washington, D.C., and watched a nest of madmen change the
course of nation-states. In subsequent calls for revenge and retaliation, the
culpability of nations and states became topical for current and former
politicians, varied experts, and news anchors around the world. One act
begets another. One act is connected to another, and another.

We possess an abundance of information about world affairs, but too
little knowledge about the interrelationships of phenomena. In the nineteenth and twentieth centuries, economic theory helped us gain some understanding about the relationships among natural resources, human labor,
and wealth. But, according to the American novelist Richard Powers,
"Economic theory stopped too soon, reducing the world's mad exchange to

mere Supply, Demand, and Price. The result resembled the Budapest Quarter nobly sawing away at a transcription of Mahler's Eighth."[2] As four musicians cannot perform a work intended for a symphony orchestra, a discipline that reduces human interaction to monetary exchanges can only explain limited aspects of the human conditions. Ecological theory, especially as it includes people, can help us better grasp "the world's mad exchange," its complexity and apparent contradictions.

The Gaia hypothesis offers an ecological explanation for global systems. According to the theory's creator, James Lovelock, "the biosphere is a self-regulating entity with the capacity to keep our planet healthy by controlling the chemical and physical environment."[3] This definition of Gaia indicates that the biosphere has the "capacity" to sustain the health of the planet. We humans play the pivotal role in determining that capacity. If we draw too much from the biosphere or overburden it with our waste, then its ability to provide the essentials for life is hampered.

Ecological thinking on the global level presents a daunting challenge. Continental associations of nations, such as the European Union and the cooperation resulting from the North American Free Trade Agreement, suggest possibilities for international interactions. Computer, satellite, and telecommunication technology provide tools to monitor global processes. It has been said that we are living in a Computer Age or, more broadly, an Information Age, that information represents power. Our challenge is to make sense of that information. Ecology helps us make connections, reveal relationships. If the interrelationships among bits of information can be understood to produce better knowledge about the world we live in, then we can inhabit an Ecological Age. If so, we need to aspire to an ecological literacy to complement our electronic literacy.

LANDING ON DISTANT SPHERES

"In Wildness is the preservation of the world," Thoreau declared. Earth is alive. We went into space to discover the obvious. Danilo Palazzo, planning professor at Milan Polytechnic, notes that when we could see for the first time the whole Earth from space, our perspective of our planet was altered forever.[4] Václav Havel reflects that the 1969 moon landing marked the end of the modern age, when "a new age in the life of humanity can be dated."[5] As Aldo Leopold observed, "Possibly, in our intuitive perceptions, we realize the invisibility of the earth—its soil, mountains, rivers, forests, climate, plants, and animals, and respect it collectively not only as a useful servant, but as a living being."[6] Leopold, McHarg, and others provided observations about Earth as a living entity that set the stage for the Gaia hypothesis.

Lovelock provides a succinct explanation of the hypothesis:

> The entire range of living matter on Earth, from whales to viruses, and from oaks to algae, could be regarded as a single living entity, capable of manipulating the Earth's atmosphere to suit its overall needs and endowed with faculties and powers far beyond those of its constituent parts.[7]

In 1974, Professors Gerald Young and Tom Bartuska of Washington State University described a framework for understanding global structure and functions. Young's academic background was in forest ecology and geography, while Bartuska's was in architecture. Together, they were instrumental in shaping the innovative, multidisciplinary environmental science and regional planning programs at WSU. Bartuska and Young observed that "earth's varied environments . . . exhibit a high-level conceptual unity and integration."[8] They borrow from ecologist Paul Sears the idea of the sphere as a unifying device:

> A unifying concept is inherent in use of the familiar combining form "sphere" from the Latin *sphaera*; e.g., in conjunction with a descriptive term such as the Greek *atmos* for vapor, it forms atmosphere. Other such terms as biosphere, hydrosphere, and lithosphere are commonly found in science literature and widely understood by laymen.[9]

Sears suggested the use of lithosphere, atmosphere, hydrosphere, biosphere, and psychosphere as an organizing structure. He had been influenced by the Russian biochemist Vladimir Vernadsky, who had published a study of the planet Earth as *The Biosphere* in 1926. Young and Bartuska recommended the substitution of Vernadsky's "noosphere" for Sears's psychosphere,[10] which I will return to later in this chapter. Young and Bartuska further refined the Sears-Vernadsky ordering scheme for the environment and proposed the following system:

> *The Lithosphere.* From *lithos*, the Greek word for stone, the outer part of the solid earth in some usages; or the entire solid or stone sphere of the earth.
>
> *The Hydrosphere.* From *hydro*, Greek for water, the earth's water environment; all of the earth's water, including oceans, lakes, streams, underground water, and vapor in the atmosphere; noted by the hydrologic cycle.
>
> *The Pedosphere.* From *pedon*, the Greek for ground or soil, the "true soil"

that upper part including the A and B horizons and most directly reflecting the processes by which soils are formed; the generic soil.

The Biosphere. From *bios*, the Greek word for life; the earth's area or layer of life; all life, the earth's biomass, including people.

The Atmosphere. From *atmo*(s), Greek for air or vapor; the gaseous envelope surrounding the earth.[11]

Gerald Young and Tom Bartuska used "ecosphere" from LaMont Cole as an overarching sphere.[12] As an ecosystem is more complex than an individual species, and an ecoregion more complex than a bioregion, the ecosphere concept is larger than the biosphere. The ecosphere combines the layer of life with the physical processes that fuel it. The ecosphere is "the sum total of life on earth together with the global environment and the earth's total resources."[13] The ecosphere is, thus, the world's "largest possible ecosystem."[14]

The framework conceived by Bartuska and Young helps us conceive global processes. We inhabit a big rock, the lithosphere, floating in space, surrounded by gas, the atmosphere. Water and soil systems create the platform for a thin layer of life, the biosphere. By conceiving Earth as this series of spheres, we can connect our local surroundings to global processes. We look out to our backyard garden where trees, shrubs, and flowers are part of both our habitat and the biosphere.

GLOBAL WARMING

Is there a global language, some form of communication that unites us as a species? The language of science crosses national borders and regional barriers. The science of climatology provides a global perspective. The increased interest in global climate change, coupled with more sophisticated monitoring devices, has advanced our understanding of weather systems. While we debate the extent of global warming, and whether it poses a problem, we undeniably know more about the planet's climate and understand its climate has changed and is changing.

We can watch hurricanes collide with Caribbean islands in real time on CNN or a specialized weather station on the television in Warsaw or New Orleans or Abu Dhabi. Or we can click into the Internet to receive current information about temperature and storm fronts for any place in the world. Satellites provide a perspective unavailable, even unthinkable, to previous generations.

Climatologists understand global weather patterns well. Air pressures affect air movements and winds. As a result, "air moves from high pressure regions to regions of low pressure," according to Forman, who further observes, "because of the Earth's rotation, air movement also has a strong east-west directionality."[15] These patterns result in distinct climatic zones that help shape the structures and characters of regions and landscapes.

The sun drives weather on Earth. The sun heats the surface of the planet, which in turn, radiates energy back into space. Atmospheric gases trap some of this outgoing energy, retaining some heat. The analogy of the glass panels of a greenhouse has been used to describe this process, and, hence, the term "greenhouse effect" is used. The natural greenhouse effect produces a temperature that makes life possible.

However, since the beginning of the industrial revolution in the nineteenth century, the atmospheric concentrations of greenhouse gases—primarily carbon dioxide, methane, and nitrous oxide—have been increasing. Human activities, such as the combustion of fossil fuels, are responsible for these increases. Industry, agriculture, and other human activities, coupled with an expanding world population, contribute to the processes of global change. This change may significantly alter Earth's habitat within a few generations.

Climate change affects the whole planet. Never before have people been able to detect change at this scale and, furthermore, attribute ourselves to be responsible. As a result, through national and international organizations, we have begun to take action. Worldwide observations result in global measurements and improved records of changes. This monitoring aids in the understanding of the physical, chemical, and biological processes responsible for changes in Earth's system on all relevant spatial and time scales. In many nations, scientists document global change and study past fluctuations. These studies enable forecasts of possible futures.

AGENTS OF CHANGE

Natural global processes and systems are dynamic, but remain relatively stable over long periods of time. Global cultural systems experience greater dynamism, but, as global warming and El Niño illustrate, even natural global systems can exhibit dramatic variability. However, dramatic cultural swings seem to occur more frequently than in the past. An international banker speculating on "hedge funds" anywhere in the world can bring down whole national economies, as examples from Asia in the late 1990s demonstrated.

Computer technologies, in particular, are changing international cultures from banking and business to construction and design.

Change doesn't just happen. A variety of economic, social, and technological forces *drive* change. What drivers of change influence, or might influence, the continued development of communities and regions around the world? Some possibilities include the following:

- Population dynamics and consumption
- Urbanization
- Connectivity and networks
- Technology, economics, and politics
- Culture and the arts
- Education and human services
- Global and regional environmental processes

Population growth and migration include those factors that will change the demographic structure of the planet. Over 6 billion people currently inhabit the planet. The United Nations projects the world's population to plateau at 9.4 billion by the year 2050 then creep up to 10.4 billion by 2100.[16] This translates into some 12.6 billion more folks joining us over the next century.[17] Half of the world's population lives in cities. In the future, even more people will move to urban regions. Global urban populations are expected to double by 2030.[18] By 2050 two-thirds of the people in the world will be living in urban regions. Various estimates exist about trends in birth and life structure as well as the distribution of income and property.

Population growth drives change because everyone requires water, food, shelter, clothing, and energy. However, levels of consumption vary. The United Nations notes that globalization tends to separate the costs from the benefits because "consumers derive goods and services from ecosystems around the world. . . . This tends to hide the environmental costs of increased consumption from those doing the consuming."[19] Our desires to consume the basics and the amenities of life affect the level of resources necessary to fulfill those demands.

Population changes—such as growth and migration—and consumption are related to urbanization. The movement of people to cities and metropolitan regions involves the transformation of spaces from rural and natural to urban and suburban, the urbanization of the wild, the abandonment of the rural, and the recovery of the core city and older suburban neighborhoods. Here are some key questions related to both population growth and urbanization:

Why do people choose to live where they do?
What policies direct/affect growth and development?
What are the long-term impacts of these policies?

Connectivity involves the ways that new networks and information systems will alter communities, transfer of knowledge, time, social relationships, and education. Connecting technologies—the automobile and the Internet—may also divide people and, thus, further fragment communities. We constantly attempt to connect through information and transportation technologies. Connectivity will continue to transform human society, but how? Some queries we could use to find answers are the following:

What will communities look like when people don't have to be next to each other for commercial reasons?
How will business, educational, and public institutions be affected?
How will connectivity affect use, knowledge, experience, and perception of place?

Connectivity and networks from new technologies are likely to drive global changes. Technological change is often linked to politics. Examples of technological and political linkages include war, energy policy, and scientific advances, such as space exploration and biotechnology. Changes in the gross national and domestic products, extractive enterprises, industry and manufacturing, food and fiber, tourism, and transportation drive economics, too.

Changing technologies affect politics. Scientists seeking to make ranching more economical tinkered with the food supply of cattle. Recycled animals beefed up the protein and mineral content of feed; however, when unhealthy dead animals entered this food stream, mad cow disease resulted. As the disease spread in Europe, beef consumption dropped drastically. Angry Europeans demanded that feed laced with animal products be banned. As Europeans turned to seafood for relief, they found that increased levels of dioxins were appearing in fish and fish oil.

The culture and the arts also drive change. Recreation and entertainment affect our aspirations and expectations. The Beatles, for example, helped define the youth culture of the late twentieth century. "All you need is love," they proclaimed in the midst of dramatic change.

The past also helps shape the future. As a result, understanding the history and prehistory of nations, regions, and communities can help us to anticipate possible changes. For example, I introduced the prehistoric Hohokam people (from a Pima word meaning "those who have gone") in chapter 4. They built a thriving culture in the river valleys of what is now southern Arizona. Their extensive agricultural settlements depended on a clever system of canals that diverted waters from the Salt and Gila Rivers. Their culture existed from as early as 300 B.C. to around A.D. 1450 when they "disappeared" for unknown reasons. Archaeologists have speculated that their decline had to do with extended periods of drought, overuse of water, social adjustments, or some combination of these factors. The Hohokam canal system was adapted by Arizona settlers in the late nineteenth century. By understanding the Hohokam system, these settlers were able to anticipate a new network of canals. By continuing to explore why the Hohokam disappeared, perhaps we can avoid repeating the same mistake.

Historic innovations in education such as universal public primary and secondary schools and the GI Bill in the United States have resulted in dramatic transformations. Future alterations in education and other human services are likely to have similarly dramatic impacts. For example, how health care is delivered to an aging population will no doubt drive change.

The global environmental processes also drive social changes and adaptations. As noted earlier, global warming trends are well known.[20] These changes already influence the life cycles of polar bears in the Arctic. Normally, polar bears spend much of the year on the ice bulking up on enough fish to allow them to survive winter hibernation. As the winter seasons shrink and the bears are forced to spend more time on land, they have less time to build their body weight. The health of the species becomes threatened when smaller cubs are born to mothers who have less time to look after their young because of their need for food.

Already, in the South Pacific, small islands disappear as the calamities of nature increase. Rising seawater, hurricanes, beach washouts, coral destruction, fish kills, and cyclones plague these remote specks of land.

In Costa Rica, the rain forest islands around mountaintops dwindle annually with less and less cloud cover to support moisture-dependent species. These habitats occur where condensate occurs, which is the top of mountains where the air cools enough to produce clouds. As the climate warms, the temperature gradient rises up the mountain, diminishing the cloud habitat and effectively trapping the flora and fauna into extinction (such species cannot go down the mountain because it is too warm for them, nor can they "leap" to another, perhaps taller mountain). It's a dead end for them.

Meanwhile, local climate changes as a result of the urban heat island, or heat archipelago, effect. This effect involves the additional heating of the air over urban settlements as a result of the replacement of naturally vegetated surfaces with those composed of asphalt, concrete, rooftops, and other human-made materials. For example, between 1970 and 1990, summer nighttime average temperatures in the Phoenix metropolitan region increased by 2.2°C, and by 6°C between rural desert and inner urban locations.[21] Additional environmental drivers of change influencing the global commons and, to varying degrees of possibility, specific regions and landscapes include natural disasters (which create more refugees than wars), the nitrogen cycle, and energy uses and greenhouse effects.

THE COARSE PORCELAIN OF THE WORLD'S SKIN

Between the ecosphere and the other biophysical spheres, Young and Bartuska suggested the use of the noosphere and the dybosphere. The noosphere concept is traced by Young and Bartuska to antiquity, quoting Socrates, "all philosophers [have held] mind to be the king of heaven and earth."[22] Vernadsky proposed adapting the Greek *nous*, meaning "mind."[23] Thus, noosphere becomes a new earthly envelope of human intellect and ideas, "an immense and growing edifice of ideas"—a reconstruction of the biosphere in the interests of freely thinking humanity as a totality; "a global domain of reflection."[24]

The dybosphere is derived from dybology, coined by the technology writer Richard Landers in the 1960s, to designate "the realm of artificially created things which behave in a life-like manner."[25] Young and Bartuska observe that the machines we make "*are* part of our environment."[26] Another term for the same thing is technosphere. A connection between the dybosphere and its impact on human interrelationships was suggested by the Canadian communication theorists Marshall McLuhan and Quentin Fiore in the 1960s, "The medium, or process, of our time—electric technology—is reshaping and restructuring patterns of social interdependence and every aspect of our personal life. It is forcing us to reconsider and re-evaluate practically every thought, every action, and every institution formerly taken for granted."[27] McLuhan argued that electronic media—in particular, television—were creating a "global village" in which "the medium was the message." McLuhan's global village provides an example of the dybosphere.

The worlds of ideas and technology keep the people on the planet spinning. Good ideas can lie dormant for years in wait of the right techniques for their resurrection. For example, Leonardo da Vinci conceived of flying machines and automation well in advance of their realization. He based his proposals on close observations of nature, such as the wings of birds and the physics of light. Leonardo's ideas became machines comprising elements of our environment.

SPACESHIP EARTH

Central to Young and Bartuska's proposal for the use of spheres is that they be viewed as interacting systems. McHarg suggested that the phenomena that comprise these spheres—rocks, water, soils, plants, and animals—be viewed hierarchically and causally.[28] That is, older components have affected and help explain younger elements, rock formations help determine water flows, which influence soil formation, which permits certain plants to grow. In McHarg's words:

> Chronology is a very good unifying device. First, we have the scientist identify bedrock geology, which is the most ancient and enduring of all subsequent events. Next, we add geomorphology, hydrology, and physiography. And then we look at the climatic impingement that explains soils and distribution of plants and animals. Through this process, the scientist has made a layer cake of chronology helping us to better understand the place as an interacting biophysical process.[29]

Such chronological understanding can be applied to the global scale. We begin with the earth itself, the mass of rock that comprises this planet. That material, our distance from the sun, and how we rotate daily and yearly determines climatic structure. The interaction of these processes establishes the conditions necessary for life.

NASA scientists employ a similar approach in their study of life in the universe. In their quest, NASA astrobiologists ask three questions:

How does life begin and develop?
Does life exist elsewhere in the universe?
What is life's future on Earth and beyond?

To study how life begins and develops, astrobiologists seek to understand how life arose on Earth; to determine the general principles governing the organization of matter into living systems; to explore how life evolves on molecular, organism, and ecosystem levels; and to determine how the terrestrial biosphere has co-evolved with Earth. NASA astrobiologists use a hierarchical approach from the cell to the ecosystem to explore the prospects for life on other planets.

Through better understanding Earth systems, NASA scientists become better equipped to explore the existence of life elsewhere in the universe. They have established four goals to address this question: (1) to establish limits for life in environments that provide analogs for conditions on other worlds; (2) to determine what makes a planet habitable and how common these worlds are in the universe; (3) to determine how to recognize the signature of life on other worlds; and (4) to determine whether there is (or once was) life elsewhere in our solar system, particularly on Mars and Europa, a moon of Jupiter. We know liquid water once flowed on the surface of Mars and may still exist below its surface. There are also indications that liquid water may exist beneath the icy crust of Europa.

By pursuing these goals, NASA astrobiologists can analyze life's future on Earth and beyond. To do so, they need to determine how ecosystems respond to environmental change on timescales relevant to human life on Earth. Then they can attempt to understand the response of terrestrial life to conditions in space or on other planets.

Astrobiologists observe extreme environments on Earth to provide analogs for understanding possible life on other planets. Examples of extreme environments studied by NASA include Antarctica and the Arctic, glaciers and ice sheets, hot springs, hot deserts, the stratosphere, volcanoes, deep ocean hydrothermal vents and cold seep communities (places where energy-rich fluids are seeping out of the ocean floor due to the geology of the underlying sediments and rock layers), and subterranean environments and caves. The impact sites of meteorites and comets are explored, as well, because of their origins in space. As NASA continues its studies of the extreme and unusual environments of the planet, our knowledge of living systems will expand.

Ecology provides an integrating device to aid in understanding the world around us. Ecological investigations help to reveal interactions. At a global scale, natural interactions occur, such as between water flows and plant associations, as well as cultural interactions such as those between nations. Such interactions can be violent or peaceful. They can contribute to the betterment of human welfare or detract from it.

Institutions have been formed to regulate the interactions among nations. The League of Nations, founded after the First World War, was the

first institution to attempt to promote international peace. All the major
European powers joined the sixty-three-nation organization. The League
was involved in many social, economic, and political activities but faltered
and then fell apart with the rise of Fascism.

The Second World War led to the second major effort to create an international forum for peaceful interaction. In addition to its peacekeeping
efforts, the United Nations is involved in many social welfare, economic
development, and emergency relief efforts. From Nairobi, the United Nations also maintains a small environmental monitoring effort. It provides
leadership in understanding the global environment and in taking international action to improve environmental quality, as its sustainable development and global climate change initiatives indicate.

In many ways, however, global institutions lag behind our understanding of planetary systems and the technologies that permit us to communicate across boundaries. Relations even between two nations can be a challenge that is complicated by many factors, including history, language, and
economics. Technology offers the possibility for better communication between, and among, nations. The world seems to be shrinking as a result of
computer and communications technologies. As the world becomes smaller and the ability to communicate becomes easier, the potentials for international institutions grow.

BIODIVERSITY

Biological diversity, or biodiversity as it has come to be known, refers to the
number, variety, and population sizes of living species in their physical
habitats[30] and, more broadly, the variety of life on Earth.[31] Our planet is a
diverse sphere. Although NASA continues to search, we do not know if
similar globes are floating out there somewhere in the universe. We only
know about our home—its vast oceans and deserts, its precious algae and
earthworms, the productive plants and soils, which keep the whole enterprise afloat. Life flourishes even in the extreme environments studied by
the NASA astrobiologists as possible analogs of other planets. There are
other stars, we know, but are there other places where light is transformed
so efficiently?

Leonardo observed, "the earth wears away the mountains and fills up
the valleys and if it had the power it would reduce the earth to a *perfect*
sphere."[32] We are fortunate that such a transition has not occurred. In-

stead, we inhabit a sphere of infinite peaks and valleys, greens and grays, wets and dries, wines and vinegars, goods and evils, loves and hates, wars and peaces, prejudices and understandings.

The human condition of the planet is not fair. The world is divided between the "haves" and the "have-nots." Paul Hawken summarized this situation as follows: "The cornucopia of resources that are being extracted, mined, and harvested is so poorly distributed that 20 percent of the earth's people are chronically hungry or starving, while the top 20 percent of the population, largely in the north[ern Hemisphere], control and consume 80 percent of the world's wealth."[33]

The United Nations indicates that this translates into uneven consumption rates among countries: "the unevenness of consumption of ecosystem goods and services worldwide is striking. It takes roughly 5 ha [12.3 ac] of productive ecosystem to support the average U.S. citizen's consumption of goods and services versus less than 0.5 ha [1.2 ac] to support consumption levels of the average citizen in the developing world."[34] Such disparity is neither fair nor sustainable.

To create a more equitable world, we must recognize, first, the basic needs of all people and, second, the great diversity of cultures that exist on the planet. All people need to be healthy, which requires adequate water, food, and shelter. Most need clothing and energy to keep them warm at night. Beyond these basics, education is necessary to elevate and sustain a culture. Education helps people appreciate the plurality of possibilities for the human condition.

Diversity is our hope. Diverse systems have the capacity to respond to infection more quickly and more effectively than homogeneous ones. Diversity is our planetary birthright. Can we learn to emphasize the positives of variety? Can we learn to celebrate the irregular, the complex, the odd, the queer?

The health of our planet rests in part on the answer to these questions. To maintain planetary diversity, it is important that various regional and national cultures remain distinct. Cultures exist through the specific circumstances of geography and of history. Such circumstances combine to form specific characteristics. A variety of cultures, each with varying characteristics or personalities, create rich possibilities for art and music, for food and dress. Diverse cultures advance the arts and science through the infusion of new and/or different ideas, ways of thinking, and discussion into the global community.

Cultural diversity contributes to the overall biological diversity of the planet. E. O. Wilson urges that "[b]iological diversity must be treated more

seriously as a global resource, to be indexed, used, and above all, preserved."[35] More serious treatment is warranted because we humans depend
on biodiversity. Although we depend on it, we are negatively impacting
global diversity. As populations increase, communities expand, often at the
expense of ecosystem, the fraying web of life that supports us.

WISDOM SITS IN PLACES

Architecture and planning face a significant theoretical challenge in attempting to come to grips with the new world order. Planning, in particular, is a product of the modern era. Beginning with the sanitary movement
in the nineteenth century, planning was based on the premise that we could
use knowledge about our environment to improve the human condition.
Modernism provided the basis for similar optimism in architecture and the
other design arts.

But we do not inhabit a truly rational world, and the modern era in architecture has passed us by. Some planning theorists have attacked the rational model of planning but have not established a suitable alternative.
The notion of anti-rational planning is counterintuitive. Some responses in
architecture have been equally silly, such as deconstructionism.[36]

The basis for a "new rationalism" exists, in fact, it has existed for some
time. For instance, in a 1965 talk at Washington State University, economist Kenneth Boulding said,

> In the imagination of those who are sensitive to the realities of our era, the
> earth has become a space ship, and this, perhaps, is the most important sin-
> gle fact of our day. For millennia, the earth in men's minds was flat and il-
> limitable. Today, as a result of exploration, speed, and the explosion of scien-
> tific knowledge, earth has become a tiny sphere, closed, limited, crowded,
> and hurtling through space to unknown destinations. This change in man's
> image of his home affects his behavior in many ways, and is likely to affect
> it much more in the future.[37]

Boulding's spaceship Earth helps us understand that what happens in one
part of the planet can affect other places—from Chernobyl to nuclear testing in India. Chaos theory helps us realize that apparently random phenomena have order. Ecology provides a way to understand the connections
and interrelationships between living things and their environments.

And so, a humble, yet ambitious, approach to planning and design is necessary. We can make Earth a better place by making sustainable and regenerative designs and plans. A few such designs exist, mostly at site, community, and landscape levels—for example, the John T. Lyle Center for Regenerative Studies in Pomona, California; EDAW and Enric Miralles/ Benedetta Tagliabue's Parc Diagonal Mar in Barcelona; and the Alterra Institute in Wageningen, The Netherlands, designed by the German architect Stefan Behnisch and others.

The Center for Regenerative Studies grew out of course and studio projects at the California State Polytechnic University in Pomona beginning during the late 1970s and continuing through the 1980s.[38] As a result of a Kellogg Foundation grant, the center opened in 1994 to its first twenty residents and will eventually house ninety people engaged in regenerative practices and technologies. The center's founder, John Lyle, believed sustainability did not go far enough to address global environmental issues. We needed to go beyond sustaining the planet and its landscapes, we should regenerate living systems, he argued. The natural tendencies of ecosystems are to regenerate after disturbance. Left alone, a degraded place will usually regenerate itself; that is, it renews itself, returning to its original, pre-degraded state. A system that cannot regenerate itself is unhealthy. The Lyle Center emphasizes the role of design in the restoration of natural systems, while integrating the needs of the human community.

The Lyle Center provides an interdisciplinary setting at Cal Poly for education, demonstration, and research in regenerative systems. The 6.5-hectare (16-acre) site, adjacent to a capped landfill, was designed for the study of passive solar–designed buildings, renewable energy capture, water recycling, nutrient cycling, food-growing systems, aquaculture, native habitat, and human communities. Lyle Center participants seek to develop regenerative models for application at many different scales, including household, community, regional, and global levels.

The site for Diagonal Mar occupies a former industrial area in northeast Barcelona facing onto the Mediterranean Sea. The 34-hectare (84-acre) development will create a new neighborhood in Barcelona, consisting of an 87,000 m² retail center, six phases of housing containing 1,875 units, 74,000 m² for offices and hotels, and a future city congress/convention facility site. The 14-hectare (35-acre) park and green area forms a key part of the mixed-use complex, developed by the international real estate company Hines, in close cooperation with the Barcelona city government. The late Enric Miralles was an especially influential Catalan architect who contributed important urban design projects for the 1992 Barcelona Olympics. EDAW is the American landscape architecture firm that led the design of Centennial Park for the 1996 Atlanta Olympics. Parc Diagonal Mar paired designers experienced in developing places of international visibility that also reinforce regional identities.[39]

The city of Barcelona has a long history of innovation in contemporary design, as showcased at the 1992 Olympics. The city's leaders would like to maintain this position. As a result, the city hosted the European Conference for Sustainable Development in the Urban Environment in May 2000. In addition, an international exposition has been organized by the Barcelona city council, the Catalan autonomous government, and the Spanish government, with the unanimous support of UNESCO as the major partner. The "Universal Forum of Cultures-Barcelona 2004" will explore the topics of peace, cultural diversity, and sustainable development. City leaders view sustainability as crucial to their future and initiated several demonstration projects, such as the cleanup of the polluted Besòs River (which empties into the Mediterranean adjacent to Barcelona), and the modernization of the regional water treatment facilities. Universal Forum of Cultures activities will occur in and around the city, while the sustainability exhibitions will be organized around the Diagonal Mar site. In keeping with the Universal Forum of Cultures-Barcelona 2004, the city council and Hines signed an ambitious agreement in 1998 committing the developer to adopt detailed, specific actions to achieve sustainable development. For example, priority was given to the use of recycled materials, renewable energies and energy-saving, land-cleaning, and ecological planning. The project designers were obliged to follow these criteria.

The park provides the centerpiece of the development. Barcelona forms a dense urban area confined by natural boundaries, with relatively little public green space. Parc Diagonal Mar will be the third largest public green space in the city. To help Hines fulfill its agreement with the city, EDAW and Enric Miralles/Benedetta Tagliabue prepared a sustainability plan for the park.[40] This statement of environmental sustainability links the public/private goals for sustainability to specific design details. The plan illustrates how community participation, life-cycle costing, cost-benefit analysis, environmental monitoring, and ecological design have been used in the park-planning process. Like the American landscape architect Laurie Olin's Vila Olimpica work, Parc Diagonal Mar attempts to forge ties to Barcelona's art, architectural, and cultural traditions, while providing needed recreational and open space opportunities for a crowded city. The park was completed in 2002 and opened in advance of the Universal Forum of Cultures.

Two buildings form Alterra, which was created when the Staring Centre merged with the IBN-DLO Nature Institute as part of the overall reorganization of several independent governmental research centers and the former Wageningen Agricultural University into the Wageningen University and Research Centre. Alterra, the "Institute for Research of the Green World," thus represents the coalescence of the leading Dutch environmental and landscape facilities. In addition to the parking lot, the two buildings are surrounded by a garden designed by a Dutch landscape architect in collaboration with an ecologist.

The west building, the former Staring Centre, is a rather typical contemporary Dutch structure, with some nice touches, including an artist-designed elevator with glass walls. Recycling, cascading water forms the elevator wall opposite the door facing out to an atrium. On the other two walls, concrete has been shaped and colored to resemble the layers of a soil profile, with the topsoil layer appropriately at the top of the elevator shaft.

The east building, the former IBN-DLO Nature Institute, is an Eden-like marvel of green building interwoven with lush gardens. The facility resulted from a pilot project in sustainable design for the Dutch Ministry of Housing and the Environment as part of a European Union program that will monitor the building. The German architectural firm Behnisch, Behnisch & Partner won the competition for the building.[41]

The Alterra internal gardens exemplify collaboration at its best, as architecture, landscape, and art flow together seamlessly. Much credit must go to the Dutch government. Behnisch eschews the label "green architect," but he has produced a green building partially because of the sustainability goals of the government, partially because of the environmental mission of its users, and largely because of the ecological commitments of the American environmental artist Michael Singer and the Dutch landscape architects. They also credit the young, idealistic architects of Behnisch's office, who seized the green agenda.

The internal gardens are twin "green lungs." The building is arranged in a rectangular figure eight around the gardens, which sit below roofs made from simple tomato greenhouses like those in the surrounding countryside.

The internal pools help ameliorate the climate and are connected to the overall site drainage. Outside, wetlands have been constructed. These wetlands receive stormwater from the site for storage and treatment. From the pond, the water enters the west atrium pool next to the library. The water in this pool drops into a filter. From this point, the water flows underground to the east atrium, where it flows over a shallow pool planted with watercress and other water plants. The roots of these plants are held in screens. The water falls off the edges of the shallow pool into a deep cistern. The water in the cistern is kept warm and reused for irrigation of the atrium gardens.

The western atrium is more lush, the eastern more arid. Both are filled to the brim with plants.

I visited on two extremely hot, humid June days. With birds singing inside the indoor garden, and solar panels adjusting to the changing sunlight above, the climate had reached a quite pleasant level without air conditioning.

What else besides the energy sensitivity and gardens are "green"? No unhealthy building materials were used, and careful attention was paid to where the materials came from, with a preference for local and regional sources. The design emphasizes the importance of natural light, the careful consideration of color, and the provision of friendly, comfortable places for people to gather.

The hard materials, plants, and art tend to be segregated in the exterior spaces. Still, there are environmental successes such as the wonderful green parking lot designed to recharge water. At the larger scale, the landscape architect was to connect this former agricultural research plot to the adjacent university town while not disturbing the nearby farmlands and rural village. At this scale, his landscape plan works well.

The crowning touch of the east Alterra building is its roof. The landscape architects designed a series of multilayered roof gardens that recall the heath landscapes of the large nearby national park, the Hoge Veluwe. The roofs retain water, reducing on-site stormwater flows. The bright yellows and burnt reds create a landscape in the sky around the greenhouse roofs. The Dutch (and the Germans, as well) plant roofs on many buildings. In fact, they have workshops for homeowners on planting roofs. They use shallow-rooted plants such as moss and succulents in order to minimize the growing medium, a mixture of lava, compost, and clay. The plants are mainly creeping sedums (perennial plants found on rocks and walls) of many varieties, with some alliums (strong-smelling bulb plants).

"All buildings interfere with the environment," Stefan Behnisch has observed. "So each building should be worth the interference."[42] The landscape created by the Alterra east building and its gardens is indeed worthwhile. The complex provides inspiration for the researchers who work there—about the healing power of plants as well as the prospects of building, garden, and art fitting together to form a whole.

Efforts such as the Lyle Center, Parc Diagonal Mar, and the Alterra Institute indicate the potential for sustainable development but are not global in their scope. Ian McHarg consistently advocated a global approach to ecological planning.[43] All the environmental data collected by various national and international agencies worldwide could and should be compiled in a global geographic information system. These data would continually be updated and refined. They would be available to the public for planning and design decision making.

A global, interactive environmental database would provide a foundation for research, decision making, and international negotiation. Issues such as global climate change, fisheries decline, ocean pollution, rain forest loss, desertification, megacity growth, and the conversion of prime farmlands could be studied and discussed. In addition, local examples, such as the John T. Lyle Center for Regenerative Studies, Parc Diagonal Mar, and the Alterra Institute, can be disseminated to planners, designers, policy makers, and average citizens worldwide.

OUR GLORIOUS INSTRUMENT

I return to the question posed at the beginning of this chapter: How can landscapes adjust to global change, while retaining their fundamental natural and cultural character? Our landscapes provide barometers for assessing the appropriateness or health of our adjustments. Two concepts might help us to accommodate change, and even thrive in complex conditions.

First, we should learn what to conserve and what to preserve. *To conserve* is to keep from damage for later use, and is similar to the concept of sustainability. Many American conservationists advocate multiple use and sustained yield—that is, we can use land, water, and air for several purposes while harvesting renewable resources such as food and timber. *To preserve* is to keep safe in a current state, which implies that the place is set aside from new uses or perhaps any use. American environmentalists debate the relative merits of conservation versus preservation. Should we engage nature and be a part of it, or should we separate ourselves from natural processes with the goal of managing nature? Conservation and preservation need not be viewed as mutually exclusive. Rather, some landscapes may benefit from multiple use, while other places need to be protected from human use, and various gradations of possibilities exist in between.

Second, both governments and private businesses have limitations that hamper their ability to address pressing environmental issues, especially those related to globalization. Public entities may not possess the flexibility to creatively address issues; that is, they may be constrained by their own bureaucratic fragmentation and inertia. Private entities, on the other hand, may be so motivated by profit (and the delusion that free enterprise provides the salvation to all human problems), that both global and local negative consequences of their actions can be ignored.

In the United States, a growing number of not-for-profit, nongovernmental organizations are filling the void between the private and public sectors. Environmental groups, such as land trusts, can pursue public objectives with the flexibility of private businesses. Land trusts protect the environment through the donation and purchase of private property. Nongovernmental land trusts work with landowners who wish to donate or sell conservation easements (permanent deed restrictions that prevent harmful land uses), or by acquiring land outright to maintain as open space. Cooperative, nongovernmental organizations can maintain a worldview, while protecting local interests and valuing regional cultures.

For centuries, there have been voices arguing that we should learn to live within the limits of the planet, or suffer grave consequences. Around A.D. 200, the Roman scholar Quintus Septimius Florens Tertullianus wrote, "Resources are scarcely adequate to us, while already nature does not sustain us." It is easy to dismiss Tertullianus as a doomsayer until one realizes that the fall of Rome began soon after. Indeed, much of the civilized world then entered the Dark Ages. Rome did not fall from a single cause. Certainly, the invasions by the Huns and the Visigoths, and the sacking of Rome by the latter, contributed to the fall of the Western Empire. Among the other factors, several environmental causes have been suggested, including the use of lead pipes and utensils (which poisoned the population and lowered their birthrate) and plagues (which reduced the population and the fertility of the survivors). Although the Eastern Roman, or Byzantine, Empire persisted, it too declined, partially because of the Justinianic Plague (541–767). This first documented plague pandemic killed as many as ten thousand people a day.[44]

Malthus, too, is rejected as a doomsayer, but his predictions were followed by world wars and genocide of ghastly proportions. How many times will we be visited by threats of the Four Horsemen of the Apocalypse—famine, war, pestilence, and death—before we begin to live within our limits? Barrett and Odum warn, "Human society is rapidly approaching, and in some aspects already overshooting, global carrying capacity."[45]

We inhabit Thoreau's "most glorious instrument." Can we learn to be more than an audience to its strains and develop as musicians that can play the instrument with precision and beauty?

FOLLOWING
NATURE'S LEAD

Our attention to physical pollution may distract us from the fact that much of the debate is over the perception of moral pollution.

—NEIL EVERNDEN

OUR PLACE IN NATURE PROVIDES A CENTRAL THEME OF PHILOSOPHY and religion. All the major faiths address this fundamental relationship. According to Abraham J. Heschel, who was a professor of ethics and mysticism at the Jewish Theological Seminary of America, "Biblical thinking has concentrated, in discussing Nature, primarily upon the sublimity of Nature. Perhaps no other literature in the world has paid so much attention to what is sublime about Nature."[1] Furthermore, the Bible provides guidance about how we should treat our environment. Heschel observed, "the idea of the Sabbath is the central idea in the Bible. . . . What is the idea of the Sabbath? First of all, to abstain from labor, to stop exploiting Nature. Six days a week we are given the right to labor, we have the privilege and duty to labor. Even to master the forces of Nature. On the seventh day that right has been suspended."[2] The Bible also includes provisions about the seventh year, the sabbatical, "in which it is forbidden to sow, to reap. This is the Sabbath of Nature, the Sabbath of the soil. It is the year in which man must abstain from exploiting nature."[3]

The Jewish Old Testament was, of course, accepted by the Christians, and additional ideas about people and their environments were introduced in the New Testament. According to the Protestant theologian Paul Tillich, people both control nature and participate with nature.[4] Tillich observed that in Judeo-Christian tradition the "controlling attitude" about nature is found "everywhere."[5] But he finds the "participating attitude . . . equally strong."[6] According to Tillich, there is a prevailing "idea of the participation of nature in man and his history—in the great drama of Creation, Fall, and Salvation. All nature participates in this. On the other hand, the Bible knows that man controls nature."[7]

Historian Lynn White Jr. and Ian McHarg wrote articles in the 1960s blaming Christianity for the environmental degradation of the modern era. White wrote that Christianity "not only established a dualism of man and nature but also insisted that it is God's will that man exploit nature for his proper ends."[8] In his usual straightforward manner, McHarg observed, "The inheritors of the Judaic-Christian-Humanist tradition have received their injunction from Genesis, a man-oriented universe, man exclusively made in the image of God, given dominion over all life and non-life, enjoined to subdue the earth."[9]

Biblical scholar James Barr, for one, disputes the multiply-and-subdue position, asserting, "The Jewish-Christian doctrine of creation is . . . much less responsible for the ecological crisis than is suggested by arguments such as those of Lynn White. On the contrary, the biblical foundations of that doctrine would tend in the opposite direction, away from a license to exploit and towards a duty to respect and to protect."[10]

Some Christian theologians, such as Sallie McFague, recommend that Christianity should be viewed in an ecological context.[11] McFague makes parallels between "God's body" and "the universe."[12] John Cobb draws another analogy: "Human beings are placed in a position in relation to other creatures much like that of God in relation to the whole of creation."[13]

A few examples exist where Christians have created places of worship from nature. Near Kraków, Poles have mined the Kopalnia Soli in the town of Wieliczka since the early thirteenth century. The mine reaches depths of 330 meters (1,082 feet), with over 200 kilometers (124 miles) of tunnels. Polish miners sculpted walls from the salt, making statues of heroes, kings, queens, mythical figures, and saints. They also made a magnificent cathedral, complete with altars, religious figures, and reliefs depicting Biblical scenes—all carved from salt.

A priest in Switzerland, Probst Xaver Niklaus Krus, decided to build a cathedral in the forest near Beromünster in 1790.[14] It took some time for his church of white beeches and chestnuts to grow, and during this time, the forest-cathedral went unnoticed by the church hierarchy. When the church did take note, Probst Krus's vision was not appreciated, and the forest cathedral was abandoned. Today, even a non-Christian can be moved in the cathedral cavern of salt below the Polish landscape and by the green basilica in the Swiss countryside. These exceptions reinforce the more prevalent Christian separation from nature. Or perhaps they, too, illustrate a controlling attitude, a dominion over nature, yet many people still feel a closer connection in these places of worship than in a Baroque cathedral.

In Islam, perhaps, the participation view occupies a stronger position than the "controlling attitude" of the Judaic-Christian tradition. Nature is revered. The garden is sacred. In the garden, people manipulate natural forces and natural materials. Animal and human images are also viewed as sacred and cannot be represented in Islamic art. The resulting artworks appear more organic and more abstract than traditional Western representational images.

Hindu theology stresses "oneness" among the natural, the human, and the divine. At the base of the Hindu pyramid of reality is the physical universe, at its apex the godhead. In between, infinite ecological relationships exist. As with the biological sciences, Hinduism recognizes unity in diversity. Complexity is acknowledged and celebrated. In Hinduism, nature is "a living presence revealing the majesty of God."[15]

In Taoism, as in most Indian and Chinese philosophy, the universe-nature is thought to perform like a play. The negative and the positive in Chinese philosophy, the yang and the yin, had their origins in the south and the north sides of a mountain: the south, or yang, toward the sun; and the north, or yin, in the shadows.[16] In Zen Buddhism, people are not separate from their environments. Alan Watts, the English-born interpreter of Eastern philosophies for the West, contrasted the western view of God as "the architect of the universe" or "as One outside it who plans it and builds it and puts it together as a construct" with the eastern view of God as "the way of things" where the view "is not the idea of construction but rather of growing."[17] As a result, God becomes the grower of things.

Each culture defines its relationship with the land in its own specific manner, giving rise to characteristic settlement patterns, economic structures, laws or rules, and land ethics. For example, the Navajo, who call themselves Diné (meaning "the People"), relate to the land as their mother, believing they are an extension of Mother Earth. As a result, people are part of the Earth's beauty. They also contend that land was created by God for everyone's use and, therefore, that land should not be bought or sold. They believe that if land is owned by one person, then it will be wanted by someone else and conflict will result. The Iroquois people maintain that every human action should consider its impact on the seventh generation in the future.

Religion provides ethical glue to stick us to each other and to the Earth. Religion attempts to link us to our pasts and futures.

To consider our impacts on future generations, we should try to understand the world around us. Young and Bartuska remarked, "the transcendental belief [is] that each part of the environment is, or can be, an emblem, symbol, or analogue of an incorporate or intellectual truth."[18] We have developed sciences and arts to provide such emblems, symbols, and analogs. Human ecology is as much a way of thinking as is a precise science, but it is not a way of thinking that rejects science. Rather, science provides many of the metaphors for understanding our ecology.

The key concepts from ecology include function, structure, and change; edges, boundaries, and ecotones; interaction, integration, and institution; diversity; and adaptation. People seek ways to function in their environments; they structure organizations and space to function effectively. Their functional and structural social and spatial organizations can and do change, but they also resist change. Our social and spatial organizations have edges and boundaries, which can overlap. The ecotones between human systems are rich, dynamic, and interesting places and spaces. Such spaces are ripe for interaction and integration and can exhibit great diversity. Diversity is especially significant for our species, but also quite challenging.

Our species adapts to different places and many situations. Our challenge is to develop adapting mechanisms that achieve Lynch's "adequate diversity." Such adaptation would recognize that diverse systems are healthy ones. Healthy systems sustain themselves, and sustainability depends on how we choose to live. As Beatley and Manning observe, "questions of ecological sustainability are fundamentally and inextricably tied to patterns of human settlement."[19]

Sustainable settlements would provide a necessary start. However, we ought to transcend merely maintaining the status quo and create regenerative settlements as John Lyle suggested. Regeneration implies self-organizing, self-renewing, and self-maintaining human settlements. Such places would acknowledge complexity, in fact embrace it, while encouraging choice, but choice based on knowledge and creativity rather than whimsy or fashion.

Regenerative design and planning needs to be pursued at all scales from the habitat to the globe. We must start where we live, our habitats. How might we redesign our homes and workplaces in a more regenerative manner? My former Arizona State University colleagues David Pijawka and Kim Shetter suggest that we should "bring the environment home."[20] The future of our planet begins at home. To create a sustainable future, we must meet our current housing needs while also ensuring that resources will be available for the habitats of subsequent generations. Our households connect us to Earth's natural processes. Each house has a foundation, constructed of materials from Earth. A frame rises from that foundation, built from timber or metal and covered with wood, bricks, or other natural substances from the ground.

Materials flow into our homes from our surroundings. Water, energy, food, tools, clothing—the necessities of human life—all need to be regenerated. Without an adequate supply of high-quality water, energy to warm and to cool us, and food to sustain our bodies, we perish.

Wastes flow out of our homes, created by the production of energy or left over from the amenities of our dwellings. Such wastes are shipped to places often unknown or unacknowledged by those who produce them. Much of what we currently call "waste" could be viewed as a valuable resource if conserved and reused.

If we and our neighbors take too much from our surroundings, or dispose too much material that cannot be recycled or that contains dangerous chemicals, the environment is degraded. Little by little, small individual decisions concerning our homes and workplaces combine to have deleterious, cumulating consequences. So we should ask questions about the sources of our foundations and walls, our food and clothing, our heating and cooling, as well as our packaging and tools. We should be curious about where our wastes go. The ability of future generations to live and prosper depends on it.

The building of community poses many basic questions. With whom do we wish to associate and why? Where do we choose to live and why? Do we have a choice about with whom we associate and where we live? If we have some choices, what determines them? Do the choices we make limit those of others? The organization of community prompts many questions about fairness and justice.

Leading environmentalist Donella Meadows summarized the issues facing communities: "The problem of the 21st century is how to live good and just lives within limits, in harmony with the earth and each other. Great cities can rise out of cruelty, deviousness, and a refusal to be bounded. Livable cities can only be sustained out of humility, compassion, and acceptance of the concept of 'enough.'"[21]

Reading the landscapes we travel through can reveal much about livability. We gaze out the window of a train or a plane or an auto. What does what we see say about the people who live there? What portraits have they constructed of themselves? How are the portraits of us perceived by others? Do we truly understand what we see from our view out the window? We may know more than we realize. "That's beautiful," we may remark of, say, a glimpse of Tuscany. Indeed, it may be beautiful and healthy. "Oh, my God!" we exclaim, considering blocks of abandoned neighborhoods in Detroit or East St. Louis. These places are probably unhealthy and unsafe, for the visitor and for whatever residents are forced to inhabit them. Sustainability can be viewed as a visual exercise.

We are visual animals and we should learn to trust what we see. Landscapes provide much information about how people are interacting with each other and their environments.

We wake up in Milan, the financial capital of Italy, then travel by train to Rome, the nation's capital and spiritual heart, for lunch. Historic, sunny Rome is clearly different than industrial, often overcast Milan, and the area in between different from both. The focused hustle and bustle of Milan differs from the more relaxed atmosphere of Rome. The light differs and, as a result, so do the shadows. Or we travel to Bologna or Florence. Like Milan, Bologna sits between the plain and the mountains; but Milan is businesslike, well, downright capitalistic, whereas Bologna leans much further to the left. Florence is charming but struggles to accommodate hordes of tourists; Rome has endured invasions by barbarians for centuries, and they have become incorporated, even celebrated, within the region. An intellectual Pole can become the pope (at least once in a millennium).

Of course, Kraków is hardly a barbarian hearth. In addition to a pope, several saints, and Nobel laureates, its Jagiellonian University also produced Copernicus, who altered our view of our relationship with our universe. You can wake up in Kraków, take the train to Warsaw, and drink a beer there in its Stare Miasto (Old Town). Drinking that beer and reflecting on the trip by train, you realize Warsaw is quite different than Kraków and the places in between different than both cities. Who created the differences? Was it the barbarians from outside Poland—those Germans, Russians, and Austrians, similar nemeses to the Italians?

Poland remained a nation even when it was not a state, as did Italy, Germany, and Israel. Do we need to be divided before we can see our unity? Can we capture a globalism as strong as the nationalism of the Poles or the Japanese? Must we endure tragedy and oppression as a species before we can create a global culture? To an outsider, the Irish and the British, the Indians and the Pakistanis, the Palestinians and the Israelis, the Poles and the Russians, the Germans and the Dutch, the Tutsis and the Hutus, the Croats and the Serbs, the Sunni and the Shiites, the Japanese and the Koreans, the Chinese and the Vietnamese, we Americans and everyone else seem pretty similar. Is an African American living in Harlem more likely to be similar to a WASP from the Main Line in Philadelphia or a bureaucrat from Abuja? Most probably, the Harlem resident would be similar to both the Main Line Philadelphian and the Nigerian civil servant, while remaining distinct from both. (The question is further complicated by the fact that Main Line WASPs helped design Nigeria's new capital city, Abuja.) The point is, we need to concentrate on what makes us similar rather than what differentiates us. We really have no other option. If we continue to be obsessed with our differences, we will destroy ourselves and much of the life of the planet in the process.

Havel summarizes the current state of human affairs as being "where everything is possible and almost nothing is certain" and where the "single planetary civilization to which we all belong confronts us with global challenges."[22] Among those challenges is the rate of change. Havel has also remarked, "We are living in extraordinary times. The human face of the world is changing so rapidly that none of the familiar political speedometers are adequate."[23] The world is changing so fast, we don't have time to be astounded.

Human nature, including our interactions with each other in a changing world, remains an unfinished topic. Yet, it is one we must confront. J. B. Jackson reflected, "Thoreau and Jefferson were poles apart in their definitions of human nature but they agreed completely as to the possibility of defining it; and, having once defined it, of creating a suitable environment for it."[24] Both Thoreau and Jefferson grounded their vision of human nature in the earth. As Douglas Paterson notes, "Humanity is, by definition, of the earth, as in *humus*."[25] Or, as McHarg quipped, "Nature has been in the business of form since the beginning, and man is only one of its products."[26]

We are a product of nature, yet the concept of nature is a social creation. The forces of nature—from the winds across the steppes to the tides of the sea—are real phenomena. So, we continue to refine and redefine our relationships with our surroundings, which, in turn, continue to exert influences on how we live.

Life, the English novelist and essayist John Fowles reminds us, or at least the "ordinary experience" of life, "from waking second to second, is in fact highly synthetic (in the sense of combinative or constructive), and made of a complexity of strands, past memories and present perceptions, times and places, private and public history. . . ."[27]

And so, I close this exploration of human ecology with a synthetic ordinary experience: a cab ride through Rome in mid-May. The cab sails through "the diamond light and timeless air of the Roman spring," as Gabriel García Márquez described it.[28] The cab driver is equipped with both a walkie-talkie and a *telefonino*. A constant stream of instructions and queries in rapid Italian fills our space. The *telefonino* rings and is wedged between shoulder and ear for conversation. The driver frequently consults his street map book, for Rome is a complex city to navigate. Perhaps he's learning English or French or Japanese or Arabic, or trying to improve his Italian. And so, our journey becomes a language seminar. The driver reveals a long-ago trip to North America. "Where have you been?" "What do you mean 'been'?" "Visited, *visitare*." Impressions are offered of the most beautiful cities (San Francisco, Vancouver), and the most frightening (almost all of the United States) and the most spectacular landscapes (the coasts of Oregon, Washington, British Columbia, and Alaska; the deserts of Arizona; the mountains of Colorado) as well as the dullest. The language seminar becomes a discussion of landscapes and communities, regions and nations.

The cab moves along, slicing through strata of time, geologic and human. One can touch time here. The Tiber flows parallel to the road; it moves toward the sea below the grade of the streets where the traffic flows in two opposite one-way directions on the parallel banks. Plane trees form galleries along the roads and the Tiber. Long branches dive down toward the river. A roof of limbs filters the light, forming long, sharp shadows across the road. At a traffic light, and between pauses of a jackhammer, birds chirp from somewhere in the canopy, then the whir of helicopter blades above in the sky, perhaps the pope, *il papa*.

Cars and cabs compete for limited space with trolleys, tour buses, *motorini*, and feet. Each jockeys for position. Journeys are delayed, swarms of *motorini* advance. Our cab finds space and proceeds, quickly. The driver shouts and gestures to others who cut in front of our path. The other drivers move ahead without a glance or an interruption. A woman in an espresso-colored suit, baseball cap, and dark glasses glides by on her *motorino* with a medium-sized brown terrier between her feet. A motorist says "*buon giorno*" to another driver with two toots of his horn. A *carabiniere* leans against his patrol car with machine gun pointed toward the street, while his partner snoozes behind the wheel.

Drying laundry spans balconies of tall buildings lining narrow streets that break off in all directions. A troop of pigeons in a piazza march toward a pair of tourists who are likely to have food. Several pilgrims pause at the piazza to study a map, their eyes tearing from pollen and pollution. Monuments of the ancients, the Renaissance, the Baroque are shrouded by scaffolding; "Roma per Roma," the signs read, a city in a constant state of reconstruction. A Roman ruin on the right; poster boards for sunglasses, a political party rally, and a rock concert on the left. The posters are torn and tagged with graffiti—they will not achieve ruin status. Trails of snails weave up and down the walls over and under their markings. Our cab passes part of an ancient Roman *insulae*, an apartment house, layers of time and earth below the modern city. A forum, an ancient marketplace, is nearby. Modern *farmacie*, bars, *tabaccherie*, *panetterie*, restaurants, *pizzerie*, and an assortment of other small businesses are abundant. A fountain spouts between the *insulae* and the forum. It, too, dates from Roman time. For centuries the fountain has been a terminus for water brought from nearby mountains, originally via aqueducts but now by pipes. One modern Roman fills a jug with water while another washes his small Fiat.

The sun casts dramatic shadows on the walls and buildings. All the colors—the blood oranges, ochers, lemon yellows, poppy reds, and rouges of the structures, the verdant plants, and the azure skies—are intense.

Rome lives. People interact with each other and with their physical and biological environments.

We learn from Rome, we can learn from all places. We connect to what's around us. From within, we try to make sense of it. We categorize stuff: the physical, the living, the living organisms like us—well, almost like us—this one older, that one younger, this one a boy, that one a girl. We attempt to relate to them, we interact, we engage in these exchanges in the world around us. We are ecological creatures in that we interact with each other and our worlds.

ACKNOWLEDGMENTS

THE CONCEPTION OF THIS BOOK OCCURRED WELL OVER TWENTY-FIVE years ago. As a result, it experienced a rather long gestation. In the mid-1970s, I was a graduate student in a landscape architecture and planning department chaired by Ian McHarg. After the publication of his book *Design with Nature*, which focused on the biophysical imperatives for design, McHarg turned his attention and considerable energy to human ecology. He believed anthropologists were the most compatible social scientists to an ecological view. (Unfortunately, in my opinion, he overlooked geographers, who did not have a strong presence at the University of Pennsylvania.) In any case, I benefited from generous guidance in ecological anthropology and ethnography by Yehudi Cohen, Dan Rose, and Setha Low, as well as enthusiastic experimentation in applied human ecology by Jon Berger. The wonderful designers Laurie Olin and Bob Hanna collaborated with Setha Low, linking their social art with her social science. Models for applying ecology to planning and design were abundant at the University of Pennsylvania, commonly called Penn. The Penn environment continued to be under the spell of the legendary Lewis Mumford, and, thanks to Nick Muhlenberg, the ideas of Benton MacKaye and Aldo Leopold were familiar.

After graduation, I was fortunate to join the faculty of Washington State University (WSU). There, I became a colleague of the great human ecologist Jerry Young, who had founded the WSU program in environmental science and regional planning. The indefatigable Young—a productive scholar and an invaluable mentor—exerted a considerable influence on this book. My other WSU ecological colleagues also were important, especially fellow McHarg protégé Bill Budd, as well as Jack Kartez, Tom Bartuska, Ken Brooks, Julie McQuary, Eldon Franz, John Reganold, and William Catton. Bill and Jack provided helpful comments on drafts of portions of this manuscript, while Jerry helped me track down several key publications.

Penn provided the seed, WSU the nurturing.

Then I moved away from an explicit involvement with human ecology, although it was always on my mind. In 1997, I was fortunate to be selected for the National Endowment for the Arts Rome Prize Fellowship in Historic Preservation and Conservation. What better city than Rome to consider the possibilities of the ecologies of our species?

It was John Meunier's urging that prompted me to apply for a sabbatical. His support and encouragement are most appreciated. He is the wisest, and most intelligent, dean that I have had the privilege to work with, and I have worked for several wonderful deans. Also at Arizona State University (ASU), I especially appreciate the support of my friend David Pijawka. Laurel McSherry, Subhro Guhathakurta, Rebecca Fish Ewan, and John Blair read sections of this book in draft and offered keen insights and constructive suggestions. Other ASU colleagues who have been especially supportive of my work are Ward Brady, John Brock, Theresa Cameron, Jeff Cook, Nan Ellin, Joe Ewan, Bill Kasson, Mary Kihl, Gerry McSheffrey, Laura Musacchio, Alvin Mushkatel, Chuck Redmond, Kim Shetter, Michael Underhill, and Max Underwood. Many former students also influenced my thinking. In particular, I am indebted to Anthony Farier for introducing me to the concept that a difference is a difference only when it makes a difference, to Michael Rushman for reminding me that the law evolves, and to Melissa Lind for the idea that a dwelling could be a fingerprint for values.

Early ideas for chapter 3, "Community," were first presented in the 1997 Howland lecture for the Department of Landscape Architecture, University of Virginia. I thank Beth Meyer for inviting me to Charlottesville. Likewise, an earlier version of chapter 7, "The Green Chaos of the Planet," was prepared for a conference organized by the Warsaw Agricultural University, and I thank Przemyslaw Wolski and Agata Cieszewska in this regard. Richard Forman, Bob Yaro, Ignacio Bunster, Jeffrey

Olson, Forster Ndubisi, Ingrid Duchhart, Jusuck Koh, John Simpson, Andrew Light, Paul Gabriel, Salila Vanka, and Anuradha Parmar offered advice and assistance, for which I'm grateful.

The American Academy in Rome is an idyllic scholarly institution. I very much appreciate the letters of recommendation for the Rome Prize from Mark Johnson, Ron McCoy, and Laurie Olin. As well, I thank the selection jury for the fellowship. At the Academy, Adele Chatfield-Taylor, Peter Boswell, Caroline Bruzelius, and the rest of the administrative and support staff both in Rome and New York contributed to make my stay particularly productive and enjoyable. My fellow Fellows, residents, and partners were wonderful, and listing them all would consume several pages. In particular, Rich Haag and Cheryl Trivison, Malcolm and Joan Campbell, Doug Argue, Roberto Behar, Elise Brewster and Paul Smith, Danny Caster, Isotta Cortesi, Alison Frazier, Mia Fuller and Brien Garnand, Mary Margaret Jones, Charles LeDray, John Marciari, Tod Marder, Myles McDonnell, Fae Myenne Ng, P. Q. Phan, Samina Quraeshi and Richard Shepard, Mark Schimmenti, Vincent Scully, Catherine Seavitt, David Stone and Linda Pellecchia, Laura and Richard Wittman, Lila Yawn, Carmen Vega, and Steve Lowenstam had a strong influence on my thoughts about this book. I deeply appreciate their fellowship, collegiality, and encouragement.

In addition to the Americans in Rome, several Italian scholars were helpful and influential, especially Danilo Palazzo, Maria Cristina Treu, Marcello Magoni, Vittoria Calzolari, Mario Ghio, Paola Falini, Silvia Macchi, Enzo Scandurra, Stefano Aragona, and Ornella Piscopo. Danilo Palazzo helped both with the Italian spelling as well as with information about the history of the travertine quarries between Rome and Tivoli.

Back in Tempe, Arizona, I finished the manuscript while on assignment to the ASU Vice Provost for Research Jonathan Fink. With other colleagues, the geologist Jon Fink conceived the need to coalesce the knowledge of the university to provide a vision for the Phoenix metropolitan region. He tapped me to launch the Greater Phoenix 2100 project. I appreciate his support because it forced me to think deeply about the possible applications of human ecology. ASU anthropology graduate student Kristin Sullivan contributed quick and efficient research assistance on several occasions. Chris Duplissa word-processed the manuscript for this book. Her standards for excellence are unparalleled. I appreciate her diligence and commitment to quality. Mack White of the University of Texas at Austin helped process the final revisions and his contribution is valued, too. University of Texas architecture graduate student Carolyn Roosen assisted with securing permissions for quotation and spotted a couple lingering typos in the process, as did Kosciuszko Foundation scholar Ewa Kaliszuk.

At Island Press, I value my continued association with Heather Boyer, Dan Sayre, Chuck Savitt, James Nuzum, Kristy Manning, Chace Caven, and Brighid Willson. Heather's editorial guidance and advice proved to be especially useful. The Island team provides wonderful collaborators in the adventure of publishing.

Anna Ostrowska Steiner selflessly encouraged me to go to Rome and personally oversaw the remodeling of a bathroom in my absence. I love her for many reasons, including her Polish sense of good and evil, right and wrong. Our children, Andrew and Halina, also put up with not having a dad around for a couple months. Their understanding is valued, and their letters provided insights into the importance of human relationships.

NOTES

INTRODUCTION: THE SUBVERSIVE SUBJECT

1. Paul B. Sears, "Ecology—A Subversive Subject," *BioScience* 14, no. 7 (July, 1964):11.
2. Eugene P. Odum, "Ecology as a Science," *The Encyclopedia of the Environment*, eds. Ruth A. Eblen and William R. Eblen (Boston: Houghton Mifflin, 1994), p. 171.
3. Gerald L. Young, "Human Ecology," *The Encyclopedia of the Environment*, eds. Eblen and Eblen, p. 339.
4. Paul Shepard, "Ecology as a Perspective," *The Encyclopedia of the Environment*, eds. Eblen and Eblen, p. 169. See also, Paul Shepard, "Introduction: Ecology and Man—A Viewpoint," *The Subversive Science: Essays toward an Ecology of Man*, eds. Paul Shepard and Daniel McKinley (Boston: Houghton Mifflin, 1969), pp. 1–10.

   Paul Shepard (1925–1996) was Avery Professor of Human Ecology and Natural Philosophy at Pitzer College. Generally regarded as a pioneer in modern ecology, he wrote about how humans perceive and interact with the natural world.
5. For examples of social scientists with deep environmental interests, see Gerald L. Young, "Environment: Term and Concept in the Social Sciences," *Social Science Information* 25, no. 1 (1986):83–124; William R. Catton Jr., *Overshoot: The Ecological Basis for Evolutionary Change* (Urbana: University of Illinois Press, 1980); and Karl S. Zimmerer, "Human Geography and the

'New Ecology': The Prospect and Promise of Integration," *Annals of the Association of American Geographers* 84, no. 1 (1994):108–125. Edward O. Wilson provides an example of a prominent biologist interested in social systems. For instance, see his *In Search of Nature* (Washington, D.C.: Island Press/Shearwater Books, 1996).

6. Among ecologists who address human communities, see especially, Daniel B. Botkin, *Discordant Harmonies: A New Ecology for the Twenty-First Century* (New York: Oxford University Press, 1990), and Richard T. T. Forman, *Land Mosaics: The Ecology of Landsapes and Regions* (Cambridge, England: Cambridge University Press, 1995). Important planning and design works in this regard include: Ian L. McHarg, *Design with Nature* (Garden City, New York: Natural History Press/Doubleday, 1969); Anne Whiston Spirn, *The Granite Garden: Urban Nature and Human Design* (New York: Basic Books, 1984); John Tillman Lyle, *Design for Human Ecosystems* (New York: Van Nostrand Reinhold, 1985); Timothy Beatley, *Ethical Land Use: Principles of Policy and Planning* (Baltimore: Johns Hopkins University Press, 1994); Doug Aberley, ed., *Futures by Design: The Practice of Ecological Planning* (Gabriola Island, British Columbia: New Society Publishers, 1994); Rutherford H. Platt, Rowan A. Rowntree, and Pamela C. Muick, eds., *The Ecological City: Preserving and Restoring Urban Biodiversity* (Amherst: University of Massachusetts Press, 1994); Joan Iverson Nassauer, ed., *Placing Nature: Culture and Landscape Ecology* (Washington, D.C.: Island Press, 1997); and Bart R. Johnson and Kristina Hill, eds., *Ecology and Design: Frameworks for Learning* (Washington, D.C.: Island Press, 2002).

7. For example, see Botkin, *Discordant Harmonies.*

8. A 1997 issue of *Science* included a series of articles related to this topic, including: F. Stuart Chapin III, Brian H. Walker, Richard J. Hobbs, David U. Hooper, John H. Lawton, Osvaldo E. Sala, and David Tilman, "Biotic Control over the Functioning of Ecosystems," *Science* 277 (1997):500–504; Andy P. Dobson, A. D. Bradshaw, and A. J. M. Baker, "Hopes for the Future: Restoration Ecology and Conservation Biology," *Science* 277 (1997):515–522; and Peter M. Vitousek, Harold A. Mooney, Jane Lubchenco, and Jerry M. Melillo, "Human Domination of Earth's Ecosystems," *Science* 277 (1997):494–499.

9. Zimmerer, "Human Geography and the 'New Ecology,'" p. 108.

10. H. Ronald Pulliam and Bart R. Johnson, "Ecology's New Paradigm: What Does It Offer to Designers and Planners?" *Ecology and Design,* eds. Johnson and Hill, p. 51.

11. Roy A. Rappaport, *Ecology, Meaning and Religion* (Berkeley, California: North Atlantic Books, 1979).

12. Ibid., p. 58.

13. A few, diverse examples of these changing views of people and their environments include: John W. Bennett, *The Ecological Transition: Cultural Anthropology and Human Adaptation* (New York and London: Pergamon,

1976); Torsten Malmberg, *Human Territoriality: Survey of Behavioural Territories in Man with Preliminary Analysis and Discussion of Meaning* (The Hague, The Netherlands: Mouton, 1980); Yi-Fu Tuan, *Escapism* (Baltimore: Johns Hopkins University Press, 1998); and Martin V. Melosi, *The Sanitary City: Urban Infrastructure in America from Colonial Times to the Present* (Baltimore: Johns Hopkins University Press, 2000).

14. Botkin, *Discordant Harmonies*, p. 129. Both aspects have been restated by Reed Noss and his colleagues as follows: first, "ecosystems not only are more complex than we think, but more complex than we can think" and, second, "nature is full of surprises." Reed F. Noss, Michael A. O'Connell, and Dennis D. Murphy, *The Science of Conservation Planning: Habitat Conservation under the Endangered Species Act* (Washington, D.C.: Island Press, 1997), pp. 76–77.

15. See, for example, Carl Steinitz, "GIS: A Personal Historical Perspective," GIS Europe 46 (June, 1993):19–22; Steinitz, "A Framework for Theory and Practice in Landscape Planning," *GIS Europe* 46 (July, 1993):42–45; Steinitz, "The Changing Face of GIS from 1965–1993," *GIS Europe* 46 (September, 1993):38–40; Julius Gy. Fabos, *Planning the Total Landscape* (Boulder, Colorado: Westview Press, 1979); and Ian L. McHarg, *A Quest for Life* (New York: John Wiley & Sons, 1996). One can sense why the early pioneers did not use the acronym for "planning information systems," but one wonders why "landscape information systems" was not adopted, because in many ways it is a more accurate reflection of the systems than GIS.

16. From within geography, Michael Goodchild provides considerable leadership; see: Michael Goodchild and Sucharita Gopal, eds., *The Accuracy of Spatial Databases* (London and New York: Taylor & Francis, 1989), and Goodchild, Bradley O. Parks, and Louis T. Steyaert, eds., *Environmental Modeling with GIS* (New York: Oxford University Press, 1993). For the landscape architectural leaders, see Eddie Nickens, "Map Maker," *Landscape Architecture* 86, no. 12 (1996):74–79, 88, and David F. Sinton, *Reflections on 25 Years of GIS* (Huntsville, Alabama: Intergraph, 1991).

17. Anne Vernez Moudon, "Urban Morphology as an Emerging Interdisciplinary Field," *Urban Morphology* 1 (1997):3–10. See, for example, M. R. G. Conzen's *Alnwick, Northumberland: A Study in Town-Plan Analysis* (Institute of British Geographers Publication 27) (London: George Philip, 1960).

    Dutch designers and planners also use the tissue concept when referring to urban settlement connections. Their word for tissue is weefsel.

18. Moudon, "Urban Morphology as an Emerging Interdisciplinary Field," p. 7.

19. Ibid., p. 4.

20. Carolyn Merchant, *Ecological Revolutions: Nature, Science and Gender in New England* (Chapel Hill: University of North Carolina Press, 1989); George F. Thompson, ed., Landscape in America (Austin: University of Texas Press, 1995); William Cronon, ed., *Uncommon Ground: Toward Reinventing Nature* (New York: W. W. Norton, 1995, republished in 1996 with the subtitle

Rethinking the Human Place in Nature); Paul Groth and Todd W. Bressi, eds., *Understanding Ordinary Landscapes* (New Haven and London: Yale University Press, 1997); and John Warfield Simpson, *Visions of Paradise: Glimpses of Our Landscape's Legacy* (Berkeley: University of California Press, 1999).

21. Simon Schama, *Landscape and Memory* (New York: Alfred A. Knopf, 1995); John R. Stilgoe, *Common Landscape of America, 1580–1845* (New Haven: Yale University Press, 1982); Stephen J. Pyne, *Fire in America: A Cultural History of Wildland and Rural Fire* (Princeton: Princeton University Press, 1982); William Cronon, *Changes in the Land: Indians, Colonists, and the Ecology of New England* (New York: Hill and Wang, 1983); and Cronon, *Nature's Metropolis: Chicago and the Great West* (New York: W. W. Norton, 1992).

22. John Opie, *Nature's Nation: An Environmental History of the United States* (Fort Worth, Texas: Harcourt Brace College Publishers, 1998).

23. The *Annales* school is exemplified by Fernand Braudel, *The Structures of Everyday Life: Civilization and Capitalism, 15th–18th Century* (translated from French by Siân Reynolds, New York: Harper & Row, 1981), and Emmanuel Le Roy Ladurie, *Carnival in Romans* (translated from French by Mary Feeney, New York: George Braziller, 1979).

24. Oliver Rackham, *The Illustrated History of the Countryside* (London: George and Nicole Weindenfeld, 1994).

25. For example, see Wallace Stegner's *Where the Bluebird Sings to the Lemonade Springs* (New York: Penguin, 1992), and Barbara Kingsolver's *High Tide in Tucson* (New York: HarperCollins, 1995). Harvard English professor Lawrence Buell makes a strong case for a green thread throughout American literature in *Writing for an Endangered World: Literature, Culture, and Environment in the U.S. and Beyond* (Cambridge, Massachusetts: The Belknap Press of Harvard University Press, 2001).

26. Alan Paton, *Cry, The Beloved Country* (New York: Charles Scribner's Sons, 1948), and Knut Hamsun, *Growth of the Soil* (New York: Alfred A. Knopf, 1921).

27. Mike Davis, *City of Quartz: Excavating the Future in Los Angeles* (London: Verso, 1990), and *Ecology of Fear: Los Angeles and the Imagination of Disaster* (New York: Metropolitan Books, 1998).

28. Terry Tempest Williams, *Refuge* (New York: Pantheon Books, 1991).

29. Neil Evernden, *The Social Creation of Nature* (Baltimore: Johns Hopkins University Press, 1992).

30. Ibid., p. 24.

31. Noss et al., *The Science of Conservation Planning*, and Gary Paul Nabhan, *Cultures of Habitat: On Nature, Culture, and Story* (Washington, D.C.: Counterpoint, 1997).

32. Richard T. T. Forman and Michel Godron, *Landscape Ecology* (New York: John Wiley & Sons, 1986), p. 595. This material is used by permission of John Wiley & Sons, Inc. See also, Z. Naveh and A. Lieberman, *Landscape Ecology: Theory and Applications* (New York: Springer-Verlag, 1984).

33. Edward Cook and Joan Hirschman, eds., "Special Issue: Landscape Ecology," *Landscape and Urban Planning* 21, nos. 1–2 (1991):1–46, and Forester Ndubisi, "Landscape Ecological Planning," *Ecological Design and Planning*, eds. George F. Thompson and Frederick R. Steiner (New York: John Wiley & Sons, 1997), pp. 9–44.

34. Anna Hersperger, "Landscape Ecology and Its Potential Application to Planning," *Journal of Planning Literature* 9, no. 1 (1994):14–29; Jill Grant, Patricia Manuel, and Darrell Joudrey, "A Framework for Planning Sustainable Residential Landscapes," *Journal of the American Planning Association* 62, no. 3 (1996):331–344; and Danilo Palazzo, Sulle spalle di giganti: Le matrici della pianificazione ambietale negli Stati Uniti (Milano: Francoangeli/DST, 1997).

35. Lowell W. Adams and Louise E. Dove, *Wildlife Reserves and Corridors in the Urban Environment* (Columbia, Maryland: National Institute for Urban Wildlife, 1989), and Reed F. Noss, "The Wildlands Project: Land Conservation Strategy," *Futures by Design*, ed. Aberley, pp. 127–165.

36. Daniel S. Smith and Paul Cawood Hellmund, eds., *Ecology of Greenways* (Minneapolis: University of Minnesota Press, 1993), and Jack Ahern, *Greenways as Strategic Landscape Planning: Theory and Application* (Wageningen, The Netherlands: Wageningen University, 2002).

37. Ken Yeang, *The Green Skyscraper: The Basis for Designing Sustainable Intensive Buildings* (Munich: Prestel-Verlag, 1999), and "The Ecological (or Green) Approach to Design," *Eco Enea* 148 (May, 2000):6–11.

38. Yeang, "The Ecological (or Green) Approach to Design," p. 9.

39. Ibid.

40. George Hersey, *The Monumental Impulse: Architecture's Biological Roots* (Cambridge: MIT Press, 1999), and Grant Hildebrand, *Origins of Architectural Pleasure* (Berkeley: University of California Press, 1999).

41. As quoted by Terry Tempest Williams in *Leap* (New York: Pantheon Books, 2000).

42. Artfully recreated by Don DeLillo in *Underworld* (New York: Scribner, 1997).

43. Ilya Prigogine and Isabelle Stengers, *Order Out of Chaos: Man's New Dialogue with Nature* (Toronto, Ontario: Bantam Books, 1984), p. 9.

    Ilya Prigonine Prigogine was born in Moscow on the eve of the Russian revolution in 1917. His family migrated to Belgium in 1929, where he received his education and became a citizen. Prigogine was awarded the 1977 Nobel Prize in chemistry. The Université Libre de Bruxelles and The University of Texas at Austin are his academic homes. His chaos theory collaborator, Isabelle Stengers, was born in Bruxelles in 1949 and received her education in the philosophy of science.

44. Ibid., 292.

45. Ibid.

46. Laurie Olin, *Across the Open Field: Essays Drawn from English Landscapes* (Philadelphia: University of Pennsylvania Press, 2000), p. 43.

47. D. B. Botkin and C. E. Beveridge, "Cities as Environments," *Urban*

Ecosystems 1 (1997):3–19; Steward T. Pickett, William R. Burch Jr., Shawn E. Dalton, Timothy W. Foresman, J. Morgan Grove, and Rowan Rowntree, "A Conceptual Framework for the Study of Human Ecosystems in Urban Areas," *Urban Ecosystems* 1 (1997):185–199; Nancy E. Grimm, J. Morgan Grove, Steward T. A. Pickett, and Charles L. Redman, "Integrated Approaches to Long-Term Studies of Ecological Systems," *BioScience* 50, no. 7 (2000):571–584; and James P. Collins, Ann Kinzig, Nancy B. Grimm, William F. Fagan, Diane Hope, Jiango Wu, and Elizabeth T. Borer, "A New Urban Ecology," *American Scientist* 88, no. 5 (September–October, 2000):416–425.

48. Grimm et al., "Integrated Approaches to Long-Term Studies of Ecological Systems," p. 571.

49. Richard Sandbrook, "From Stockholm to Rio," *Earth Summit '92*, ed. Joyce Quarrie (London: The Regency Press, 1992), p. 16.

50. Grant et al., "A Framework for Planning Sustainable Residential Landscapes," p. 332. Reprinted by permission of the *Journal of the American Planning Association* 63, no. 3 (1996).

51. Sheila Peck, *Planning for Biodiversity* (Washington, D.C.: Island Press, 1998), p. 12.

52. Eugene P. Odum, *Fundamentals of Ecology* (Philadelphia: W. B. Saunders, 1971), and Reed F. Noss, "Indicators for Monitoring Biodiversity: A Hierarchical Approach," *Conservation Biology* 4, no. 4 (1990):355–364.

53. Moudon, "Urban Morphology as an Emerging Interdisciplinary Field," p. 7.

54. As quoted by Myles McDonnell in a 1998 talk at the American Academy in Rome, "Public Life and *Patria Potestas.*" See Marcus Tullius Cicero, *De Officiis* 1.53–55, xvii.

55. As quoted by Rachel Fletcher, "Proportioning Systems and the Timber Framer," *Journal of the Timber Framing Guild* 18 (December, 1990):8–9.

56. Alice Jones, "The Psychology of Sustainability: What Planners Can Learn from Attitude Research," *Journal of Planning Education and Research* 16, no. 1 (1996):59.

57. Ibid.

58. Ibid.

59. See, for example, Gerald L. Young, "Hierarchy and Central Place: Some Questions of More General Theory," *Geografiska Annaler* 60B (1978):71–78, and Gerald Young, Frederick Steiner, Kenneth Brooks, and Kenneth Struckmeyer, "Planning the Built Environment: Determining the Regional Context," *The Built Environment: A Creative Inquiry into Design and Planning,* eds. Tom J. Bartuska and Gerald L. Young (Menlo Park, California: Crisp Publications, 1994), pp. 305–317.

60. Gerald L. Young, "A Conceptual Framework for an Interdisciplinary Human Ecology," *Acta Oecologiae Hominis* 1 (1989):28.

61. C. S. Holling, "What Barriers? What Bridges?" *Barriers and Bridges to the Renewal of Ecosystems and Institutions,* eds. Lance H. Gunderson, C. S. Holling, and Stephen S. Light (New York: Columbia University Press, 1995), p. 24.

62. Ibid.

63. Ibid.
64. Evernden, *The Social Creation of Nature*, p. 42.
65. Jiango Wu and Orie L. Loucks, "From Balance of Nature to Hierarchical Patch Dynamics: A Paradigm Shift in Ecology," *The Quarterly Review of Biology* 70, no. 4 (1995):439.
66. Ibid.
67. The hierarchical organization evolved in part from Bartuska and Young, eds., *The Built Environment*. That book resulted from a multidisciplinary course taught by several of us on the Washington State University (WSU) faculty. In the early 1980s, Tom Bartuska and Jerry Young organized faculty from architecture, landscape architecture, planning, environmental science, and interior design spread across campus in several WSU colleges as well as design faculty from the nearby University of Idaho to offer the course. Subsequently, they edited the volume of our collected papers including their own important contributions. (With Wendy McClure of the University of Idaho faculty, Bartuska and Young are currently preparing a revised edition of the book.) The hierarchy used in *The Built Environment* was environment, products, interiors, structures, landscapes, cities, regions, and earth–planet. The organization used here retains some of those elements, combines others, and adds nation-state. Additional influences for this hierarchical organization come from the disciplines of landscape ecology and planning.

1. FUNDAMENTAL PRINCIPLES OF HUMAN ECOLOGY

1. Yehudi A. Cohen, ed., *Man in Adaptation: The Cultural Present* (Chicago: Aldine, 1974), p. 1. Reprinted with permission from Yehudi A. Cohen, *Man in Adaptation: The Cultural Present* (New York: Aldine de Gruyter), copyright © 1968, 1974 by Yehudi A. Cohen.
2. Roy A. Rappaport, *Ecology, Meaning and Religion* (Berkeley, California: North Atlantic Books, 1979), pp. 59–60.
   Rappaport (1926–1997) studied the religious aspects of society through an ecological lens. He earned his Ph.D. from Columbia University and taught at the University of Michigan.
3. Young et al., "Planning the Built Environment: Determining the Regional Context," *The Built Environment: A Creative Inquiry into Design and Planning*, eds. Tom J. Bartuska and Gerald L. Young (Menlo Park, California: Crisp Publications, 1994), and Howard T. Odum, *Systems Ecology: An Introduction* (New York: John Wiley & Sons, 1983).
4. See especially Young's "Environment: Term and Concept in the Social Sciences," *Social Science Information* 25, no. 1 (1996); his edited volume *Origins of Human Ecology* (Stroudsburg, Pennsylvania: Hutchinson Ross Publishing Company, 1983); and his "The Case for a 'Catholic' Ecology," *Human Ecology Review* 1, no.

2 (1994):310–319. Works expanding Young's already comprehensive conceptual vision include: Hersperger, "Landscape Ecology and Its Potential Application to Planning," *Journal of Planning Literature* 9, no. 1 (1986); Donna L. Hall and William W. Budd, "Landscape Ecology and Landscape Planning," Human Systems Ecology, eds. Rusong Wang, Jingzhu Zhao, and Zhiyun Ouyang (Beijing: China Science and Technology Press, 1991), pp. 51–62; and Frank B. Golley, *A Primer for Environmental Literacy* (New Haven: Yale University Press, 1998).

5. Daniel B. Botkin and Edward A. Keller, *Environmental Science: Earth as a Living Planet* (New York: John Wiley & Sons, 1998), p. 35. This matieral is used by permission of John Wiley & Sons, Inc.

    In general systems terms, "a system is an aggregation of living and/or non-living entities." John P. van Gigch, *Applied General Systems Theory* (New York: Harper & Row, 1974), p. 3.

6. Young et al., "Planning the Built Environment," and Odum, *Systems Ecology: An Introduction.*

7. Angus M. Woodbury, *Principles of General Ecology* (New York: The Blakiston Company, 1954).

    Ernst Haeckel (1834–1919) was trained as a physician, but abandoned his medical practice after reading Charles Darwin's *Origin of the Species*. Haeckel pursued studies that overlapped biology, anthropology, and philosophy.

8. Ibid., p. 7.

9. Roy A. Rappaport, *Pigs for the Ancestors* (New Haven: Yale University Press, 1968).

10. Ludwig Von Bertalanffy, *General Systems Theory* (New York: George Braziller, 1968).

11. Julian H. Steward, *A Theory of Cultural Change* (Urbana: University of Illinois Press, 1955).

12. As explained by Jonathan Berger, "Landscape Patterns of Local Social Organization and Their Importance for Land Use Planning," *Landscape Planning* 8 (1980):199. Reprinted from *Landscape Planning* with permission from Elsevier Science.

    In addition to Steward, cited above, see Clifford J. Geertz, *Agricultural Involution* (Berkeley: University of California Press, 1963).

13. The classic statement on the topic was provided by Floyd Hunter in *Community Power Structure* (Chapel Hill: University of North Carolina Press, 1953). See also, Dan Rose, Frederick Steiner, and Joanne Jackson, "An Applied Human Ecological Approach to Regional Planning," *Landscape Planning* 5 (1978–79):241–261.

14. Von Bertalanffy, *General Systems Theory.*

15. William Ophuls, *Ecology and the Politics of Scarcity* (San Francisco: W. H. Freeman, 1977), p. 11.

16. Golley, *A Primer for Environmental Literacy*, p. 10.

17. Ibid., p. 11.

18. As quoted by Betty Jean Craige, "The Holistic Vision of Eugene Odum, Ecologist and Environmentalist" (manuscript) (Athens: The Center for Humanities and the Arts, University of Georgia, 1998), pp. 1–2.

19. Niraj Verma, *Similarities, Connections, and Systems* (Lanham, Maryland: Lexington Books, 1998), pp. 10–11.

20. Golley, *A Primer for Environmental Literacy*, p. 225.

21. Ibid., p. 226.

22. Pickett et al., "A Conceptual Framework for the Study of Human Ecosystems in Urban Areas," *Urban Ecosystems* 1 (1997), p. 185.

23. Golley, *A Primer for Environmental Literacy*, p. 227.

24. Gerald L.Young, "A Conceptual Framework for an Interdisciplinary Human Ecology," *Acta Oecologiae Hominis* 1 (1989), and Young et al., "Planning the Built Environment."

25. Richard T. T. Forman and Michel Godron, *Landscape Ecology* (New York: John Wiley & Sons, 1986), and Hersperger, "Landscape Ecology and Its Potential Application to Planning."

26. Anne Vernez Moudon, "Urban Morphology as an Emerging Interdisciplinary Field," *Urban Morphology* 1 (1997), p. 7.

27. Forman and Godron, *Landscape Ecology*.

28. Hersperger, "Landscape Ecology and Its Potential Application to Planning," p. 17.

29. Ibid.

30. Forman and Godron, *Landscape Ecology*.

31. Moudon, "Urban Morphology as an Emerging Interdisciplinary Field," p. 7.

32. Eugene P. Odum, *Ecology and Our Endangered Life Support System* (Sunderland, Massachusetts: Sinauer, 1993), p. 49.

33. Wenche E. Dramstad, James D. Olson, and Richard T. T. Forman, *Landscape Ecology Principles in Landscape Architecture and Land-Use Planning* (Washington, D.C.: Island Press, Harvard University, and American Society of Landscape Architects, 1996), p. 27.

34. Ibid.

35. Ibid.

36. M. Suzanne Sontag and Margaret M. Bubolz, *Families on Small Farms: Case Studies in Human Ecology* (East Lansing: Michigan State University Press, 1996), p. 21.

37. See Lynch's *Collected Works*, for example, Tridib Banerjee and Michael Southworth, eds., City Sense and City Design: Writings and Projects of Kevin Lynch (Cambridge, Massachusetts: MIT Press, 1990).

    Kevin Lynch (1918–1984) studied architecture with Frank Lloyd Wright at Taliesin and then planning at the Massachusetts Institute of Technology, where he subsequently served on the faculty.

38. James Cowan, *A Mapmaker's Dream: The Meditations of Fra Mauro, Cartographer to the Court of Venice* (New York: Warner Books, 1996).

39. Daniel B. Botkin and Edward A. Keller, *Environmental Science: Earth as a Living Planet* (New York: John Wiley & Sons, 1998), p. 121.

40. Ibid.

41. Ibid.

42. Marston Bates, "Process," *Man's Role in Changing the Face of the Earth*, ed. William L. Thomas Jr. (Chicago: University of Chicago Press, 1956), pp. 1136–1140.

43. Gerald L. Young, "Human Ecology as an Interdisciplinary Domain: A Critical Inquiry," *Advances in Ecological Research* 8 (1974):1–105, and "Interaction as a Concept Basic to Human Ecology: An Exploration and Synthesis," *Advances in Human Ecology* 5 (1998):313–365.

44. Young, "A Conceptual Framework for an Interdisciplinary Human Ecology," p. 3.

45. Jon C. Teaford, *The Twentieth-Century City* (Baltimore: Johns Hopkins University Press, 1986), p. 6.

46. Seymour J. Mandelbaum, *Open Moral Communities* (Cambridge, Massachusetts: MIT Press, 2000), p. 9.

47. Young, "A Conceptual Framework for an Interdisciplinary Human Ecology," p. 84.

48. Ibid., pp. 86–87.

49. Ibid., p. 84.

50. Cohen, *Man in Adaptation*, p. 3. Reprinted with permission from Yehudi A. Cohen, copyright © 1968, 1974 by Yehudi A. Cohen.

51. Clifford Geertz, *Available Light: Anthropological Reflections on Philosophical Topics* (Princeton, New Jersey: Princeton University Press, 2000), p. 15.

52. Stewart Brand, *The Clock of the Long Now: Time and Responsibility* (New York: Basic Books, 1999), p. 42.

53. William Wistar Comfort, *Just Among Friends: The Quaker Way of Life* (Philadelphia: American Friends Service Committee, 1968), p. 20. Reprinted with permission from the American Friends Service Committee.

54. Odum, *Ecology and Our Endangered Life Support System.*

55. Botkin and Keller, *Environmental Science.*

56. See Geertz, *Available Light,* for example.

57. Gary Paul Nabhan, *Cultures of Habitat: On Nature, Culture, and Story* (Washington, D.C.: Counterpoint, 1997), p. 5.

58. Timothy Beatley and Kristy Manning, *The Ecology of Place* (Washington, D.C.: Island Press, 1997), p. 36, adapted from Timothy Beatley, "Urban Policy and Fair Equality of Opportunity," *Shaping a National Agenda,* eds. Gene Grigsby and David Godschalk (Los Angeles: Los Angeles Center for Afro-American Studies, University of California, 1993).

59. Aldo Leopold, *A Sand County Almanac and Sketches Here and There* (London: Oxford University Press, 1949).

60. Pierre Dansereau, *Biogeography: An Ecological Perspective* (New York: Ronald Press, 1957), p. 318.

61. Richard T. T. Forman, *Land Mosaics: The Ecology of Landscapes and Regions* (Cambridge, England: Cambridge University Press, 1995), p. 502. Reprinted with permission of Cambridge University Press.

62. Dansereau, *Biogeography,* p. 205.

63. Sontag and Bubolz, *Families on Small Farms,* p. 23.

64. John W. Bennett, *The Northern Plainsmen* (Chicago: Aldine, 1969).

65. Paul Hawken, "A Declaration of Sustainability," *Utne Reader* (September/October 1993):57. Reprinted with permission from *Utne Reader.*

66. Ibid.

67. Ibid., p. 58.
68. Cohen, *Man in Adaptation,* p. 4. Reprinted with permission from Yehudi A. Cohen, copyright © 1968, 1974 by Yehudi A. Cohen.
69. Yi-Fu Tuan, *Escapism* (Baltimore: Johns Hopkins University Press, 1998), p. 6.
70. Arthur Koestler, *The Ghost in the Machine* (New York: Macmillan, 1967). In *The Ghost in the Machine,* Koestler (1905–1983) presents a set of principles that attempted to unify theories of complex systems. See Young, *Origins of Human Ecology,* as well as Gerald Young, Frederick Steiner, Kenneth Brooks, and Kenneth Struckmeyer, "Determining the Regional Context for Landscape Planning," *Landscape Planning* 10 (1983):269–296.
71. Hersperger, "Landscape Ecology and Its Potential Application to Planning," p. 19 citing Jan C. Smuts, *Holism and Evolution* (London: Macmillan, 1926).
72. Young, "A Conceptual Framework for an Interdisciplinary Human Ecology," p. 38.
73. Ibid., p. 39.
74. Ibid., p. 37. See also, Gerald L. Young, "Holism: Writ and Riposte in Ecology and Human Ecology," *Advances in Human Ecology* 7 (1998):313–365, and Gerald L. Young, "A Piece of the Main: Parts and Wholes in Human Ecology," *Advances in Human Ecology* 8 (1999):1–31.
75. Hersperger, "Landscape Ecology and Its Potential Application to Planning," p. 19 building on I. S. Zonneveld, "Scope and Concepts of Landscape Ecology as an Emerging Science," *Changing Landscapes: An Ecological Perspective,* eds. I. S. Zonneveld and R. T. T. Forman (New York: Springer-Verlag, 1990).
76. Neil Evernden, *The Social Creation of Nature* (Baltimore: Johns Hopkins University Press, 1992), p. 40.

2. HABITAT

1. Vitruvius, *On Architecture* (translated from Latin by Frank Granger, Cambridge, Massachusetts: Harvard University, 1931), Book I, Chapter IV, pp. 39–40.
2. Ibid., Book I, Chapter II, p. 31.
3. Anne Vernez Moudon, "Urban Morphology as an Emerging Interdisciplinary Field," *Urban Morphology* 1 (1997) p. 7.
4. Ibid.
5. May Theilgaard Watts, *Reading the Landscape: An Adventure in Ecology* (New York: The Macmillan Company, 1957).
6. Gary Paul Nabhan, *Cultures of Habitat: On Nature, Culture, and Story* (Washington, D.C.: Counterpoint, 1997), p. 3.
7. Pierre Dansereau, *Biogeography: An Ecological Perspective* (New York: Ronald Press, 1957), p. 325.
8. Reed F. Noss et al., *The Science of Conservation Planning: Habitat Conservation under the Endangered Species Act* (Washington, D.C.: Island Press, 1997), p. xv.
9. Frank R. Abate, ed.-in-chief, *The Oxford Desk Dictionary and Thesaurus* (New York: Oxford University Press, 1997), p. 348.

10. Paul B. Sears, "The Process of Environmental Change by Man," *Man's Role in Changing the Face of the Earth,* ed. William L.Thomas Jr. (Chicago: University of Chicago Press, 1956), p. 472.

11. Noss et al., *The Science of Conservation Planning,* p. 3.

12. Eugene P. Odum, *Ecology and Our Endangered Life Support System* (Sunderland, Massachusetts: Sinauer, 1993), p. 50. See also, Charles Elton, *Animal Ecology* (New York: Macmillan, 1927).

13. M. Suzanne Sontag and Margaret M. Bubolz, *Families on Small Farms: Case Studies in Human Ecology* (East Lansing: Michigan State University Press, 1996).

14. Ibid., p. 25.

15. Ibid.

16. Gaston Bachelard, *The Poetics of Space* (translated from French by Maria Jolas, New York: The Orion Press, 1964), p. 17. Bachelard (1884–1962) studied poetic language, the daydream, and phenomenology.

17. Dankmar Adler, "Function and Environment," *Roots of Contemporary Architecture,* ed. Lewis Mumford (New York: Dover, 1972), p. 249. Alder (1844–1900) was a partner of Louis Sullivan and a pioneer in the development of steel-framed skyscrapers.

18. See, for example, Nan Ellin's wonderful review and synthesis *Postmodern Urbanism* (Cambridge, Massachusetts: Blackwell Publishers, 1996).

19. Christopher Alexander, Sara Ishikawa, Murray Silverstein, Max Jacobson, Ingrid Fiksdahl-King, and Shloma Angel, *A Pattern Language: Towns, Buildings, Construction* (New York: Oxford University Press, 1977). Another voice for a more place-based approach within architecture was provided by Charles Moore. See his selected essays: Kevin Keim, ed., *You Have to Pay for the Public Life: Selected Essays of Charles W. Moore* (Cambridge, Massachusetts: The MIT Press, 2001).

20. Vincent Scully, *Architecture: The Natural and the Manmade* (New York: St. Martin's Press, 1991), p. 208.

21. Steven A. Moore, "Reproducing the Local," *Platform* (Spring, 1999):8.

22. Liza Oz-Golden, "Increasing Outdoor Comfort in the Sonoran Desert: An Analysis of the Hayden Ferry Site, Tempe, Arizona" (Tempe: School of Planning and Landscape Architecture, Arizona State University, 1999).

23. Lewis Mumford wrote a 1967 review of Albert Mayer's book *The Urgent Future* in *Architecture Record.* This review was reprinted with the title "Trend Is Not Destiny" in *Lewis Mumford, Architecture as a Home for Man: Essays for Architecture Record,* ed. Jeanne M. Davern (New York: Architectural Record Books, 1975), pp. 201–206. Mumford took the title from the trend-is-not-destiny admonition in Mayer's book. Mumford argued that the admonition "should be on the walls of every planning office" (p. 203). The destiny quote has also been attributed to René Dubos. The earliest use of the phrase that I am aware of is by Paul Valéry.

24. Gerald L. Young, "A Conceptual Framework for an Interdisciplinary Human Ecology," *Acta Oecologiae Hominis* 1 (1989), pp. 50–51 referring to Kurt Lewin, *Field Theory in Social Science: Selected Theoretical Papers* (New York: Harper & Row, 1951).

25. Reinhold Niebuhr, *The Nature and Destiny of Man* (New York: Charles Scribner's Sons, 1943), p. 252. Niebuhr (1892–1971) was born in Missouri of German parents. A professor of theology at the Union Theological Seminary in New York, Niebuhr was a social activist and a writer on ethics, history, and politics.

26. Alexander et al., *A Pattern Language,* p. 469.

27. David Hancocks, *A Different Nature: The Paradoxical World of Zoos and Their Uncertain Future* (Berkeley: University of California Press, 2001), pp. 6–7. Copyright © 2001, The Regents of the University of California.

28. Gabriel García Márquez, *One Hundred Years of Solitude* (translated from Spanish by Gregory Rabassa, New York: Harper & Row, 1970).

29. McDonnell, "Public Life and Patria Potestas, The Extended Patriarchal Roman Family Revised." Paper presented at the American Academy in Rome, March 5, 1998.

30. Clifford Geertz, "The Impact of the Concept of Culture on the Concept of Man," *Man in Adaptation: The Cultural Present,* ed. Yehudi A. Cohen (Chicago: Aldine, 1974), pp. 19–32.

31. Sontag and Bubolz, *Families on Small Farms,* p. 26.

32. Fae Myenne Ng, *Bone* (New York: HarperCollins, 1993), p. 3.

33. Winston Churchill, Speech to the House of Commons, October 28, 1943.

34. Vitruvius, Book II, Chapter I, p. 77.

35. Ibid., p. 79.

36. Ibid.

37. Andrea Palladio, *The Four Books on Architecture* (translated by Robert Tavernor and Richard Schofield, Cambridge, Massachusetts: MIT Press, 1997), p. 45.

38. Richard Powers, *Plowing the Dark* (New York: Farrar, Straus and Giroux, 2000), p. 167.

3. COMMUNITY

1. James Howard Kunstler, "Home from Nowhere: How to Make Our Cities and Towns Livable," *The Atlantic Monthly* (September, 1996), 43–66.

2. Seymour J. Mandelbaum, *Open Moral Communities* (Cambridge, Massachusetts: MIT Press, 2000), p. ix.

3. Moura Quayle and Tilo C. Driessen van der Lieck, "Growing Community: A Case for Hybrid Landscapes," *Landscape and Urban Planning* 39, no. 2–3 (1997):99. Reprinted from *Landscape and Urban Planning* with permission from Elsevier Science.

4. Alex Marshall, *How Cities Work: Suburbs, Sprawl, and Roads Not Taken* (Austin: University of Texas Press, 2000), p. xvi.

5. Robert E. Ricklefs, *Ecology* (Newton, Massachusetts: Chiron Press, 1973), p. 783.

6. Eugene P. Odum, *Fundamentals of Ecology* (Philadelphia: W. B. Saunders, 1971), p. 145.

7. Elizabeth Morris, "Community in Theory and Practice: A Framework for Intellectual Renewal," *Journal of Planning Literature* 11, no. 1 (1996):128.

8. Ibid.

9. Ibid.

10. Neil Evernden, *The Social Creation of Nature* (Baltimore: Johns Hopkins University Press, 1992).

11. Robert Park and Ernest Burgess, *The City* (Chicago: University of Chicago Press, 1925).

12. Morris, "Community in Theory and Practice," p. 137.

13. Robert Fishman, "The Mumford-Jacobs Debate," *Planning History Studies* 10, no. 1–2 (1996):3–11.

14. Philip Selznick, "In Search of Community," *Rooted in the Land: Essays on Community and Place*, eds. William Vitek and Wes Jackson (New Haven: Yale University Press, 1996), p. 195.

15. Ibid.

16. See: www.talossa.net.

17. M. R. G. Conzen, *Alnwick, Northumberland: A Study in Town-Plan Analysis* (London: George Philip, 1960). For further elaborations of Conzen's ideas, see J. W. R. Whitehand, ed., *The Urban Landscape: Historical Development and Management* (London: Academic Press, 1981); T. R. Slater, ed., *The Built Form of Western Cities* (Leicester, England: Leicester University Press, 1990); Michael Joseph Schmandt, "Postmodernism and the Southwest Urban Landscape" (Tempe, Arizona: Department of Geography, Arizona State University, 1995); and Michael J. Schmandt, "The Importance of History and Context in the Postmodern Urban Landscape," *Landscape Journal* 18, no. 2 (1999):157–165.

18. Schmandt, "Postmodernism and the Southwest Urban Landscape," p. 13.

19. Ibid.

20. Anne Vernez Moudon, "Urban Morphology as an Emerging Interdisciplinary Field," *Urban Morphology* 1 (1997) p. 7.

21. Daniel Taylor-Ide and Carl E. Taylor, *Just and Lasting Change: When Communities Own Their Futures* (Baltimore: Johns Hopkins University Press, 2002).

22. Richard Buckminster Fuller, *Synergetics: Explorations in the Geometry of Thinking* (with E. J. Applewhite) (New York: Macmillan, 1975), p. 372.

23. Presentation at the American Academy in Rome by Robeto Behar on February 19, 1998. See also, Roberto M. Behar, "Little Guatemala and the Invention of Miami," *The New City* 2 (1994):105–115.

24. Such communities resulted because of common heritages and also discrimination by the larger population. As Gail Lee Dubrow reminds us about the Asian-American communities in the West,

> These Chinatowns, Little Tokyos, Little Manilas, and Koreatowns embody patterns of segregation that are not merely social phenomena; they might also be understood as spatial expressions of racialized relations inscribed upon the urban landscape. These ethnic enclaves, in part the expression of community identity founded on common culture and language, also were forged as a result of restrictive immigration policies and pervasive discrimination in the sale and rental of property.

Dubrow, "Asian American Imprints on the Western Landscape," *Preserving Cultural Landscapes in America,* eds. Arnold R. Alanen and Robert Z. Melnick (Baltimore: Johns Hopkins University Press, 2000), p. 144.

25. Primo Levi, *The Drowned and the Saved* (London: Abacus, 1989), p. 44.

26. Herbert Gans, *The Levittowners: Ways of Life and Politics in a New Suburban Community* (New York: Alfred A. Knopf, 1967).

27. Don Luymes, "The Fortification of Suburbia: Investigating the Rise of Enclave Communities," *Landscape and Urban Planning* 39, nos. 2–3 (1997):188. Reprinted from *Landscape and Urban Planning* with permission from Elsevier Science.

28. Ibid., p. 191.

29. John Brinckerhoff Jackson, *Discovering the Vernacular Landscape* (New Haven: Yale University Press, 1984), p. 45. See also, Paul Smith Jr., *The Poetics of Landscape* (Berkeley: Department of Landscape Architecture, University of California, 1992).

30. John Dixon Hunt, *Greater Perfections: The Practice of Garden Theory* (Philadelphia: University of Pennsylvania Press, 2000).

31. Robert D. Putnam, *Bowling Alone: The Collapse and Revival of American Community* (New York: Simon & Schuster, 2000).

32. Douglas D. Paterson, "Community Building and the Necessity for Radical Revision," *Landscape and Urban Planning* 39, nos. 2–3 (1997):86. Reprinted from *Landscape and Urban Planning* with permission from Elsevier Science.

33. Ibid.

34. William Vitek and Wes Jackson, eds., *Rooted in the Land: Essays on Community and Place* (New Haven: Yale University Press, 1996).

35. John B. Cobb Jr., "Defining Normative Community," *Rooted in the Land,* eds. Vitek and Jackson, p. 190.

36. Ibid., p. 191.

37. Wallace Stegner, *Where the Bluebird Sings to the Lemonade Springs* (New York: Penguin, 1992), p. 201.

38. Rachel Fletcher, "Proportioning Systems and the Timber Framer," *Journal of the Timber Framing Guild* 18 (December, 1990): p. 8.

39. John W. Reps, *The Making of Urban America: A History of City Planning in the United States* (Princeton: Princeton University Press, 1965), p. 29.

40. Ibid., p. 160.

41. Anthony N. B. Garvan, "Proprietary Philadelphia as Artifact," *The Historian and the City,* eds. Oscar Handlin and John Burchard (Cambridge, Massachusetts: MIT Press, 1963), pp. 177–201.

42. A. E. J. Morris, *The History of Urban Form, Prehistory to Renaissance* (London: George Goodwin Limited, 1979), p. 265–266.

43. Ibid.

44. Reps, *The Making of Urban America.*

45. Morris, *The History of Urban Form.*

46. James Coke, "Antecedents to Local Planning," *Principles and Practices of Urban Planning,* eds. William I. Goodman and Eric C. Freund (Washington, D.C.: International City Management Association, 1968).

47. Ibid., p. 9.
48. Peter Calthrope and William Fulton, *The Regional City* (Washington, D.C.: Island Press, 2001), p. 279. Of the various publications about this movement, including those by the protagonists themselves, one of the best is provided by journalist Philip Langdon, *A Better Place to Live: Reshaping the American Suburb* (Amherst: University of Massachusetts Press, 1994).
49. Andres Duany, Elizabeth Plater-Zyberk, and Jeff Speck, *Suburban Nation: The Rise of Sprawl and the Decline of the American Dream* (New York: North Point Press, 2001), pp. 11–12.
50. Peter Calthorpe, *The Next American Metropolis: Ecology, Community and the American Dream* (New York: Princeton Architectural Press, 1993), pp. 11–12.
51. William E. Rees, "Globalization and Sustainability: Conflict or Convergence?" *Bulletin of Science, Technology and Society* 22, no. 4 (2002):249–268. See also, William E. Rees, "Is 'Sustainable City' an Oxymoron?" Local Environment 2, no. 3 (1997):303–310; William E. Rees, "Ecological Footprints and Appropriated Carrying Capacity: What Urban Economics Leaves Out," *Environment and Urbanization* 4, no. 2 (1992):121–130; and Mathis Wackernagel and William Rees, *Our Ecological Footprint: Reducing Human Impact on the Earth* (Gabriola Island, British Columbia: New Society Publishers, 1996).
52. Timothy Beatley and Kristy Manning, *The Ecology of Place* (Washington, D.C.: Island Press, 1997).
53. Rees, "Is 'Sustainable City' an Oxymoron?" p. 307.
54. Paterson, "Community Building and the Necessity for Radical Revision," p. 83. Reprinted from *Landscape and Urban Planning* with permission from Elsevier Science.
55. Ibid.
56. Selznick, "In Search of Community," p. 197.
57. Ibid., p. 199.
58. Mark Luccarelli, *Lewis Mumford and the Ecological Region* (New York: The Guilford Press, 1995), p. 22.
59. The President's Council on Sustainable Development, *Sustainable Development: A New Consensus* (Washington, D.C.: U.S. Government Printing Office, 1996), p. 12.
60. Cobb, "Defining Normative Community," p. 192.

4. LANDSCAPE

1. These relationships are a central focus of cultural geography. See, for example, William Norton, *Human Geography* (Toronto: Oxford University Press, 1998).
2. D. W. Meinig, ed., *The Interpretation of Ordinary Landscapes* (New York: Oxford University Press, 1979), p. 2.
3. Steven C. Bourassa, *The Aesthetics of Landscape* (London: Belhaven, 1991), p. 21.
4. As quoted by D. W. Meinig, "Reading the Landscape: An Appreciation of W. G. Hoskins and J. B. Jackson," *The Interpretation of Ordinary Landscapes,* ed. Meinig, p. 220. See also, J. B. Jackson, "The Order of a Landscape" in the same book.

5. Nina Leopold Bradley, "14th H. Wayne Pritchard Lecture," Soil and Water Conservation Society Annual Meeting, Lexington, Kentucky, 1991.

6. Yi-Fu Tuan, *Topophilia: A Study of Environmental Perception, Attitudes, and Values* (Englewood Cliffs, New Jersey: Prentice-Hall, 1974), p. 133.

7. John R. Stilgoe, *Common Landscape of America, 1580–1845* (New Haven, Connecticut: Yale University Press, 1982), p. 12.

8. Tuan, *Topophilia*, p. 133.

9. For example, see Richard T. T. Forman and Michel Godron, *Landscape Ecology* (New York: John Wiley & Sons, 1986); Richard T. T. Forman, *Land Mosaics: The Ecology of Landscapes and Regions* (Cambridge, England: Cambridge University Press, 1995); and Sheila Peck, *Planning for Biodiversity* (Washington, D.C.: Island Press, 1998).

10. Joan Iverson Nassauer, ed. *Placing Nature: Culture and Landscape Ecology* (Washington, D.C.: Island Press, 1997), p. 10.

11. Anne Whiston Spirn, *The Language of Landscape* (New Haven: Yale University Press, 1998).

12. Ibid., p. 185.

13. Ibid., p. 133.

14. Ibid., p. 158.

15. Ibid., p. 262.

16. See Kevin Lynch and Gary Hack, *Site Planning* (Cambridge, Massachusetts: MIT Press, 1984). Lynch's standard site planning was published in three editions. The third was co-authored by Lynch's MIT colleague Gary Hack, the current dean of the Graduate School of Fine Arts at the University of Pennsylvania.

17. Paul Shepard, *Man in the Landscape* (College Station: Texas A&M University Press, 1991), p. 139.

18. Paul van der Ree, Gerrit Smienk, and Clemens Steenbergen, *Italian Villas and Gardens* (Amsterdam: Thoth, 1992), p. 229.

19. James S. Ackerman, *The Villa: Form and Ideology of Country Houses* (Princeton: Princeton University Press, 1990).

20. Van der Ree et al., *Italian Villas and Gardens*, p. 229.

21. Ibid. See also, Clemens Steenbergen and Wouter Reh, *Architecture and Landscape* (Amsterdam: Thoth, 1996).

22. Shepard, *Man in the Landscape*, p. 139.

23. Thomas Jefferson to James Madison, 1785.

24. Curt Meine, "Inherit the Grid," *Placing Nature*, ed. Nassauer, pp. 45–62.

25. Ibid.

26. Horace Walpole, *The History of the Modern Taste in Gardening* (London: John Major, 1827), p. 264.

27. Forman, *Land Mosaics*, p. 21. Reprinted with permission of Cambridge University Press.

28. Ibid., p. 25.

29. Ibid.

30. Ibid., p. 26.

31. Ervin H. Zube, James L. Sell, and Jonathan G. Taylor, "Landscape Perception: Research, Application, and Theory," *Landscape Planning* 9, no. 1 (1982):22.

32. Tuan, *Topophilia*.

33. Simon Schama, *Landscape and Memory* (New York: Alfred A. Knopf, 1995), p. 61.

34. Ian L. McHarg, "Ecology and Design," *Ecological Design and Planning*, eds. George F. Thompson and Frederick R. Steiner (New York: John Wiley & Sons, 1997), p. 321. This material is used by permission of John Wiley & Sons, Inc.

35. Ibid.

36. For example, McHarg, "Ecology and Design" and *Design with Nature* (Garden City, New York: Natural History Press/Doubleday, 1969); Frederick Steiner, "The Aesthetics of Soil Conservation," presentation at Malabar Farm, Ohio, October 27, 1988, and "Earth Medicine," *GSD News* (Fall, 1996):8–9; John W. Simpson, "Landscape Medicine: A Timely Treatment," *Journal of Soil and Water Conservation* 44, no. 6 (November–December, 1989):577–579; Bruce K. Ferguson, "The Concept of Landscape Health," *Journal of Environmental Management* 40 (1994):129–137, and "The Maintenance of Landscape Health in the Midst of Land Use Change," *Journal of Environmental Management* 48 (1996):387–395, and Kristina Hill, "Design and Planning as Healing Arts: The Broader Context of Health and Environment," *Ecology and Design: Frameworks for Learning*, eds. Bart R. Johnson and Kristina Hill (Washington, D.C.: Island Press, 2002), pp. 203–214.

37. Ferguson, "The Maintenance of Landscape Health in the Midst of Land Use Change," p. 387.

38. Timothy Beatley and Kristy Manning, *The Ecology of Place* (Washington, D.C.: Island Press, 1997), p. 86.

39. See: Forman and Godron, *Landscape Ecology*; I. S. Zonneveld and Richard T. T. Forman, eds., *Changing Landscapes: An Ecological Perspective* (New York: Springer-Verlag, 1990); Forman, *Land Mosaics*; Wenche E. Dramstad, James D. Olson, and Richard T. T. Forman, *Landscape Ecology Principles in Landscape Architecture and Land-Use Planning* (Washington, D.C.: Island Press, Harvard University, and American Society of Landscape Architects, 1996); and Richard T. T. Forman and Anna M. Hersperger, "Ecologia del paesaggio e planificazione: una potente combinazione," *Urbanistica* 108 (gennaio–giugno, 1997):61–66.

40. Dramstad et al., *Landscape Ecology Principles in Landscape Architecture and Land-Use Planning*, p. 7.

41. Robert Smithson, "A Sedimentation of the Mind: Earth Projects," *The Writings of Robert Smithson*, ed. Nancy Holt (New York: New York University Press, 1989), p. 82. The most recent edition is *Robert Smithson: The Collected Writings*, ed. Jack Flam (Berkeley: University of California), p. 100.

42. For example, George F. Thompson and Frederick R. Steiner, eds., *Ecological Design and Planning* (New York: John Wiley & Sons, 1997), and James Corner, ed., *Recovering Landscape: Essays in Contemporary Landscape Architecture* (New York: Princeton Architectural Press, 1999).

43. Aldo Leopold, *Round River: From the Journals of Aldo Leopold*, ed. Luna B. Leopold (Minocqua, Wisconsin: North Word Press, 1991), p. 237.

44. Forman and Godron, *Landscape Ecology*; Zonneveld and Forman, eds., *Changing Landscapes*; Forman, Land Mosaics; and Dramstad et al., *Landscape Ecology Principles in Landscape Architecture and Land-Use Planning*, for example.

45. Forman, *Land Mosaics*.

46. Theodore Roethke, "The Lost Son," *The Collected Poems of Theodore Roethke* (New York: Doubleday, 1966), p. 58.

47. Wallace Stegner, *Where the Bluebird Sings to the Lemonade Springs* (New York: Penguin, 1992), p. 45.

48. Ibid., p. xv.

5. THE ECOLOGICAL REGION

1. Preston E. James, *All Possible Worlds* (Indianapolis: Odyssey Press, 1972).

2. Robert G. Bailey, *Ecoregions: The Ecosystem Geography of the Oceans and Continents* (New York: Springer-Verlag, 1998), p. 2.

3. Benton MacKaye, "Regional Planning and Ecology," *Ecological Monographs* 10 (1940):351.

4. Ibid., p. 350.

5. Ibid., p. 351.

6. Mark Luccarelli, *Lewis Mumford and the Ecological Region* (New York: The Guilford Press, 1995), and Robert Wojtowicz, *Lewis Mumford and American Modernism: Eutopian Theories for Architecture and Urban Planning* (Cambridge: Cambridge University Press, 1996).

7. Lawrence Buell makes an especially compelling case for centrality of Whitman and William Carlos Williams in this tradition, identifying the latter as a "bioregionalist," in *Writing for an Endangered World: Literature, Culture, and Environment in the U.S. and Beyond* (Cambridge, Massachusetts: The Belknap Press of Harvard University Press, 2001), pp. 109–120.

8. Philip Boardman, *The Worlds of Patrick Geddes: Biologist, Town Planner, Re-educator, Peace-warrior* (London: Routledge & Kegan Paul, 1978), p. 141.

9. Patrick Geddes, *Cities in Evolution: An Introduction to the Town Planning Movement and to the Study of Civics* (London: Williams & Norgate, 1915) as cited in Marshall Stalley, ed., *Patrick Geddes: Spokesman for the Environment* (New Brunswick, New Jersey: Rutgers University Press, 1972), p. 6.

10. Marcella Hazan, *Essentials of Classic Italian Cooking* (New York: Alfred A. Knopf, 1995), p. 3.

11. Regione Lombardia Assessorato all' Urbanistica, *Il Recupero Paesistico dell' Adda di Leonardo* (Milano: Bollettino Ufficiale, Regione Lombardia, 1998), pp. 99–100. Joseph Rykwert links the rise of the Milan *navigli* to "the invention of the lock in Italy [which] made it possible to move vessels up and down hills, transforming water transport." *The Seduction of Place: The City in the Twenty-First Century* (New York: Pantheon, 2000), p. 32.

12. Carl Frederick Kraenzel, *The Great Plains in Transition* (Norman: University of Oklahoma Press, 1955), p. 292.

13. Howard W. Odum in Howard W. Odum and Katharine Jocher, eds., *In Search of the Regional Balance of America* (Westport, Connecticut: Greenwood Press, 1945), p. 3.

14. Howard W. Odum, *The Way of the South: Toward the Regional Balance of America* (New York: The Macmillan Company, 1947), p. 3.

15. Peter Calthorpe and William Fulton, *The Regional City* (Washington, D.C.: Island Press, 2001), p. 10.

16. For example, see Charles B. Hunt, *Physiography of the United States* (San Francisco: W. H. Freeman, 1967); Robert G. Bailey, *Ecoregions of the United States* (Ogden, Utah: U.S. Forest Service, 1978); Robert G. Bailey, *Ecosystem Geography* (New York: Springer-Verlag, 1996); Lewis M. Cowardin, Virginia Carter, Francis C. Golet, and Edward T. LaRoe, *Classification of Wetlands and Deepwater Habitats in the United States* (Washington, D.C.: U.S. Government Printing Office, 1979); and Young et al., "Planning the Built Environment."

17. Bailey, *Ecoregions*, p. 7.

18. Wilbur Zelinsky, "North America's Vernacular Regions," *Annals of the Association of American Geographers* 70 (1980):1–16.

19. Ernest Callenbach, *Ecotopia* (Berkeley, California: Banyan Tree, 1975).

20. Joel Garreau, *The Nine Nations of North America* (Boston: Houghton Mifflin, 1981).

21. T. S. Eliot, *Notes toward the Definition of Culture* (New York: Harcourt, Brace, 1949). I first learned of Eliot's book from Jerry Young when we were writing a paper with our colleagues Kenneth Brooks and Kenneth Struckmeyer (Young et al., "Determining the Regional Context for Landscape Planning"). That paper evolved into a subsequent book chapter (Young et al., "Planning the Built Environment"). Portions of this chapter originated from that work. That material has been rewritten and expanded here.

22. Wendell Berry, *A Continuous Harmony: Essays Cultural and Agricultural* (New York: A Harvest/HBJ Book, 1975).

23. Gary Snyder, *The Real Work* (New York: New Directions Books, 1980).

24. Buell, *Writing for an Endangered World*.

25. Buell, *Writing for an Endangered World*, p. 116, quoting Gary Snyder, *The Practice of the Wild* (San Francisco: North Point Press, 1990), p. 27.

26. For example, see Thomas Berry, "Bioregions: The Context for Reinhabiting the Earth," *The Dream of the Earth*, ed. Barbara Dean (San Francisco: Sierra Club Books, 1988).

27. Clair Reiniger, "Bioregional Planning and Ecosystem Protection," *Ecological Design and Planning*, eds. George F. Thompson and Frederick R. Steiner (New York: John Wiley & Sons, 1997), p. 185. This material used by permission of John Wiley & Sons, Inc.

28. Kirkpatrick Sale, *Dwellers in the Land: The Bioregional Vision* (San Francisco: Sierra Club Books, 1985), p. 55.

29. National Research Council, *New Strategies for America's Watersheds* (Washington, D.C.: National Academy Press, 1999), p. 1.

30. Michael Hough, *Out of Place: Restoring Identity to the Regional Landscape* (New Haven: Yale University Press, 1990).

31. Gerald Young et al., "Planning the Built Environment: Determining the Regional Context," *The Built Environment: A Creative Inquiry into Design and Planning,* eds., Young and Bartuska (Menlo Park, California: Crisp Publications, 1994).

32. G. L. Young, "Environmental Law: Perspectives from Human Ecology," *Environmental Law* 6 (1976):294.

33. Lynch in Tridib Banerjee and Michael Southworth, eds., *City Sense and City Design: Writings and Projects of Kevin Lynch* (Cambridge, Massachusetts: MIT Press, 1990), p. 68.

34. Ibid.

35. Howard W. Odum, "The Promise of Regionalism," *Regionalism in America,* ed. Merrill Jensen (Madison: University of Wisconsin Press, 1965), p. 403.

36. Ibid., p. 397.

37. TVA's first board of directors included Arthur Morgan, Harcourt Morgan, and David Lilienthal.

38. Arthur E. Morgan, *The Miami Conservancy District* (New York: McGraw-Hill, 1951), and *Dams and Other Disasters* (Boston: Porter Sargent, 1971).

39. Tennessee Valley Authority, "A Short History of TVA: From the New Deal to a New Century" (http://www.tva.gov/abouttva/history.htm).

40. Yahaya Doka, "Policy Objectives, Land Tenure, and Settlement Performance: Implications for Equity and Economic Efficiency in the Columbia Basin Irrigation Project" (Pullman: Department of Agricultural Economics, Washington State University, 1979).

41. David Myhra, "Rexford Guy Tugwell: Initiator of America's Greenbelt New Towns, 1935 to 1936," *Journal of the American Institute of Planners* 40 (1974):176–187.

42. See Benton MacKaye, *The New Exploration* (New York: Harcourt Brace, 1928), and Peter Hall, *Cities of Tomorrow* (Oxford: Basil Blackwell, 1988).

43. Arnold R. Alanen and Joseph A. Eden, *Main Street Ready-Made: The New Deal Community of Glendale, Wisconsin* (Madison: The State Historical Society of Wisconsin, 1987), p. 8.

John Nolen (1869–1937) has been called the "father of American town planning." Educated first in business at the University of Pennsylvania's Wharton School and then in landscape architecture at Harvard University, Nolen prepared city plans for Savannah, Georgia (1906); Roanoke, Virginia (1907); Montclair, New Jersey (1908); Glen Ridge, New Jersey (1908); and San Diego (1908 and 1925–1926). His San Diego work led to a master plan for Balboa Park (1927). He also designed several new towns, including Kingsport, Tennessee; Mariemont, Ohio; and Venice, Florida. Nolen helped establish the city planning profession in the United States and wrote and edited several books.

44. Myhra, "Rexford Guy Tugwell"; Frederick R. Steiner, *The Politics of New Town Planning* (Athens: Ohio University Press, 1981); Zane L. Miller, *Suburb: Neighborhood and Community in Forest Park, Ohio, 1935–1976* (Knoxville: University of Tennessee Press, 1981); and Cathy D. Knepper, *Greenbelt, Maryland* (Baltimore: Johns Hopkins University Press, 2001).

45. Hubert N. van Lier and Frederick R. Steiner, "A Review of the Zuiderzee Reclamation Works: An Example of Dutch Physical Planning," *Landscape Planning* 9 (1982):35–59.

46. Coen van der Wal, *In Praise of Common Sense: Planning the Ordinary. A Physical Planning History of the New Towns in the IJsselmeerpolders* (Rotterdam: 010 Publishers, 1997).

47. John Friedmann and William Alonso, eds., *Regional Development and Planning* (Cambridge, Massachusetts: MIT Press, 1964).

48. John Friedmann, *Retracking America* (Garden City, New York: Anchor Press/Doubleday, 1973), and Ian McHarg, *Design with Nature* (Garden City, New York: Natural History Press/Doubleday, 1969).

49. Friedmann, *Retracking America*, p. 63.

50. McHarg, *Design with Nature*, p. 153. This material is used with permission of John Wiley & Sons, Inc.

51. John Friedmann, "Regional Planning as a Field of Study," *Regional Development and Planning*, eds. Friedmann and Alonso, pp. 63–64.

52. As quoted by Gerald Young, "Human Ecology as an Interdisciplinary Domain: A Critical Inquiry," *Advances in Ecological Research* 8 (1974): p. 46.

53. Carl F. Kraenzel, "Principles of Regional Planning: As Applied to the Northwest," *Social Forces* 25 (1947):376.

54. Frederick Steiner, "Regional Planning in the United States: Historic and Contemporary Examples," *Landscape Planning* 10 (1983):297–315, and Tom Bartuska and Gerald Young, eds., *The Built Environment: A Creative Inquiry into Design and Planning* (Menlo Park, California: Crisp Publications, 1994).

55. Robert Estall, "Planning in Appalachia: An Examination of the Appalachian Regional Development Programme and Its Implications for the Future of American Regional Planning Commissions," *Institute of British Geographers* 7 (1982):52.

56. Ibid.

57. Alan J. Hahn and Cynthia D. Dyballa, "State Environmental Planning and Local Influence," *Journal of the American Planning Association* 47 (1981):324–335.

58. Tad Widby, "Trouble in Tahoe," *Planning* 46, no. 3 (1980):6–7, and Hal Rubin, "Lake Tahoe: A Tale of Two States," *Sierra* 66, no.6 (1981):43–47.

59. U.S. Congress, *Tahoe Regional Planning Compact* (Public Law 96-551), 1980.

60. Pinelands Commission, *New Jersey Pinelands Comprehensive Management Plan* (New Lisbon, New Jersey, 1980). See also, Jonathan Berger and John W. Sinton, *Water, Earth, and Fire* (Baltimore: Johns Hopkins University Press, 1985).

61. Jack Ahern, *Greenways as Strategic Landscape Planning: Theory and Application* (Wageningen, The Netherlands: Wageningen University, 2002).

62. Robert D. Yaro and Tony Hiss, *A Region at Risk: The Third Regional Plan for the New York–New Jersey–Connecticut Metropolitan Area* (Washington, D.C.: Island Press, 1996).

63. Ibid., p. 1. See also, John Thomas, "Holding the Middle Ground," *The American Planning Tradition*, ed. Robert Fishman (Washington, D.C.: The Woodrow Wilson Center Press, 2000), pp. 33–63.

64. Yaro and Hiss, *A Region at Risk*, p. 2.

65. Eugenie Ladner Birch, "The Big Picture People," *Planning* 66, no. 3 (2000):22.

66. Giovanna Fossa, Robert Lane, Danilo Palazzo, and Robert Pirani, eds., *Transforming the Places of Production. Trasformare i luoghi della Produzione* (Milano: Edizioni Olivares, 2002).

67. Ibid. Work on one of the Italian sites, an abandoned slaughterhouse in the town of Monza, continued and resulted in a plan for its renovation. Danilo Palazzo, *Master Plan dell' area dell' ex macello a Monza* (Milano: Politecnico di Milano, 2001).

68. Frederick Law Olmsted, *A Journey through Texas: Or, A Saddle Trip on the Southwestern Frontier* (New York: Dix, Edwards & Co., 1857), p. 110.

69. Ibid., p. 111.

6. NATION, STATE, AND NATION-STATE

1. Walter Whitman, *Leaves of Grass* (Brooklyn, New York, 1855), p. iv.

2. Yehudi A. Cohen, ed., *Man in Adaptation: The Cultural Present* (Chicago: Aldine, 1974), p. 54. Reprinted with permission from Yehudi A. Cohen, copyright © 1968, 1974 by Yehudi A. Cohen.

3. Jacob Burckhardt, *The Civilization of the Renaissance in Italy* (translated by S. G. C. Middlemore, New York: Harper, 1958). The Swiss historian Burckhardt (1818–1892) was one of the founders of the cultural interpretation of history.

4. John Le Carré, *The Constant Gardener* (New York: Scribner, 2001), p. 137.

5. Harry Mulisch, *The Discovery of Heaven* (translated by Paul Vincent, New York: Viking Penguin, 1996), p. 556.

6. A. E. J. Morris, *The History of Urban Form: Prehistory to Renaissance* (London: George Goodwin Limited, 1979), p. 19.

7. Ibid., p. 20.

8. Plato, *Timaeus and Critias* (translated by D. Lee, Middlesex, England: Penguin Books, 1971).

9. William Norton, *Explorations in the Understanding of Landscape: A Cultural Geography* (New York: Greenwood Press, 1989), p. 123.

10. John G. Neihardt, *Black Elk Speaks: Being the Life Story of a Holy Man of the Oglala Sioux* (Lincoln: University of Nebraska Press, 2000, originally 1932), p. 125. Used with permission of the University of Nebraska Press.

11. Norton, *Explorations in the Understanding of Landscape*, p. 125.

12. Plato, *Timaeus and Critias*.

13. Cohen, *Man in Adaptation*, p. 55. Reprinted with permission from Yehudi A. Cohen, copyright © 1968, 1974 by Yehudi A. Cohen.

14. David Hancocks, *A Different Nature: The Paradoxical World of Zoos and Their Uncertain Future* (Berkeley: University of California Press, 2001), p. 41. Copyright © The Regents of the University of California.

15. As quoted by Hancocks in *A Different Nature*, p. 91.
16. Hancocks, *A Different Nature*, p. 92.
17. Simon Schama, *The Embarrassment of Riches: An Interpretation of Dutch Culture in the Golden Age* (Berkeley: University of California Press, 1988), p. 34.
18. Ibid., p. 35.
19. Cohen, *Man in Adaptation*, pp. 401–402. Reprinted with permission from Yehudi A. Cohen, copyright © 1968, 1974 by Yehudi A. Cohen.
20. Niccolò Machiavelli, *The Prince* (New York: Cambridge University Press, 1988, originally published in 1513). Reprinted with the permission of Cambridge University Press.
21. Thomas L. Friedman, "Foreign Affairs: Two Sick Nations, One Cure," *New York Times* (July 25, 1998):8. (Originally published in the *New York Times*, July 25, 1998.)
22. See, for instance, Frederick Steiner, John Blair, Laurel McSherry, Subhrajit Guhathakurta, Joaquin Marruffo, and Matthew Holm, "A Watershed at a Watershed: The Potential for Environmentally Sensitive Area Protection in the Upper San Pedro Drainage Basin (Mexico and USA)," *Landscape and Urban Planning* 49 (2000):129–148.
23. Paul Ganster, general ed., *San Diego–Tijuana International Border Area Planning Atlas* (San Diego: San Diego State University Press and Institute for Regional Studies of the Californias, 2000), p. vii.
24. Tim Parks, *Italian Neighbors or a Lapsed Anglo-Saxon in Verona* (New York: Fawcett Columbine, 1992), p. 21.
25. Don DeLillo, *Underworld* (New York: Scribner, 1997), p. 11.
26. Julian P. Boyd, ed., Mina R. Bryan and Elizabeth L. Hunter, associate eds., *The Papers of Thomas Jefferson* (Volume 6, May 21, 1781, to March 1784, Princeton: Princeton University Press, 1952), p. 581.
27. Ibid., p. 604.
28. Ibid., p. 598.
29. Ibid.
30. Václav Havel, Address of the President of the Czech Republic on the Occasion of the Liberty Medal Ceremony, Philadelphia, Pennsylvania (July 4, 1994), p. 5.

7. THE GREEN CHAOS OF THE PLANET

1. Richard T. T. Forman, *Land Mosaics: The Ecology of Landscapes and Regions* (Cambridge, England: Cambridge University Press, 1995), p. 435. Reprinted with the permission of Cambridge University Press.
2. Richard Powers, *Plowing the Dark* (New York: Farrar, Straus and Giroux, 2000), p. 77.
3. James E. Lovelock, *Gaia: A New Look at Life on Earth* (Oxford, England: Oxford University Press, 1982), p. xii. See also, James E. Lovelock, *The Ages of Gaia: A Biography of Our Living Earth* (New York: Norton, 1988).

4. Danilo Palazzo, "La terra dalla luna, ovvero come la paura della bomba ha aiutato (negli Stati Uniti) la pianificazione ecologica," *Oikos* 2 (1997):59–84.
5. Václav Havel, Address of the President of the Czech Republic on the Occasion of the Liberty Medal Ceremony, Philadelphia, Pennsylvania (July 4, 1994), p. 1.
6. As quoted by David Rains Wallace, "Sand County's Conservation Prophet," *Sierra* (November/December 1987):62–67.
7. Lovelock, *Gaia*, p. 9.
8. Gerald L. Young and Tom J. Bartuska, "Sphere: Term and Concept as an Integrative Device Toward Understanding Environmental Unity," *General Systems* XIX (1974):219.
9. Ibid., p. 214, borrowing from Paul Sears, *The Ecology of Man* (Eugene: Oregon State System of Higher Education, 1959).
10. Ibid., adapted from V. I. Vernadsky, "The Biosphere and the Noosphere," *American Scientist* 33, no. 1 (January, 1945):483–517.
11. Adapted from Young and Bartuska, "Sphere: Term and Concept as an Integrative Device Toward Understanding Environmental Unity," pp. 222–225.
12. Ibid., using LaMont C. Cole, "The Ecosphere," *Scientific American* 198, no. 4 (April, 1958):83–92.
13. Cole, "The Ecosphere," p. 85.
14. Ibid.
15. Forman, *Land Mosaics,* p. 323. Reprinted with the permission of Cambridge University Press.
16. Gary W. Barrett and Eugene P. Odum, "The Twenty-First Century: The World at Carrying-Capacity," *BioScience* 50, no. 4 (2000):363–368 using United Nations, *World Population Prospects: The 1996 Revisions* (New York: United Nations, 1998).
17. Stewart Brand, *The Clock of the Long Now: Time and Responsibility* (New York: Basic Books, 1999).
18. United Nations Development Programme, United Nations Environment Program, World Bank, World Resources Institute, *World Resources 2000–2001, People and Ecosystems, The Fraying Web of Life* (Amsterdam: Elsevier, 2000).
19. Ibid., p. 23. Reprinted from *World Resources 2000–2001* with permission from Elsevier Science.
20. For example, see Paul Harrison and Fred Pearce, *AAA Atlas of Population & Environment* (Berkeley: University of California Press, 2000).
21. Anthony Brazel, Nancy Selover, Russell Vose, and Gordon Heisler, "The Tale of Two Climates—Baltimore and Phoenix LTER Sites," *Climate Research* 15 (2000):123–135.
22. Young and Bartuska, "Sphere," p. 226.
23. Vernadsky, "The Biosphere and the Noosphere."
24. From Young and Bartuska, "Sphere," p. 226, based on Vernadsky and on Pierre Teilhard de Chardin, "The Antiquity and World Expansion of Human Culture," *Man's Role in Changing the Face of the Earth,* ed. Thomas, pp. 103–112.
25. Richard R. Landers, *Man's Place in the Dybosphere* (Englewood Cliffs, New Jersey: Prentice-Hall, 1966), p. 4.
26. Young and Bartuska, "Sphere," p. 226.

27. Marshall McLuhan and Quentin Fiore, *The Medium is the Massage* (New York: Bantam Books, 1967), no page numbers.

Canadian communications theorist and educator Marshall McLuhan (1911–1980) gained popularity and fame in the 1960s with his ideas about the impact of electronic media on culture.

28. McHarg, *Design with Nature,* "Ecology and Design," and with Frederick R. Steiner, eds., *To Heal the Earth: The Selected Writings of Ian McHarg* (Washington, D.C.: Island Press, 1998).

29. McHarg in McHarg and Steiner, *To Heal the Earth,* p. 136.

30. David E. Alexander, "Biological Diversity (Biodiversity)," *Encyclopedia of Environmental Science,* eds. David E. Alexander and Rhodes W. Fairbridge (Dordrecht, The Netherlands: Kluwer Academic Publishers, 1999), pp. 46–51.

31. Thomas E. Lovejoy, "Biodiversity," *The Encyclopedia of the Environment,* eds. Eblen and Eblen, pp. 60–61.

32. As quoted in Tom J. Bartuska and Gerald L. Young, "Aesthetics and Ecology: Notes on the Circle and the Sphere," *The Journal of Aesthetic Education* 9, no. 3 (1975):82.

33. Hawken, "A Declaration of Sustainability," p. 54. Reprinted with permission from the *Utne Reader* (September/October 1993).

34. United Nations Environment Programme et al., *World Resources 2000–2001,* p. 23. Reprinted from *World Resources 2000–2001* with permission from Elsevier Science.

35. E. O. Wilson, "The Current State of Biological Diversity," , *Biodiversity,* ed. E. O. Wilson (Washington, D.C.: National Academy Press, 1988), p. 3.

36. Deconstruction is a term very closely linked with postmodernism. The French philosopher Jacque Derrida proposed deconstructionism as a strategy of analysis applied to linguistics. Deconstructionists attempt to understand the ideological biases through the reading of texts. All life is viewed as texts, including architecture.

After the decline of modernism in architecture, architects went searching for a new style. Several advocated postmodernism, others deconstructionism, and still others some combination. Deconstructionist buildings reject their context both natural and built. They appear fragmented with no clear order.

37. Kenneth E. Boulding, "Earth as a Space Ship" (Talk to Committee on Space Sciences, Washington State University, Pullman, Washington, May 10, 1965).

Boulding (1910–1993) was born in Liverpool, England, was educated at Oxford, and taught at several American universities before settling at the University of Colorado at Boulder in 1967. He possessed a broad view of economics, fusing it with biology in his work on evolutionary economics.

38. Professors John Lyle and Jeff Olson led these studios, and, when Lyle died in 1998, the center was named after him. The center's director, Joan Safford, had been a graduate research assistant for the Kellogg-sponsored grant.

39. Frederick Steiner, "American Landscape Architecture: Leaping Continental Divides," *Rassegna di Architettura e Urbanistica* (Rome: University of Rome, 1998), and Enric Miralles, Benedetta Tagliabue, EDAW, and Frederick

Steiner, *Parc Diagonal Mar Sustainability: Statement of Environmental Sustainability* (Barcelona: Hines, 1998).

40. Miralles et al., *Parc Diagonal Mar Sustainability*.
41. Originally, landscape architect Thijs van Hees was to work with Stefan Behnisch, the partner-in-charge, on the design of both the exterior and interior landscapes. Instead, van Hees collaborated with the ecologist Ger Londo on the lands around the building while Behnisch worked with American artist Michael Singer and Dutch landscape architecture firm Copijn Tuin-en Landschapsarchitectuur on the dual internal gardens of the Alterra building. Singer designed much of the interior gardens with Copijn: the water features, sculptural elements, pavilion, and pavers. The Copijn team included Hyco Verhaagen, the partner-in-charge who worked directly with the architects of Behnisch's office; Charlotte Korthals-Altes, who led plant selection and coordinated design development with Singer; and Luc van Dam, who performed the site engineering.
42. Frederick Steiner, "Natural Interferences," *Landscape Architecture* 90, no. 11 (November, 2000), p. 92. See also, Egbert Koster, *Natuur onder architectuur/Architecture for nature* (Haarlem: Schuyt & Co., 1998).
43. McHarg, *A Quest for Life*, and McHarg and Steiner, *To Heal the Earth*.
44. Daniel Del Castillo, "A Long-Ignored Plague Gets Its Due," *The Chronicle for Higher Education* XLVIII, no. 23 (February 15, 2002), pp. A22–A23.
45. Barrett and Odum, "The Twenty-First Century," p. 366.

8. FOLLOWING NATURE'S LEAD

1. From a transcript of a television interview with Abraham J. Heschel broadcast on WCAU-TV (CBS), Channel 10, Philadelphia, Sunday, November 13, 1960. The program was part of *The House We Live In* series hosted by Ian McHarg, who edited the transcripts, p. 2.
2. Ibid., p. 3.
3. Ibid.
4. Paul Tillich, *The House We Live In* transcript from November 20, 1960, ed. McHarg.
5. Ibid., p. 4.
6. Ibid., p. 5.
7. Ibid.
8. Lynn White Jr. "The Historical Roots of Our Ecological Crisis," *Science* 155 (March 10, 1967):1205.

White (1907–1987) was a medieval scholar specializing in the technology of the Middle Ages and the religious background of industrialism. He taught at Princeton, Stanford, and UCLA and was president of Mills College. His *Science* essay is generally considered to be a classic in environmental ethics.
9. McHarg from McHarg and Steiner, eds., *To Heal the Earth*, p. 12, originally

in *The Urban Condition*, eds. Leonard J. Duhl and John Powell (New York: Basic Books, 1963).

10. James Barr, "Man and Nature: The Ecological Controversy and the Old Testament," *Ecology and Religion in History*, eds. David Spring and Eileen Spring (New York: Harper & Row, 1974), p. 73. See other essays in *Ecology and Religion in History*, too.

11. Sallie McFague, *The Body of God: An Ecological Theology* (Minneapolis: Fortress Press, 1993).

12. Ibid., p. 83.

13. John B. Cobb Jr. "A Christian View of Biodiversity," *Biodiversity*, ed. Wilson, p. 484.

14. Verena Eggman and Bernd Steiner, *Baumzeit* (Zürich: Werd Verlag, 1995).

15. Swami Nikhilananda, *The House We Live In* transcript from December 4, 1960, ed. McHarg, p. 2.

16. Alan Watts, *The House We Live In* transcript from December 11, 1960, ed. McHarg.

   Alan Watts (1915–1973) wrote over twenty books and numerous articles about the teachings of Eastern and Western religions and philosophy.

17. Ibid., p. 8.

18. Young and Bartuska, "Sphere," p. 220.

19. Beatley and Manning, *Ecology of Place*, p. 2.

20. K. David Pijawka and Kim Shetter, *The Environment Comes Home* (Tempe: Herberger Center for Design Excellence, Arizona State University, 1995).

21. As quoted by Beatley and Manning, *Ecology of Place*, p. 1. Donella Meadows (1941–2001) was best known as the co-author of the 1972 international best-seller *The Limits to Growth*. She also taught environmental studies at Dartmouth College and was a leading voice in the sustainability movement.

22. Havel, Address of the President of the Czech Republic on the Occasion of the Liberty Medal Ceremony, p. 4.

23. Address of the President of Czechoslovakia Václav Havel to a Joint Session of the United States Congress, Washington, D.C., February 21, 1990.

24. J. B. Jackson in Ervin Zube, ed., *Landscapes: Selected Writings of J. B. Jackson* (Amherst: University of Massachusetts Press, 1970), p. 9.

25. Paterson, "Community Building and the Necessity for Radical Revision," p. 88. Reprinted from *Landscape and Urban Planning* with permission from Elsevier Science.

26. McHarg and Steiner, *To Heal the Earth*, p. 64.

27. John Fowles, "Seeing Nature Whole," *Harper's* 259 (November 1979):53.

28. Márquez, *One Hundred Years of Solitude*, p. 374.

BIBLIOGRAPHY

Abate, Frank R., ed.-in-chief, *The Oxford Desk Dictionary and Thesaurus* (New York: Oxford University Press, 1997).

Aberley, Doug, ed., *Futures by Design: The Practice of Ecological Planning* (Gabriola Island, British Columbia: New Society Publishers, 1994).

Ackerman, James S., *The Villa: Form and Ideology of Country Houses* (Princeton: Princeton University Press, 1990).

Adams, Lowell W., and Louise E. Dove, *Wildlife Reserves and Corridors in the Urban Environment* (Columbia, Maryland: National Institute for Urban Wildlife, 1989).

Adler, Dankmar, "Function and Environment." In Lewis Mumford, ed., *Roots of Contemporary Architecture* (Third Edition) (New York: Dover, 1972), pp. 243–250.

Ahern, Jack, *Greenways as Strategic Landscape Planning: Theory and Application* (Wageningen, The Netherlands: Wageningen University, 2002).

Alanen, Arnold R., and Joseph A. Eden, *Main Street Ready-Made: The New Deal Community of Glendale, Wisconsin* (Madison: The State Historical Society of Wisconsin, 1987).

Alanen, Arnold R., and Robert Z. Melnick, eds., *Preserving Cultural Landscapes in America* (Baltimore: Johns Hopkins University Press, 2000).

Alexander, Christopher, Sara Ishikawa, Murray Silverstein, Max Jacobson, Ingrid Fiksdahl-King, and Shloma Angel, *A Pattern Language: Towns, Buildings, Construction* (New York: Oxford University Press, 1977).

Alexander, David E. "Biological Diversity (Biodiversity)." In David E. Alexander and Rhodes W. Fairbridge, eds., *Encyclopedia of Environmental Science* (Dordrecht, The Netherlands: Kluwer Academic Publishers, 1999), pp. 46–51.

Alexander, David E., and Rhodes W. Fairbridge, eds., *Encyclopedia of Environmental Science* (Dordrecht, The Netherlands: Kluwer Academic Publishers, 1999).

Bachelard, Gaston, *The Poetics of Space* (translated from French by Maria Jolas). (New York: The Orion Press, 1964).

Bailey, Robert G., *Ecoregions of the United States* (Ogden, Utah: U.S. Forest Service, 1978).

Bailey, Robert G., *Ecoregions: The Ecosystem Geography of the Oceans and Continents* (New York: Springer-Verlag, 1998).

Bailey, Robert G., *Ecosystem Geography* (New York: Springer-Verlag, 1996).

Banerjee, Tridib, and Michael Southworth, eds., *City Sense and City Design: Writings and Projects of Kevin Lynch* (Cambridge, Massachusetts: MIT Press, 1990).

Barr, James, "Man and Nature: The Ecological Controversy and the Old Testament." In David Spring and Eileen Spring, eds., *Ecology and Religion in History* (New York: Harper & Row, 1974), pp. 48–75.

Barrett, Gary W., and Eugene P. Odum, "The Twenty-First Century: The World at Carrying Capacity," *BioScience* 50(4, 2000),363–368.

Bartuska, Tom J., and Gerald L. Young, "Aesthetics and Ecology: Notes on the Circle and the Sphere," *The Journal of Aesthetic Education* 9(3, 1975),78–91.

Bartuska, Tom J., and Gerald L. Young, eds., *The Built Environment: A Creative Inquiry into Design and Planning* (Menlo Park, California: Crisp Publications, 1994).

Bates, Marston, "Process." In William L. Thomas Jr. ed., *Man's Role in Changing the Face of the Earth* (Chicago: University of Chicago Press, 1956), pp. 1136–1140.

Beatley, Timothy, *Ethical Land Use: Principles of Policy and Planning* (Baltimore: Johns Hopkins University Press, 1994).

Beatley, Timothy, "Urban Policy and Fair Equality of Opportunity." In Gene Grigsby and David Godschalk, eds., *Shaping a National Agenda* (Los Angeles: Los Angeles Center for Afro-American Studies, University of California, 1993).

Beatley, Timothy, and Kristy Manning, *The Ecology of Place* (Washington, D.C.: Island Press, 1997).

Behar, Roberto, Presentation at the American Academy in Rome, February 19, 1998. Rome, Italy.

Behar, Roberto M., "Little Guatemala and the Invention of Miami," *The New City* 2 (The American City [special edition], 1994), pp. 105–115.

Bennett, John W., *The Ecological Transition: Cultural Anthropology and Human Adaptation* (New York and London: Pergamon, 1976).

Bennett, John W., *The Northern Plainsmen* (Chicago: Aldine, 1969).

Berger, Jonathan, "Landscape Patterns of Local Social Organization and Their Importance for Land Use Planning," *Landscape Planning* 8(1980):193–232.

Berger, Jonathan, and John W. Sinton, *Water, Earth, and Fire* (Baltimore: Johns Hopkins University Press, 1985).

Berry, Thomas, "Bioregions: The Context for Reinhabiting the Earth." In Barbara Dean, ed., *The Dream of the Earth* (San Francisco: Sierra Club Books, 1988).

Berry, Wendell, *A Continuous Harmony: Essays Cultural and Agricultural* (New York: A Harvest/HBJ Book, 1975).

Birch, Eugenie Ladner, "The Big Picture People," *Planning* 66(3, 2000):20–25.

Boardman, Philip, *The Worlds of Patrick Geddes: Biologist, Town Planner, Re-educator, Peace-warrior* (London: Routledge & Kegan Paul, 1978).

Botkin, D. B., and C. E. Beveridge, "Cities as Environments," *Urban Ecosystems* 1(1997):3–19.

Botkin, Daniel B., *Discordant Harmonies: A New Ecology for the Twenty-First Century* (New York: Oxford University Press, 1990).

Botkin, Daniel B., and Edward A. Keller, *Environmental Science: Earth as a Living Planet* (New York: John Wiley & Sons, 1998).

Boulding, Kenneth E., "Earth as a Space Ship" (Talk to Committee on Space Sciences, Washington State University, Pullman, Washington, May 10, 1965).

Bourassa, Steven C., *The Aesthetics of Landscape* (London: Belhaven, 1991).

Boyd, Julian P., ed., Mina R. Bryan and Elizabeth L. Hunter, associate eds., *The Papers of Thomas Jefferson* (volume 6, May 21, 1781, to March 1784). (Princeton, New Jersey: Princeton University Press, 1952).

Bradley, Nina Leopold, "14th H. Wayne Pritchard Lecture." Soil and Water Conservation Society Annual Meeting, Lexington, Kentucky, 1991.

Brand, Stewart, *The Clock of the Long Now: Time and Responsibility* (New York: Basic Books, 1999).

Braudel, Fernand, *The Structures of Everyday Life: Civilization and Capitalism, 15th–18th Century* (translated from French by Siân Reynolds). (New York: Harper & Row, 1981).

Brazel, Anthony, Nancy Selover, Russell Vose, and Gordon Heisler, "The Tale of Two Climates—Baltimore and Phoenix LTER Sites," *Climate Research* 15(2000):123–135.

Buell, Lawrence, *Writing for an Endangered World: Literature, Culture, and Environment in the U.S. and Beyond* (Cambridge, Massachusetts: The Belknap Press of Harvard University Press, 2001).

Burckhardt, Jacob, *The Civilization of the Renaissance in Italy* (translated by S. G. C. Middlemore). (New York: Harper, 1958).

Callenbach, Ernest, *Ecotopia* (Berkeley, California: Banyan Tree, 1975).

Calthorpe, Peter, *The Next American Metropolis: Ecology, Community and the American Dream* (New York: Princeton Architectural Press, 1993).

Calthorpe, Peter, and William Fulton, *The Regional City* (Washington, D.C.: Island Press, 2001).

Cartwright, D., ed., *Field Theory in Social Science: Selected Theoretical Papers* (New York: Harper & Row, 1951).

Cather, Willa, *My Ántonia* (Boston: Houghton Mifflin Company, 1995, originally published in 1918).

Catton, William R., Jr., *Overshoot: The Ecological Basis for Evolutionary Change* (Urbana: University of Illinois Press, 1980).

Chapin, F. Stuart III, Brian H. Walker, Richard J. Hobbs, David U. Hooper, John H. Lawton, Osvaldo E. Sala, and David Tilman, "Biotic Control over the Functioning of Ecosystems," *Science* 277(1997):500–504.

Cicero, Marcus Tullius, *De Officiis* 1.53–55, xvii.

Cobb, John B., Jr., "A Christian View of Biodiversity." In E. O. Wilson, ed., *Biodiversity* (Washington, D.C.: National Academy Press, 1988), pp. 481–485.

Cobb, John B., Jr., "Defining Normative Community." In William Vitek and Wes Jackson, eds., *Rooted in the Land: Essays on Community and Place* (New Haven, Connecticut: Yale University Press, 1996), pp. 185–194.

Cohen, Yehudi A., ed., *Man in Adaptation: The Cultural Present* (Second Edition). (Chicago: Aldine, 1974).

Coke, James, "Antecedents to Local Planning." In William I. Goodman and Eric C. Freund, eds., *Principles and Practices of Urban Planning* (Washington, D.C.: International City Management Association, 1968), pp. 7–28.

Cole, LaMont C., "The Ecosphere," *Scientific American* 198(4, April, 1958):83–92.

Collins, James P., Ann Kinzig, Nancy B. Grimm, William F. Fagan, Diane Hope, Jiango Wu, and Elizabeth T. Borer, "A New Urban Ecology," *American Scientist* 88(5, September–October, 2000):416–425.

Comfort, William Wistar, *Just Among Friends: The Quaker Way of Life* (Philadelphia: American Friends Service Committee, 1968).

Conzen, M. R. G., *Alnwick, Northumberland: A Study in Town-Plan Analysis* (Institute of British Geographers Publication 27). (London: George Philip, 1960).

Cook, Edward, and Joan Hirschman, eds., "Special Issue: Landscape Ecology," *Landscape and Urban Planning* 21(1–2, 1991):1–46.

Corner, James, ed., *Recovering Landscape: Essays in Contemporary Landscape Architecture* (New York: Princeton Architectural Press, 1999).

Cowan, James, *A Mapmaker's Dream: The Meditations of Fra Mauro, Cartographer to the Court of Venice* (New York: Warner Books, 1996).

Cowardin, Lewis M., Virginia Carter, Francis C. Golet, and Edward T. LaRoe, *Classification of Wetlands and Deepwater Habitats in the United States* (Washington, D.C.: U.S. Government Printing Office, 1979).

Craige, Betty Jean, "The Holistic Vision of Eugene Odum, Ecologist and Environmentalist" (manuscript). (Athens: The Center for Humanities and the Arts, University of Georgia, 1998).

Cronon, William, *Changes in the Land: Indians, Colonists, and the Ecology of New England* (New York: Hill and Wang, 1983).

Cronon, William, *Nature's Metropolis: Chicago and the Great West* (New York: W. W. Norton, 1992).

Cronon, William, ed., *Uncommon Ground: Rethinking the Human Place in Nature* (New York: W. W. Norton, 1996).

Cronon, William, ed., *Uncommon Ground: Toward Reinventing Nature* (New York: W. W. Norton, 1995).

Dansereau, Pierre, *Biogeography: An Ecological Perspective* (New York: Ronald Press, 1957).

Davern, Jeanne M., ed., *Lewis Mumford, Architecture as a Home for Man: Essays for Architectural Record* (New York: Architectural Record Books, 1975).

Davis, Mike, *City of Quartz: Excavating the Future in Los Angeles* (London: Verso, 1990).

Davis, Mike, *Ecology of Fear: Los Angeles and the Imagination of Disaster* (New York: Metropolitan Books, 1998).

Del Castillo, Daniel, "A Long-Ignored Plague Gets Its Due," *The Chronicle for Higher Education* XLVIII(23, February 15, 2002):A22–A23.

DeLillo, Don, *Underworld* (New York: Scribner, 1997).

Dobson, Andy P., A. D. Bradshaw, and A. J. M. Baker, "Hopes for the Future: Restoration Ecology and Conservation Biology," *Science* 277(1997):515–522.

Doka, Yahaya, "Policy Objectives, Land Tenure, and Settlement Performance: Implications for Equity and Economic Efficiency in the Columbia Basin Irrigation Project" (Ph.D. dissertation). (Pullman: Department of Agricultural Economics, Washington State University, 1979).

Dramstad, Wenche E., James D. Olson, and Richard T. T. Forman, *Landscape Ecology Principles in Landscape Architecture and Land-Use Planning* (Washington, D.C.: Island Press, Harvard University, and American Society of Landscape Architects, 1996).

Duany, Andres, Elizabeth Plater-Zyberk, and Jeff Speck, *Suburban Nation: The Rise of Sprawl and the Decline of the American Dream* (New York: North Point Press, 2001).

Dubrow, Gail Lee, "Asian American Imprints on the Western Landscape." In Arnold R. Alanen and Robert Z. Melnick, eds., *Preserving Cultural Landscapes in America* (Baltimore: Johns Hopkins University Press, 2000), pp. 143–168.

Duhl, Leonard J., and John Powell, eds., *The Urban Condition* (New York: Basic Books, 1963).

Eblen, Ruth A., and William R. Eblen, eds., *The Encyclopedia of the Environment* (Boston: Houghton Mifflin, 1994).

Eggman, Verena, and Bernd Steiner, *Baumzeit* (Zürich: Werd Verlag, 1995).

Eliot, T. S., *Notes toward the Definition of Culture* (New York: Harcourt, Brace, 1949).

Ellin, Nan, *Postmodern Urbanism* (Cambridge, Massachusetts: Blackwell Publishers, 1996).

Elton, Charles, *Animal Ecology* (New York: Macmillan, 1927).

Estall, Robert, "Planning in Appalachia: An Examination of the Appalachian Regional Development Programme and Its Implications for the Future of American Regional Planning Commissions," *Institute of British Geographers*, Transaction New Series, 7(1982):35–58.

Evernden, Neil, *The Social Creation of Nature* (Baltimore: Johns Hopkins University Press, 1992).

Fabos, Julius Gy., *Planning the Total Landscape* (Boulder, Colorado: Westview Press, 1979).

Ferguson, Bruce K., "The Concept of Landscape Health," *Journal of Environmental Management* 40(1994):129–137.

Ferguson, Bruce K., "The Maintenance of Landscape Health in the Midst of Land Use Change," *Journal of Environmental Management* 48(1996):387–395.

Fishman, Robert, "The Mumford-Jacobs Debate," *Planning History Studies* 10(1–2, 1996):3–11.

Fishman, Robert, ed., *The American Planning Tradition* (Washington, D.C.: The Woodrow Wilson Center Press, 2000).

Fletcher, Rachel, "Proportioning Systems and the Timber Framer," *Journal of the Timber Framing Guild* 18(December, 1990):8–9.

Forman, Richard T. T., *Land Mosaics: The Ecology of Landscapes and Regions* (Cambridge, England: Cambridge University Press, 1995).

Forman, Richard T. T., and Michel Godron, *Landscape Ecology* (New York: John Wiley & Sons, 1986).

Forman, Richard T. T., and Anna M. Hersperger, "Ecologia del paesaggio e planificazione: una potente combinazione," *Urbanistica* 108(gennaio–giugno, 1997):61–66.

Fossa, Giovanna, Robert Lane, Danilo Palazzo, and Robert Pirani, eds., *Transforming the Places of Production. Trasformare i luoghi della Produzione* (Milano: Edizioni Olivares, 2002).

Fowles, John, "Seeing Nature Whole," *Harper's* 259(November 1979):49–68.

Friedman, Thomas L., "Foreign Affairs: Two Sick Nations, One Cure." *New York Times* (July 25, 1998):8.

Friedmann, John, "Regional Planning as a Field of Study." In John Friedmann and William Alonso, eds., *Regional Development and Planning* (Cambridge, Massachusetts: MIT Press, 1964).

Friedmann, John, *Retracking America* (Garden City, New York: Anchor Press/Doubleday, 1973).

Friedmann, John, and William Alonso, eds., *Regional Development and Planning* (Cambridge, Massachusetts: MIT Press, 1964).

Fuller, Richard Buckminster, *Synergetics: Explorations in the Geometry of Thinking* (with E. J. Applewhite). (New York: Macmillan, 1975).

Gans, Herbert, *The Levittowners: Ways of Life and Politics in a New Suburban Community* (New York: Alfred A. Knopf, 1967).

Ganster, Paul, general ed., *San Diego–Tijuana International Border Area Planning Atlas/Atlas de Planeación del área Fronteriza Internacional Tijuana–San Diego* (San Diego: San Diego State University Press and Institute for Regional Studies of the Californias, 2000).

Garreau, Joel, *The Nine Nations of North America* (Boston: Houghton Mifflin, 1981).

Garvan, Anthony N. B., "Proprietary Philadelphia as Artifact." In Oscar Handlin and John Burchard, eds., *The Historian and the City* (Cambridge, Massachusetts: MIT Press, 1963), pp. 177–201.

Geddes, Patrick, *Cities in Evolution: An Introduction to the Town Planning Movement and to the Study of Civics* (London: Williams & Norgate, 1915).

Geertz, Clifford J., *Agriculture Involution* (Berkeley: University of California Press, 1963).

Geertz, Clifford, *Available Light: Anthropological Reflections on Philosophical Topics* (Princeton, New Jersey: Princeton University Press, 2000).

Geertz, Clifford, "The Impact of the Concept of Culture on the Concept of Man." In Yehudi A. Cohen, ed., *Man in Adaptation: The Cultural Present* (Second Edition). (Chicago: Aldine, 1974), pp. 19–32. (Originally in John R. Platt, ed., *New Views of the Nature of Man*. Chicago: University of Chicago Press, 1965).

Golley, Frank B., *A Primer for Environmental Literacy* (New Haven, Connecticut: Yale University Press, 1998).

Goodchild, Michael, and Sucharita Gopal, eds., *The Accuracy of Spatial Databases* (London and New York: Taylor & Francis, 1989).

Goodchild, Michael F., Bradley O. Parks, and Louis T. Steyaert, eds., *Environmental Modeling with GIS* (New York: Oxford University Press, 1993).

Goodman, William I., and Eric C. Freund, eds., *Principles and Practices of Urban Planning* (Washington, D.C.: International City Management Association, 1968).

Grant, Jill, Patricia Manuel, and Darrell Joudrey, "A Framework for Planning Sustainable Residential Landscapes," *Journal of the American Planning Association* 62(3, 1996):331–344.

Grigsby, Gene, and David Godschalk, eds., *Shaping a National Agenda* (Los Angeles: Los Angeles Center for Afro-American Studies, University of California, 1993).

Grimm, Nancy E., J. Morgan Grove, Steward T. A. Pickett, and Charles L. Redman, "Integrated Approaches to Long-Term Studies of Ecological Systems," *BioScience* 50(7, 2000):571–584.

Groth, Paul, and Todd W. Bressi, eds., *Understanding Ordinary Landscapes* (New Haven and London: Yale University Press, 1997).

Gunderson, Lance H., C. S. Holling, and Stephen S. Light, eds., *Barriers and Bridges to the Renewal of Ecosystems and Institutions* (New York: Columbia University Press, 1995).

Hahn, Alan J., and Cynthia D. Dyballa, "State Environmental Planning and Local Influence," *Journal of the American Planning Association* 47(1981):324–335.

Hall, Donna L., and William W. Budd, "Landscape Ecology and Landscape Planning." In Rusong Wang, Jingzhu Zhao, and Zhiyun Ouyang, eds., *Human Systems Ecology* (Beijing: China Science and Technology Press, 1991), pp. 51–62.

Hall, Peter, *Cities of Tomorrow* (Oxford: Basil Blackwell, 1988).

Hamsun, Knut, *Growth of the Soil* (New York: Alfred A. Knopf, 1921).

Hancocks, David, *A Different Nature: The Paradoxical World of Zoos and Their Uncertain Future* (Berkeley: University of California Press, 2001).

Handlin, Oscar, and John Burchard, eds., *The Historian and the City* (Cambridge, Massachusetts: MIT Press, 1963).

Harrison, Paul, and Fred Pearce, *AAA Atlas of Population & Environment* (Berkeley: University of California Press, 2000).

Havel, Václav, Address of the President of Czechoslovakia to a Joint Session of the United States Congress, Washington, D.C. (February 21, 1990).

Havel, Václav, Address of the President of the Czech Republic, His Excellency Václav Havel, on the Occasion of the Liberty Medal Ceremony. Philadelphia, Pennsylvania (July 4, 1994).

Hawken, Paul, "A Declaration of Sustainability," *Utne Reader* (September/October, 1993):54–61.

Hazan, Marcella, *Essentials of Classic Italian Cooking* (New York: Alfred A. Knopf, 1995).

Hersey, George, *The Monumental Impulse: Architecture's Biological Roots* (Cambridge: MIT Press, 1999).

Hersperger, Anna, "Landscape Ecology and Its Potential Application to Planning," *Journal of Planning Literature* 9(1, 1994):14–29.

Heschel, Abraham J., *The House We Live In*. Transcript of the program broadcast on WCAU-TV (CBS), Channel 10, Philadelphia, Sunday, November 13, 1960, hosted and edited by Ian McHarg.

Hildebrand, Grant, *Origins of Architectural Pleasure* (Berkeley: University of California Press, 1999).

Hill, Kristina, "Design and Planning as Healing Arts: The Broader Context of Health and Environment." In Bart R. Johnson and Kristina Hill, eds., *Ecology and Design: Frameworks for Learning* (Washington, D.C.: Island Press, 2002), pp. 203–214.

Holling, C. S., "What Barriers? What Bridges?" In Lance H. Gunderson, C. S. Holling, and Stephen S. Light, eds., *Barriers and Bridges to the Renewal of Ecosystems and Institutions* (New York: Columbia University Press, 1995), pp. 3–34.

Holt, Nancy, ed., *The Writings of Robert Smithson* (New York: New York University Press, 1989).

Hough, Michael, *Out of Place: Restoring Identity to the Regional Landscape* (New Haven, Connecticut: Yale University Press, 1990).

Hunt, Charles B., *Physiography of the United States* (San Francisco: W. H. Freeman, 1967).

Hunt, John Dixon, *Greater Perfections: The Practice of Garden Theory* (Philadelphia: University of Pennsylvania Press, 2000).

Hunter, Floyd, *Community Power Structure* (Chapel Hill: University of North Carolina Press, 1953).

Jackson, J. B., "The Order of a Landscape." In D. W. Meinig, ed., *The Interpretation of Ordinary Landscapes* (New York: Oxford University Press, 1979), pp. 153–163.

Jackson, John Brinckerhoff, *Discovering the Vernacular Landscape* (New Haven, Connecticut: Yale University Press, 1984).

James, Preston E., *All Possible Worlds* (Indianapolis: Odyssey Press, 1972).

Jensen, Merrill, ed., *Regionalism in America* (Madison: University of Wisconsin Press, 1965).

Johnson, Bart R., and Kristina Hill, eds., *Ecology and Design: Frameworks for Learning* (Washington, D.C.: Island Press, 2002).

Jones, Alice, "The Psychology of Sustainability: What Planners Can Learn from Attitude Research," *Journal of Planning Education and Research* 16(1, 1996):56–65.

Keim, Kevin, ed., *You Have to Pay for the Public Life: Selected Essays of Charles W. Moore* (Cambridge, Massachusetts: The MIT Press, 2001).

Kingsolver, Barbara, *High Tide in Tucson* (New York: HarperCollins, 1995).

Knepper, Cathy D., *Greenbelt, Maryland* (Baltimore: Johns Hopkins University Press, 2001).

Koestler, Arthur, *The Ghost in the Machine* (New York: Macmillan, 1967).

Koster, Egbert, *Natuur onder architectuur/Architecture for nature* (Haarlem: Schuyt & Co., 1998).

Kraenzel, Carl F., "Principles of Regional Planning: As Applied to the Northwest," *Social Forces* 25(1947):373–384.

Kraenzel, Carl Frederick, *The Great Plains in Transition* (Norman: University of Oklahoma Press, 1955).

Kunstler, James Howard, "Home from Nowhere: How to Make Our Cities and Towns Livable," *The Atlantic Monthly* (September, 1996):43–66.

Landers, Richard R., *Man's Place in the Dybosphere* (Englewood Cliffs, New Jersey: Prentice-Hall, 1966).

Langdon, Philip, *A Better Place to Live: Reshaping the American Suburb* (Amherst: University of Massachusetts Press, 1994).

Le Carré, John, *The Constant Gardener* (New York: Scribner, 2001).

Le Roy Ladurie, Emmanuel, *Carnival in Romans* (translated from French by Mary Feeney). (New York: George Braziller, 1979).

Leopold, Aldo, *A Sand County Almanac and Sketches Here and There* (London: Oxford University Press, 1949).

Leopold, Aldo, *Round River: From the Journals of Aldo Leopold*. Luna B. Leopold, ed. (Minocqua, Wisconsin: North Word Press, 1991).

Levi, Primo, *The Drowned and the Saved* (London: Abacus, original Giulio Einaudi editore s.p.a., 1989).

Lewin, Kurt, *Field Theory in Social Science: Selected Theoretical Papers*. D. Cartwright, ed. (New York: Harper & Row, 1951).

Lovejoy, Thomas E., "Biodiversity." In Ruth A. Eblen and William R. Eblen, eds., *The Encyclopedia of the Environment* (Boston: Houghton Mifflin, 1994), pp. 60–61.

Lovelock, James E., *The Ages of Gaia: A Biography of Our Living Earth* (New York: Norton, 1988).

Lovelock, James E., *Gaia: A New Look at Life on Earth* (Paperback Edition). (Oxford, England: Oxford University Press, 1982).

Luccarelli, Mark, *Lewis Mumford and the Ecological Region* (New York: The Guilford Press, 1995).

Luymes, Don, "The Fortification of Suburbia: Investigating the Rise of Enclave Communities," *Landscape and Urban Planning* 39(2–3, 1997):187–203.

Lyle, John Tillman, *Design for Human Ecosystems* (New York: Van Nostrand Reinhold, 1985).

Lynch, Kevin, "Design and City Appearance." In William I. Goodman and Eric C. Freund, eds., *Principles and Practices of Urban Planning* (Washington, D.C.: International City Management Association, 1968), pp. 249–276.

Lynch, Kevin, and Gary Hack, *Site Planning* (Third Edition). (Cambridge, Massachusetts: MIT Press, 1984).

Machiavelli, Niccolò, *The Prince* (New York: Cambridge University Press, 1988, originally 1513).

MacKaye, Benton, *The New Exploration* (New York: Harcourt Brace, 1928).

MacKaye, Benton, "Regional Planning and Ecology," *Ecological Monographs* 10(1940):349–353.

Malmberg, Torsten, *Human Territoriality: Survey of Behavioural Territories in Man with Preliminary Analysis and Discussion of Meaning* (The Hague, The Netherlands: Mouton, 1980).

Mandelbaum, Seymour J., *Open Moral Communities* (Cambridge, Massachusetts: MIT Press, 2000).

Márquez, Gabriel García, *Cien Años de Soledad* (Buenos Aires: Editorial Sudamericana, 1967, English translation by Gregory Rabassa, *One Hundred Years of Solitude*. New York: Harper & Row, 1970).

Marshall, Alex, *How Cities Work: Suburbs, Sprawl, and Roads Not Taken* (Austin: University of Texas Press, 2000).

McDonnell, Myles, "Public Life and *Patria Potestas*: The Extended Patriarchal Roman Family Revised." Paper presented at the American Academy in Rome, March 5, 1998. Rome, Italy.

McFague, Sallie, *The Body of God: An Ecological Theology* (Minneapolis: Fortress Press, 1993).

McHarg, Ian L., *A Quest for Life* (New York: John Wiley & Sons, 1996).

McHarg, Ian L., *Design with Nature* (Garden City, New York: Natural History Press/Doubleday, 1969).

McHarg, Ian L., "Ecology and Design." In George F. Thompson and Frederick R. Steiner, eds., *Ecological Design and Planning* (New York: John Wiley & Sons, 1997), pp. 321–332.

McHarg, Ian, *The House We Live In.*Transcripts from the programs broadcast on WCAU-TV (CBS), Channel 10, Philadelphia, 1960–1961.

McHarg, Ian L., "Man and Environment." In Ian L. McHarg and Frederick R. Steiner, eds., *To Heal the Earth: The Selected Writings of Ian McHarg* (Washington, D.C.: Island Press, 1998, pp. 10–23. Originally in Leonard J. Duhl and John Powell, eds., *The Urban Condition*. New York: Basic Books, 1963).

McHarg, Ian L., and Frederick R. Steiner, eds., *To Heal the Earth: The Selected Writings of Ian McHarg* (Washington, D.C.: Island Press, 1998).

McLuhan, Marshall, and Quentin Fiore, *The Medium Is the Massage* (New York: Bantam Books, 1967).

Meadows, Donnella, Dennis Meadows, Jorgen Randers, and William W. Behrensill, *The Limits to Growth* (New York: Universe Books, 1972).

Meine, Curt, "Inherit the Grid." In Joan Iverson Nassauer, ed., *Placing Nature: Culture and Landscape Ecology* (Washington, D.C.: Island Press, 1997), pp. 45–62.

Meinig, D. W., ed., *The Interpretation of Ordinary Landscapes* (New York: Oxford University Press, 1979).

Melosi, Martin V., *The Sanitary City: Urban Infrastructure in America from Colonial Times to the Present* (Baltimore: Johns Hopkins University Press, 2000).

Merchant, Carolyn, *Ecological Revolutions: Nature, Science and Gender in New England* (Chapel Hill: University of North Carolina Press, 1989).

Miller, Zane L., *Suburb: Neighborhood and Community in Forest Park, Ohio, 1935–1976* (Knoxville: The University of Tennessee Press, 1981).

Miralles, Enric, Benedetta Tagliabue, EDAW, and Frederick Steiner, *Parc Diagonal Mar Sustainability: Statement of Environmental Sustainability* (September). (Barcelona: Hines, 1998).

Moore, Steven A., "Reproducing the Local," *Platform* (Spring, 1999):2–3, 8–9.

Morgan, Arthur E., *Dams and Other Disasters* (Boston: Porter Sargent, 1971).

Morgan, Arthur E., *The Miami Conservancy District* (New York: McGraw-Hill, 1951).

Morris, A. E. J., *The History of Urban Form: Prehistory to Renaissance* (Second Edition). (London: George Goodwin Limited, 1979).

Morris, Elizabeth, "Community in Theory and Practice: A Framework for Intellectual Renewal" (CPL Bibliography 330). *Journal of Planning Literature* 11(1, 1996):127–150.

Moudon, Anne Vernez, "Urban Morphology as an Emerging Interdisciplinary Field," *Urban Morphology* 1(1997):3–10.

Mulisch, Harry, *The Discovery of Heaven* (translated from the Dutch by Paul Vincent). (New York: Viking Penguin, 1996).

Mumford, Lewis, ed., *Roots of Contemporary Architecture* (Third Edition). (New York: Dover, 1972).

Mumford, Lewis, "Trend Is Not Destiny." In Jeanne M. Davern, ed., *Lewis Mumford, Architecture as a Home for Man: Essays for Architectural Record* (New York: Architectural Record Books, 1975), pp. 201–206.

Myhra, David, "Rexford Guy Tugwell: Initiator of America's Greenbelt New Towns, 1935 to 1936," *Journal of the American Institute of Planners* 40(1974):176–187.

Nabhan, Gary Paul, *Cultures of Habitat: On Nature, Culture, and Story* (Washington, D.C.: Counterpoint, 1997).

Nassauer, Joan Iverson, ed., *Placing Nature: Culture and Landscape Ecology* (Washington, D.C.: Island Press, 1997).

National Research Council, *New Strategies for America's Watersheds* (Washington, D.C.: National Academy Press, 1999).

Naveh, Z., and A. Lieberman, *Landscape Ecology: Theory and Applications* (New York: Springer-Verlag, 1984).

Ndubisi, Forester, "Landscape Ecological Planning." In George F. Thompson and Frederick R. Steiner, eds., *Ecological Design and Planning* (New York: John Wiley & Sons, 1997), pp. 9–44.

Neihardt, John G., *Black Elk Speaks: Being the Life Story of a Holy Man of the Oglala Sioux* (first published in 1932). (Lincoln: University Press of Nebraska, 2000).

Ng, Fae Myenne, *Bone* (New York: HarperCollins, 1993).

Nickens, Eddie, "Map Maker," *Landscape Architecture* 86(12, 1996):74–79, 88.

Niebuhr, Reinhold, *The Nature and Destiny of Man* (volume II, Human Destiny). (New York: Charles Scribner's Sons, 1943).

Nikhilananda, Swami, *The House We Live In*. Transcript of the program broadcast on WCAU-TV (CBS), Channel 10, Philadelphia, Sunday, December 4, 1960, hosted and edited by Ian McHarg.

Norton, William, *Explorations in the Understanding of Landscape: A Cultural Geography* (New York: Greenwood Press, 1989).

Norton, William, *Human Geography* (Third Edition). (Toronto: Oxford University Press, 1998).

Noss, Reed F., "Indicators for Monitoring Biodiversity: A Hierarchical Approach," *Conservation Biology* 4(4, 1990):355–364.

Noss, Reed F., "The Wildlands Project: Land Conservation Strategy." In Doug Aberley, ed., *Futures by Design, The Practice of Ecological Planning* (Gabriola Island, British Columbia: New Society Publishers, 1994), pp. 127–165.

Noss, Reed F., Michael A. O'Connell, and Dennis D. Murphy, *The Science of Conservation Planning: Habitat Conservation under the Endangered Species Act* (Washington, D.C.: Island Press, 1997).

Odum, Eugene P., "Ecology as a Science." In Ruth A. Eblen and William R.

Eblen, eds., *The Encyclopedia of the Environment* (Boston: Houghton Mifflin, 1994), pp. 171–175.

Odum, Eugene P., *Ecology and Our Endangered Life Support System* (Second Edition). (Sunderland, Massachusetts: Sinauer, 1993).

Odum, Eugene P., *Fundamentals of Ecology* (Philadelphia: W. B. Saunders, 1971).

Odum, Howard T., *Systems Ecology: An Introduction* (New York: John Wiley & Sons, 1983).

Odum, Howard W., "The Promise of Regionalism." In Merrill Jensen, ed., *Regionalism in America* (Madison: University of Wisconsin Press, 1965), pp. 395–419.

Odum, Howard W., *The Way of the South: Toward the Regional Balance of America* (New York: The Macmillan Company, 1947).

Odum, Howard W., and Katharine Jocher, eds., *In Search of the Regional Balance of America* (Westport, Connecticut: Greenwood Press, 1945).

Olin, Laurie, *Across the Open Field: Essays Drawn from English Landscapes* (Philadelphia: University of Pennsylvania Press, 2000).

Olmsted, Frederick Law, *A Journey through Texas: Or, A Saddle Trip on the Southwestern Frontier* (New York: Dix, Edwards & Co., also, London: Sampson Low, Son & Co. and Edinburg: Thos. Constable & Co., 1857).

Ophuls, William, *Ecology and the Politics of Scarcity* (San Francisco: W. H. Freeman, 1977).

Opie, John, *Nature's Nation: An Environmental History of the United States* (Fort Worth, Texas: Harcourt Brace College Publishers, 1998).

Oz-Golden, Liza, "Increasing Outdoor Comfort in the Sonoran Desert: An Analysis of the Hayden Ferry Site, Tempe, Arizona" (Master of Environmental Planning thesis). (Tempe: School of Planning and Landscape Architecture, Arizona State University, 1999).

Palazzo, Danilo, "La terra dalla luna, ovvero come la paura della bomba ha aiutato (negli Stati Uniti) la pianificazione ecologica," *Oikos* 2(1997):59–84.

Palazzo, Danilo, *Master Plan dell' area dell' ex macello a Monza* (Milan, Italy: Politecnico di Milano, 2001).

Palazzo, Danilo, *Sulle spalle di giganti: Le matrici della pianificazione ambietale negli Stati Uniti* (Milan, Italy: Francoangeli/DST, 1997).

Palladio, Andrea, *The Four Books on Architecture* (translated by Robert Tavernor and Richard Schofield). (Cambridge, Massachusetts: MIT Press, 1997).

Park, Robert, and Ernest Burgess, *The City* (Chicago: University of Chicago Press, 1925).

Parks, Tim, *Italian Neighbors or a Lapsed Anglo-Saxon in Verona* (New York: Fawcett Columbine, 1992).

Paterson, Douglas D., "Community Building and the Necessity for Radical Revision," *Landscape and Urban Planning* 39(2–3, 1997):83–98.

Paton, Alan, *Cry, The Beloved Country* (New York: Charles Scribner's Sons, 1948).

Peck, Sheila, *Planning for Biodiversity* (Washington, D.C.: Island Press, 1998).

Penone, Giuseppe, *Giuseppe Penone* (Torino, Italy: Hopefulmonster, Galleria
    Civica di Arte Contemporanea, Trento, Italia, 1997).
Pickett, Steward T., William R. Burch Jr., Shawn E. Dalton, Timothy W.
    Foresman, J. Morgan Grove, and Rowan Rowntree, "A Conceptual
    Framework for the Study of Human Ecosystems in Urban Areas," *Urban
    Ecosystems* 1(1997):185–199.
Pijawka, K. David, and Kim Shetter, *The Environment Comes Home* (Tempe:
    Herberger Center for Design Excellence, Arizona State University, 1995).
Pinelands Commission, *New Jersey Pinelands Comprehensive Management Plan*
    (New Lisbon, New Jersey, 1980).
Plato, *Timaeus and Critias* (translated by D. Lee). (Middlesex, England: Penguin
    Books, 1971).
Platt, John R., ed., *New Views of the Nature of Man* (Chicago: University of
    Chicago Press, 1965).
Platt, Rutherford H., Rowan A. Rowntree, and Pamela C. Muick, eds., *The
    Ecological City: Preserving and Restoring Urban Biodiversity* (Amherst:
    University of Massachusetts Press, 1994).
Powers, Richard, *Plowing the Dark* (New York: Farrar, Straus and Giroux, 2000).
(The) President's Council on Sustainable Development, *Sustainable Development:
    A New Consensus* (Washington, D.C.: U.S. Government Printing Office,
    1996).
Prigogine, Ilya, and Isabelle Stengers, *Order Out of Chaos: Man's New Dialogue
    with Nature* (Toronto, Ontario: Bantam Books, 1984).
Pulliam, H. Ronald, and Bart R. Johnson, "Ecology's New Paradigm: What Does
    It Offer to Designers and Planners?" In Bart R. Johnson and Kristina Hill,
    eds., *Ecology and Design: Frameworks for Learning* (Washington, D.C.: Island
    Press, 2002), pp. 51–84.
Putnam, Robert D., *Bowling Alone: The Collapse and Revival of American
    Community* (New York: Simon & Schuster, 2000).
Pyne, Stephen J., *Fire in America: A Cultural History of Wildland and Rural Fire*
    (Princeton, New Jersey: Princeton University Press, 1982).
Quarrie, Joyce, ed., *Earth Summit '92* (London: The Regency Press, 1992).
Quayle, Moura, and Tilo C. Driessen van der Lieck, "Growing Community: A
    Case for Hybrid Landscapes," *Landscape and Urban Planning* 39(2–3,
    1997):99–107.
Rackham, Oliver, *The Illustrated History of the Countryside* (London: George and
    Nicole Weindenfeld, 1994).
Rappaport, Roy A., *Ecology, Meaning and Religion* (Berkeley, California: North
    Atlantic Books, 1979).
Rappaport, Roy A., *Pigs for the Ancestors* (New Haven, Connecticut: Yale
    University Press, 1968).
Rees, William E., "Ecological Footprints and Appropriated Carrying Capacity:
    What Urban Economics Leaves Out," *Environment and Urbanization* 4(2,
    1992):121–130.

Rees, William E., "Globalization and Sustainability: Conflict or Convergence?" *Bulletin of Science, Technology and Society* 22 (4, 2002):249–269.

Rees, William E., "Is 'Sustainable City' an Oxymoron?" *Local Environment* 2(3, 1997):303–310.

Regione Lombardia Assessorato all' Urbanistica, *Il Recupero Paesistico dell' Adda di Leonardo* (Milano: Bollettino Ufficiale, Regione Lombardia, 1998).

Reiniger, Clair, "Bioregional Planning and Ecosystem Protection." In George F. Thompson and Frederick R. Steiner, eds., *Ecological Design and Planning* (New York: John Wiley & Sons, 1997), pp. 185–200.

Reps, John W., *The Making of Urban America: A History of City Planning in the United States* (Princeton, New Jersey: Princeton University Press, 1965).

Ricklefs, Robert E., *Ecology* (Newton, Massachusetts: Chiron Press, 1973).

Roethke, Theodore, "The Lost Son." In *The Collected Poems of Theodore Roethke* (New York: Doubleday, 1966), pp. 53–58.

Rose, Dan, Frederick Steiner, and Joanne Jackson, "An Applied Human Ecological Approach to Regional Planning," *Landscape Planning* 5(1978–79):241–261.

Rubin, Hal, "Lake Tahoe: A Tale of Two States," *Sierra* 66(6, 1981):43–47.

Rykwert, Joseph, *The Seduction of Place: The City in the Twenty-First Century* (New York: Pantheon, 2001).

Sale, Kirkpatrick, *Dwellers in the Land: The Bioregional Vision* (San Francisco: Sierra Club Books, 1985).

Sandbrook, Richard, "From Stockholm to Rio." In Joyce Quarrie, ed., *Earth Summit '92* (London: The Regency Press, 1992), pp. 15–16.

Schama, Simon, *The Embarrassment of Riches: An Interpretation of Dutch Culture in the Golden Age* (Berkeley: University of California Press, 1988).

Schama, Simon, *Landscape and Memory* (New York: Alfred A. Knopf, 1995).

Schmandt, Michael J., "The Importance of History and Context in the Postmodern Urban Landscape," *Landscape Journal* 18(2, 1999):157–165.

Schmandt, Michael Joseph, "Postmodernism and the Southwest Urban Landscape" (Ph.D. dissertation). (Tempe, Arizona: Department of Geography, Arizona State University, 1995).

Scully, Vincent, *Architecture: The Natural and the Manmade* (New York: St. Martin's Press, 1991).

Sears, Paul, *The Ecology of Man* (Eugene: Oregon State System of Higher Education, 1959).

Sears, Paul B., "Ecology—A Subversive Subject," *BioScience* 14(7, July, 1964):11–13.

Sears, Paul B., "The Process of Environmental Change by Man." In: William L. Thomas Jr. ed., *Man's Role in Changing the Face of the Earth* (Chicago: University of Chicago Press, 1956), pp. 471–486.

Selznick, Philip, "In Search of Community." In William Vitek and Wes Jackson, eds., *Rooted in the Land: Essays on Community and Place* (New Haven, Connecticut: Yale University Press, 1996), pp. 195–203.

Shepard, Paul, "Ecology as a Perspective." In Ruth A. Eblen and William R.

Eblen, eds., *The Encyclopedia of the Environment* (Boston: Houghton Mifflin, 1994), pp. 169–171.

Shepard, Paul, "Introduction: Ecology and Man—A Viewpoint." In Paul Shepard and Daniel McKinley, eds., *The Subversive Science: Essays toward an Ecology of Man* (Boston: Houghton Mifflin, 1969), pp. 1–10.

Shepard, Paul, *Man in the Landscape* (Second Edition). (College Station: Texas A&M University Press, 1991).

Shepard, Paul, and Daniel McKinley, eds., *The Subversive Science: Essays toward an Ecology of Man* (Boston: Houghton Mifflin, 1969).

Simpson, John W., "Landscape Medicine: A Timely Treatment," *Journal of Soil and Water Conservation* 44(6, November–December, 1989):577–579.

Simpson, John Warfield, *Visions of Paradise: Glimpses of Our Landscape's Legacy* (Berkeley: University of California Press, 1999).

Sinton, David F., *Reflections on 25 Years of GIS* (Huntsville, Alabama: Intergraph, 1991).

Slater, T. R., ed., *The Built Form of Western Cities* (Leicester, England: Leicester University Press, 1990).

Smith, Daniel S., and Paul Cawood Hellmund, eds., *Ecology of Greenways* (Minneapolis: University of Minnesota Press, 1993).

Smith, Paul, Jr., "The Poetics of Landscape: On the Aesthetic Experience of the Ephemeral Qualities of the Landscape" (Master of Landscape Architecture thesis). (Berkeley: Department of Landscape Architecture, University of California, 1992).

Smithson, Robert, "A Sedimentation of the Mind: Earth Projects." In Nancy Holt, ed., *The Writings of Robert Smithson* (New York: New York University Press, 1989).

Smuts, Jan C., *Holism and Evolution* (London: Macmillan, 1926).

Snyder, Gary, *The Practice of the Wild* (San Francisco: North Point Press, 1990).

Snyder, Gary, *The Real Work* (New York: New Directions Books, 1980).

Sontag, M. Suzanne, and Margaret M. Bubolz, *Families on Small Farms: Case Studies in Human Ecology* (East Lansing: Michigan State University Press, 1996).

Spirn, Anne Whiston, *The Granite Garden: Urban Nature and Human Design* (New York: Basic Books, 1984).

Spirn, Anne Whiston, *The Language of Landscape* (New Haven, Connecticut: Yale University Press, 1998).

Spring, David, and Eileen Spring, eds., *Ecology and Religion in History* (New York: Harper & Row, 1974).

Stalley, Marshall, ed., *Patrick Geddes: Spokesman for the Environment* (New Brunswick, New Jersey: Rutgers University Press, 1972).

Steenbergen, Clemens, and Wouter Reh, *Architecture and Landscape* (Amsterdam: Thoth, 1996).

Stegner, Wallace, *Where the Bluebird Sings to the Lemonade Springs* (New York: Penguin, 1992).

Steiner, Frederick, "The Aesthetics of Soil Conservation," Paper presentation, Malabar Farm, Ohio, October 27, 1988.

Steiner, Frederick, "American Landscape Architecture: Leaping Continental Divides," *Rassegna di Architettura e Urbanistica* (Rome: University of Rome, 1998).

Steiner, Frederick, "Earth Medicine," *GSD News* (Fall, 1996):8–9.

Steiner, Frederick, "Natural Interferences," *Landscape Architecture* 90, no. 11 (November 2000):68–73, 91–93.

Steiner, Frederick, "Regional Planning in the United States: Historic and Contemporary Examples," *Landscape Planning* 10(1983):297–315.

Steiner, Frederick, Jóhn Blair, Laurel McSherry, Subhrajit Guhathakurta, Joaquin Marruffo, and Matthew Holm, "A Watershed at a Watershed: The Potential for Environmentally Sensitive Area Protection in the Upper San Pedro Drainage Basin (Mexico and USA)," *Landscape and Urban Planning* 49(2000):129–148.

Steiner, Frederick R., *The Politics of New Town Planning* (Athens: Ohio University Press, 1981).

Steinitz, Carl, "The Changing Face of GIS from 1965–1993," *GIS Europe* 46(September, 1993):38–40.

Steinitz, Carl, "A Framework for Theory and Practice in Landscape Planning," *GIS Europe* 46(July, 1993):42–45.

Steinitz, Carl, "GIS: A Personal Historical Perspective," *GIS Europe* 46(June, 1993):19–22.

Steward, Julian H., *A Theory of Cultural Change* (Urbana: University of Illinois Press, 1955).

Stilgoe, John R., *Common Landscape of America, 1580–1845* (New Haven, Connecticut: Yale University Press, 1982).

Taylor-Ide, Daniel, and Carl E. Taylor, *Just and Lasting Change: When Communities Own Their Futures* (Baltimore: Johns Hopkins University Press, 2002).

Teaford, John C., *The Twentieth-Century City* (Baltimore: Johns Hopkins University Press, 1986).

Teilhard de Chardin, Pierre, "The Antiquity and World Expansion of Human Culture." In William L. Thomas Jr., ed., *Man's Role in Changing the Face of the Earth* (Chicago: University of Chicago Press, 1956), pp. 103–112.

Tennessee Valley Authority, "A Short History of TVA: From the New Deal to a New Century" (http://www.tva.gov/abouttva/history.htm).

Thomas, John, "Holding the Middle Ground." In Robert Fishman, ed., *The American Planning Tradition* (Washington, D.C.: The Woodrow Wilson Center Press, 2000), pp. 33–63.

Thomas, William L., Jr., ed., *Man's Role in Changing the Face of the Earth* (Chicago: University of Chicago Press, 1956).

Thompson, George F., ed., *Landscape in America* (Austin: University of Texas Press, 1995).

Thompson, George F., and Frederick R. Steiner, eds., *Ecological Design and Planning* (New York: John Wiley & Sons, 1997).

Tillich, Paul, *The House We Live In*. Transcript of the program broadcast on WCAU-TV (CBS), Channel 10, Philadelphia, Sunday, November 20, 1960, hosted and edited by Ian McHarg.

Tuan, Yi-Fu, *Escapism* (Baltimore: Johns Hopkins University Press, 1998).

Tuan, Yi-Fu, *Topophilia: A Study of Environmental Perception, Attitudes, and Values* (Englewood Cliffs, New Jersey: Prentice-Hall, 1974).

United Nations, *World Population Prospects: The 1996 Revisions* (New York: United Nations, 1998).

United Nations Development Programme, United Nations Environment Program, World Bank, World Resources Institute, *World Resources 2000–2001, People and Ecosystems, The Fraying Web of Life* (Amsterdam: Elsevier, 2000).

U.S. Congress, *Tahoe Regional Planning Compact* (Public Law 96-551), 1980.

van der Ree, Paul, Gerrit Smienk, and Clemens Steenbergen, *Italian Villas and Gardens* (Amsterdam: Thoth, 1992).

van der Wal, Coen, *In Praise of Common Sense: Planning the Ordinary. A Physical Planning History of the New Towns in the IJsselmeerpolders* (Rotterdam: 010 Publishers, 1997).

van Gigch, John P., *Applied General Systems Theory* (New York: Harper & Row, 1974).

van Lier, Hubert N., and Frederick R. Steiner, "A Review of the Zuiderzee Reclamation Works: An Example of Dutch Physical Planning," *Landscape Planning* 9(1982):35–59.

Verma, Niraj, *Similarities, Connections, and Systems* (Lanham, Maryland: Lexington Books, 1998).

Vernadsky, Vladimir I., "The Biosphere and the Noosphere," *American Scientist* 33(1, January, 1945):483–517.

Vitek, William, and Wes Jackson, eds., *Rooted in the Land: Essays on Community and Place* (New Haven, Connecticut: Yale University Press, 1996).

Vitousek, Peter M., Harold A. Mooney, Jane Lubchenco, and Jerry M. Melillo, "Human Domination of Earth's Ecosystems," *Science* 277(1997):494–499.

Vitruvius, *On Architecture* (translated by Frank Granger). (Cambridge, Massachusetts: Harvard University, 1931).

Von Bertalanffy, Ludwig, *General Systems Theory* (New York: George Braziller, 1968).

Wackernagel, Mathis, and William Rees, *Our Ecological Footprint: Reducing Human Impact on the Earth* (Gabriola Island, British Columbia: New Society Publishers, 1996).

Wallace, David Rains, "Sand County's Conservation Prophet," *Sierra* (November/December 1987):62–67.

Walpole, Horace, *The History of the Modern Taste in Gardening* (Seventh Edition). (London: John Major, 1827).

Wang, Rusong, Jingzhu Zhao, and Zhiyun Ouyang, eds., *Human Systems Ecology* (Beijing: China Science and Technology Press, 1991).

Watts, Alan, *The House We Live In*. Transcript of the program broadcast on WCAU-TV (CBS), Channel 10, Philadelphia, Sunday, December 11, 1960, hosted and edited by Ian McHarg.

Watts, May Theilgaard, *Reading the Landscape: An Adventure in Ecology* (New York: The Macmillan Company, 1957).

White, Lynn, Jr., "The Historical Roots of Our Ecologic Crisis," *Science* 155(March 10, 1967):1203–1207.

Whitehand, J. W. R., ed., *The Urban Landscape: Historical Development and Management* (London: Academic Press, 1981).

Whitman, Walter, *Leaves of Grass* (Brooklyn, New York, 1855).

Widby, Tad, "Trouble in Tahoe," *Planning* 46(3, 1980):6–7.

Williams, Terry Tempest, *Leap* (New York: Pantheon Books, 2000).

Williams, Terry Tempest, *Refuge* (New York: Pantheon Books, 1991).

Wilson, E. O., "The Current State of Biological Diversity." In E. O. Wilson, ed., *Biodiversity* (Washington, D.C.: National Academy Press, 1988), pp. 3–18.

Wilson, E. O., ed., *Biodiversity* (Washington, D.C.: National Academy Press, 1988).

Wilson, Edward O., *In Search of Nature* (Washington, D.C.: Island Press/Shearwater Books, 1996).

Wojtowicz, Robert, *Lewis Mumford and American Modernism: Eutopian Theories for Architecture and Urban Planning* (Cambridge: Cambridge University Press, 1996).

Woodbury, Angus M., *Principles of General Ecology* (New York: The Blakiston Company, 1954).

Wu, Jiango, and Orie L. Loucks, "From Balance of Nature to Hierarchical Patch Dynamics: A Paradigm Shift in Ecology," *The Quarterly Review of Biology* 70(4, 1995):439–466.

Yaro, Robert D., and Tony Hiss, *A Region at Risk: The Third Regional Plan for the New York–New Jersey–Connecticut Metropolitan Area* (Washington, D.C.: Island Press, 1996).

Yeang, Ken, "The Ecological (or Green) Approach to Design," *Eco Enea* 148(May, 2000):6–11.

Yeang, Ken, *The Green Skyscraper: The Basis for Designing Sustainable Intensive Buildings* (Munich: Prestel-Verlag, 1999).

Young, G. L., "Environmental Law: Perspectives from Human Ecology," *Environmental Law* 6(1976):289–307.

Young, Gerald L., "A Conceptual Framework for an Interdisciplinary Human Ecology," *Acta Oecologiae Hominis* 1(1989):1–135.

Young, Gerald L., "A Piece of the Main: Parts and Wholes in Human Ecology," *Advances in Human Ecology* 8(1999):1–31.

Young, Gerald L., "The Case for a 'Catholic' Ecology," *Human Ecology Review* 1(2, 1994):310–319.

Young, Gerald L., "Environment: Term and Concept in the Social Sciences," *Social Science Information* 25(1, 1986):83–124.

Young, Gerald L., "Hierarchy and Central Place: Some Questions of More General Theory," *Geografiska Annaler* 60B(1978):71–78.

Young, Gerald L., "Holism: Writ and Riposte in Ecology and Human Ecology," *Advances in Human Ecology* 7(1998):313–365.

Young, Gerald L., "Human Ecology." In Ruth A. Eblen and William R. Eblen, eds., *The Encyclopedia of the Environment* (Boston: Houghton Mifflin, 1994), pp. 339–342.

Young, Gerald L., "Human Ecology as an Interdisciplinary Domain: A Critical Inquiry," *Advances in Ecological Research* 8(1974):1–105.

Young, Gerald L., "Interaction as a Concept Basic to Human Ecology: An Exploration and Synthesis," *Advances in Human Ecology* 5(1998):313–365.

Young, Gerald L., ed., *Origins of Human Ecology* (Stroudsburg, Pennsylvania: Hutchinson Ross Publishing Company, 1983).

Young, Gerald L., and Tom J. Bartuska, "Sphere: Term and Concept as an Integrative Device toward Understanding Environmental Unity," *General Systems* XIX(1974):219–230.

Young, Gerald, Frederick Steiner, Kenneth Brooks, and Kenneth Struckmeyer, "Determining the Regional Context for Landscape Planning," *Landscape Planning* 10(1983):269–296.

Young, Gerald, Frederick Steiner, Kenneth Brooks, and Kenneth Struckmeyer, "Planning the Built Environment: Determining the Regional Context." In Tom J. Bartuska and Gerald L. Young, eds., *The Built Environment: A Creative Inquiry into Design and Planning* (Menlo Park, California: Crisp Publications, 1994), pp. 305–317.

Zelinsky, Wilbur, "North America's Vernacular Regions," *Annals of the Association of American Geographers* 70(1980):1–16.

Zimmerer, Karl S., "Human Geography and the 'New Ecology': The Prospect and Promise of Integration," *Annals of the Association of American Geographers* 84(1, 1994):108–125.

Zonneveld, I. S., "Scope and Concepts of Landscape Ecology as an Emerging Science." In I. S. Zonneveld and R. T. T. Forman, eds., *Changing Landscapes: An Ecological Perspective* (New York: Springer-Verlag, 1990).

Zonneveld, I. S., and R. T. T. Forman, eds., *Changing Landscapes: An Ecological Perspective* (New York: Springer-Verlag, 1990).

Zube, Ervin, ed., *Landscapes: Selected Writings of J. B. Jackson* (Amherst: University of Massachusetts Press, 1970).

Zube, Ervin H., James L. Sell, and Jonathan G. Taylor, "Landscape Perception: Research, Application, and Theory," *Landscape Planning* 9(1, 1982):1–33.

INDEX

Adams, Ansel, 93
Adams, Thomas, 121
Adaptation: to cold climates, 88; communities and, 69; definitions of, 34–35; global processes and, 152, 163; to habitats, 52–53; landscapes and, 87–88, 93, 145, 163; nations and, 139–140; overview, 34–36, 170; regions and, 110–111
Adirondack Park Agency, 117, 118–119, 120
Adirondack Park Land Use and Development Plan, 118
Adler, Dankmar, 44, 192n.17
Agrarianism, 59, 66, 82–83, 84
Agriculture: habitat and, 42; regions of, 104–105
Ahern, Jack, 120–121
Alberti, 70
Alexander, Christopher, 45, 48
Allen, Woody, 30
Alterra Institute, 159, 161–163
Anastazi people, 139
Andersson, Sven-Ingvar, 80
Andrus, Cecil D., 120
Animals: cruelty prevention societies, 130; as pets, 48–49
Annales school of historiography, 7
Apartheid, 138
Appalachian Regional Commission, 117–118, 120
Appalachian Regional Development Act (1965), 117
Aquoe Albuloe, 22, 23
Architects, 58. *See also* Planning
Aristotle, 69, 96, 128
Art (earth/environmental): landscape and, 9, 10; regions and, 105–106; significance of, 90–91, 92, 93

Artbytes, 60
Atmosphere, 148
Atta, Mohammed, 138
Automobiles and settlement, 25–26, 114

Babbitt, Bruce, 126
Bachelard, Gaston, 43, 192n.16
Bacon, Francis, 82
Bailey, Robert, 95, 103–104
Balance of nature, 15. *See also* Disequilibrium
Balkans and conflict, 141
Baltimore LTER, 11
Barcelona, 159–161
Barrett, Gary W., 164
Barr, James, 168
Bartuska, Tom, 147–148, 153, 154, 170
Bates, Marston, 31
BBC radio/television, 130–131
Beatley, Timothy, 34, 90, 170
Behar, Roberto, 62
Behnisch, Stefan, 159, 161, 162, 207n.41
Benedikt, Michael, 51
Berry, Wendell, 105
Bible, 167–168
Biodiversity: overview, 33–34; SCERP and, 135–136; significance of, 156–158
Biological hierarchy, 12–13
Bioregion, 95, 106
Biosphere, 148
Biosphere, The (Vernadsky), 147
Black Elk, 129
Bloedel Reserve (Haag), 80
Bonaparte, Napoleon, 139
Borgo of Genoa, 64
Botkin, Daniel, 4, 21, 31, 33
Boulding, Kenneth, 158, 206n.37
Boundaries: community and, 64–66;

description of, 28, 29–30, 170; of habitat, 46–48; of landscapes, 84–85; of nations, 133–136; of regions, 106; rivers as, 135–136
Boyd, Julian, 140
Bradley, Nina Leopold, 77
Brand, Stewart, 32
Brandywine Valley, Pennsylvania, 109
Brown, Denise Scott, 45
Brundtland Commission, 121
Bubolz, Margaret M., 35, 42, 50
Buell, Lawrence, 105–106
Building/lot, 13
Buildings and function, 44–46
Burckhardt, Jacob, 127, 203n.3
Burgess, Ernest, 58, 59
Byrne, Brendan T., 119, 120

Callenbach, Ernest, 104
Calthorpe, Peter, 72, 73, 103
Carrying capacity, 164
Casteneda, Carlos, 61
Cell phones, 130
Central Park (NY), 29, 91
Change: in communities, 61, 62–63, 67–68; at global scale, 145, 148–153, 163–165, 173; in human systems, 27–28, 170; institutions and, 32; in landscapes, 9; nations and, 139–140; nation-states and, 133; urbanization and, 150–151
Chaos theory, 10–11, 158
Christians and nature, 167–169
Churchill, Winston, 52
Cicero, Marcus Tullius, 13
Cities: "regional city," 101–102; regionalism of, 101–102; as urban form level, 13
City-states, Greece, 126, 128
Civic places, 63. See also Institutions
Civil War, America, 139
Climate: adaptation to, 88; global warming, 148–149, 152–153; information on, 5, 6, 148–149; regional divisions by, 103–104
Cobb, John B., Jr., 68, 74, 168
Cohen, Yehudi: adaptation, 35; culture, 19–20; institutions, 32; nations/nation-states, 125, 129, 132
Coke, James, 71
Cole, LaMont, 148
Columbia Basin Act (1943), 113
Columbia Basin Irrigation Project, 113–114
Columbia Basin Joint Investigations, 113

Community: basic elements of, 59–60, 74; boundaries and, 64–66; change in, 61, 62–63, 67–68; civic places in, 63; creation of, 58, 69–73; definitions/descriptions of, 57, 59–60; density vs. dispersion, 59; development of, 73–74; diversity and, 68–69; ecological footprints of, 69–73; function of, 61–63; gated communities, 65; hierarchies and, 13; idea of, 58–59; interactions and, 66–68; language and, 60; from memory/desire, 62, 194–195n.24; overview, 13, 57–58; segregation in, 194–195n.24; structure of, 61–63; sustainability of, 74, 171; "three natures" and, 66; types of, 66
"Community of local communities," 68–69
Competition, 30, 31
Computer Age, 6, 146
Conflicts: in the Balkans, 141; diversity and, 137; human similarities and, 173; nations and, 134–135
Connectivity, 150, 151
Conservation biology, 9
Conservation vs. preservation, 163
Consumption: as agent of change, 150; differences in, 157
Conzen, M.R.G., 7, 61
Coon Creek watershed (WI), 34
Cornaro, Alvise, 83
Corridor, 27
Cowan, James, 30
Crime and communities, 65
Cronon, William, 7
Crow, Michael, 22
Cry, The Beloved Country (Paton), 7
Cultural core, 21
Cultural Revolution, China, 139
Culture: change and, 149–151; communities and, 59–60, 66; descriptions of, 19–20; diversity of, 33–34, 43–45, 157; global culture, 172–173; habitat diversity and, 51–52; landscape and, 88, 93; languages for landscape, 80; nations/nation-states and, 128–131, 131; nature link, 8; overview, 24–25; regions and, 98–100, 101–102, 104, 105, 122–123

da Vinci, Leonardo, 99–100, 154, 156
Dangermand, Jack, 5
Davis, Mike, 7
Deconstructionism, 158, 206n.36

Deeds, Edward, 112
Deep context, 79–80
Deep structure, 80, 123
de Jonge, Nico, 81–82
DeLillo, Don, 137
Descartes, René, 82
Deserts, 87–88
Discrimination and regions, 107, 108
Disequilibrium: in new ecology, 15; point of view, 3
Diversity: in communities, 68–69; of habitats, 50–52; health and, 34; of landscapes, 86–88, 92–93; in nations/states, 137–138; overview, 33–34, 170; regions and, 105, 109–110, 122–123. *See also* Biodiversity
Drainage basins. *See* Watersheds
Dramstad, Wenche E., 29
Duany, Andres, 72–73
Dubai-style house, 43–44
Du Pont, Pierre S., 109
Dybosphere, 153

Earth: change and, 145, 148–153, 163–165, 173; diversity, 156–158; global warming, 148–149; images from space, 5; as organization level, 13, 14; overview, 145–146; planning/architecture and, 158–163; resource limits of, 164; as single living entity, 146–148; spheres of, 147–148, 153–154; understanding of, 154–155. *See also* Global scale
Earth Day, 2–3
Ecological Age, 6, 146
Ecological planning/design: description, 88–89; positive trends/drawbacks, 89–92. *See also* Planning; Regional planning
Ecology: American vs. European, 8–9; overview, 2–3, 21. *See also* Human ecology
Economics: ecological view of, 1; overview, 2; politics and, 22–24; segregation and, 64–65, 138
Economic theory, 145–146
Ecoregions, 95
Ecosphere, 148
Ecosystems: definitions/descriptions, 21, 23–24; function/structure/change in, 27–28
Ecotones: communities and, 66; description

of, 28, 170; of habitats, 47–48; of landscapes, 85; between nations, 134–135
Edge effect, 29
Edges: communities and, 66; descriptions of, 9, 28, 29, 170; of habitat, 47; of landscapes, 85
Eisenhower, Dwight, 126
Eliot, Charles, 91
Eliot, T.S., 105
Emerson, Ralph Waldo, 66, 96–97
Emo villa, 70
Environmental determinism, 2, 3
Estall, Robert, 117–118
Ethics and human ecology, 167–175
Ethnicity and community, 62, 64, 194–195n.24
European Union, 134, 135, 146
Everglades, 100
Evernden, Neil, 8, 15, 37, 58

Family, 48–50
Farm Security Administration, 101
Fêng shui, 80
Ferguson, Bruce, 89
Fiore, Quentin, 153
Fletcher, Rachel, 70
Forman, Richard, 8–9, 27, 84–85, 90, 93, 145
Fowles, John, 173–174
Fox, George, 32, 33
Frampton, Kenneth, 45
Franklin, Carol, 91–92
Friedmann, John, 115–116, 121
Friedman, Thomas, 133
Fugitive, The, 101
Fuller, R. Buckminster, 61
Fulton, William, 103
Function: buildings and, 44–46; of communities, 61–63; of Earth, 147–148; in human systems, 26–28, 170; institutions and, 32; of landscapes, 82, 84

Gaia hypothesis, 146, 147
Gans, Herbert, 45, 65
Garreau, Joel, 104
Gas Works Park (Haag), 80
Gated communities, 65
Gaudí, Antoni, 110
Geddes, Patrick, 96, 97
Geertz, Clifford, 21, 32, 50
Gentrification, 67–68

Geographical information system. *See* GIS
Ghettos, 62–63
GIS (geographical information system): for global data, 163; naming of, 183n.15; uses of, 4–5, 6
Glatt, Linnea, 10
Global scale: culture, 172–173; institutions, 155–156; interactions, 146, 155–156; language, 148–149, 156. *See also* Earth
Global village, 153
Global warming: consequences of, 152–153; description of, 148–149
Godron, Michel, 8, 27
Golley, Frank, 23, 24
Grand Coulee Dam, 113
Grant, Jill, 11
Great Depression, 111, 112
Greek city-states, 126, 128
Greenbelt new towns, 114, 115
Greenhouse gases, 149
Greenways, 9, 120–121
Gridiron street system, 71
Grimm, Nancy, 11
Growth of the Soil (Hamsun), 7

Haag, Rich, 80, 91–92
Habitat: adaptations to, 52–53; boundaries and, 46–48; definitions of, 40–41; diversity of, 50–52; environment and, 43–44, 45–46, 50–51; improvements in, 53–54; interactions and, 48–50; niche vs., 41–42; overview, 13, 39–40; technology and, 42, 44, 46, 51; values and, 52–53
Haeckel, Ernst, 21, 188n.7
Halprin, Lawrence, 80, 91–92
Hamsun, Knut, 7
Hancocks, David, 48–49, 130
Havel, Václav, 140, 146, 173
Hawken, Paul, 35, 157
Hazan, Marcella, 99
Health and diversity, 34
Heat island effect, 12, 153
Hersey, George, 10
Hersperger, Anna, 27; on holism, 36
Heschel, Abraham J., 167
Hierarchy theory, 12–15, 20
Hildebrand, Grant, 10
Hillerman, Tony, 7
Hindu theology, 169
Hines real estate company, 159, 160
Hirst, Damien, 10

History: interactions and, 137; regions and, 108–109; significance of, 28, 151–152
Hohokam people, 87, 126, 152
Holism: in general systems theory, 21; overview, 13, 14, 36–37. *See also* Earth
Holling, C.S., 14
Holme, Thomas, 70, 71
Holt, Nancy, 10, 90, 92
Home and sustainability, 171
Homeostasis, 21, 89
Homestead Act (1862), 83
Hopi nation, 100, 134, 139
Howard, Ebenezer, 114
Howe, William, 109
Human ecology: concepts of, 20–21, 170; definition, 96; description, 24; ethical implications, 167–175; new human ecology, 3–12; overview, 1–16; term significance, 2; urban ecology, 4, 11
Humans: plant/animal differences from, 19–20; similarities between, 173
Hunt, John Dixon, 66
Hydrosphere, 147

Ickes, Harold, 113
Identity: nations and, 131–133; regions and, 108–109
IJssemeerpolders Development Authority, 115
Information: economy and, 121–122; as resource, 22; technology and, 5, 6, 25, 148–149
Information Age, 6, 146
Institutions: community change and, 67–68; at global scale, 155–156; nations and, 129–131; overview, 30, 31–33; regions and, 109; resource exploitation and, 21–23
Integration: landscapes and, 85–86; overview, 30, 31–33, 170; regions and, 107–109
Integrative traits: overview, 24–26. *See also* Culture; Language; Technology
Interactions: bioregions and, 106; in communities, 66–68; landscapes and, 9, 85–86; between nations, 146, 155–156; nation/state and, 126, 136–137, 141–142; in nested networks, 14; overview, 30–33, 170; significance of, 1, 175
International style (design), 45

Internet: adaptation and, 35–36; property/ copyright issues and, 47; significance of, 6; Talossa kingdom on, 60; uses, 148
Iroquois people, 132, 169–170
Islam and nature, 169
Italy: *borgo* of Genoa, 64; diversity of, 172; interactions in, 136–137; Milan, 99, 121–122, 172, 203n.67; regional culture of, 98–100; regions of, 99–100, 108, 109; Rome, 22–23, 65, 69, 164, 172, 174–175

Jackson, J.B., 45, 65–66, 77, 173
Jackson, Wes, 68
Jeffersonian grid, 82–83, 84, 126
Jefferson, Thomas: agrarianism, 59, 66, 82–83, 84; human nature, 173; impact of, 71–72, 97, 139–140; landscape grids, 82–83, 84, 126; "pursuit of happiness," 96
Jewish people: in Kraków communities, 62–63; nature and religion, 167
Johnson, Bart R., 3
Johnson, Lyndon B., 117
Joint families, 50
Jones, Alice, 14
Jones, Grant, 91–92
Jones, Inigo, 71
Joyce, James, 36

Kazimierz neighborhood, 62, 63
Keller, Edward A., 21, 31, 33
Kennedy, John F., 117, 137
Kent, William, 84
Kettering, Charles, 112
King, Martin Luther, 139
Kingsolver, Barbara, 7
Koestler, Arthur, 36, 191n.70
Korea, 135
Kraenzel, Carl Frederick, 100–101, 116
Kraków, Poland, 62–63, 168, 172
Kropotkin, Petr, 97
Krus, Probst Xaver Niklaus, 168–169
Kunstler, James Howard, 57

Landers, Richard, 153
Land Ordinance Act (1785), 83, 139, 140
Landscape architecture, 9, 91–92
Landscape ecology: considerations of, 9–10; landscape scale and, 78–79; overview, 8–10; scale of nature, 79; significance of, 90–92

Landscapes: boundaries of, 84–85; defining characteristics of, 85–86; definitions of, 77, 78–79; design/planning of, 88–92; diversity of, 86–88, 92–93; ecotones of, 85; edges of, 85; function and, 82, 84; interaction/integration and, 85–86; landscaping vs., 91, 92; languages of, 79–82; as organization level, 13, 78–79; overview, 77–78; structure of, 82–84; studies of, 7–8; watershed divisions of, 83–84
Land trusts, 164
Language: community and, 60; global language, 148–149, 156; hierarchies and, 20–21; jargons, 25; of landscape ecologists, 92–93; landscapes and, 81; nations and, 20–21, 126, 128–129; overview, 24–25; regions and, 98; states/nation-states and, 128–129
Language of Landscape, The (Spirn), 79, 80
League of Nations, 155–156
Le Carré, John, 127
Lely, Cornelis, 115
Lenni-Lenape native Americans, 100
Leopold, Aldo: community, 66, 68; Earth, 146–147; ecology, 34, 92; farms, 77, 78; "land pyramid," 97
Le Play, Frédéric, 97
Levi, Primo, 62–63
Lewin, Kurt, 46
Lewis, Phil, 91–92
Life and extreme environments, 155, 156
Life-space, 46
Lincoln, Abraham, 126
Lithosphere, 147
Locke, John, 82
Lombardy region of Italy, 99–100, 108
Loucks, Orie, 15
Lovelock, James, 21, 146, 147
LTERs (Long Term Ecological Research projects), 11
Luccarelli, Mark, 96–97
Luymes, Don, 65
Lyle Center for Regenerative Studies, 159, 163, 206n.38
Lyle, John, 91–92, 159, 170, 206n.38
Lynch, Kevin, 29, 80, 110–111, 170, 189n.37

Machiavelli, Nicoló, 133
MacKaye, Benton, 95–96, 101, 102, 111

Mad cow disease, 151
Malthus, Thomas, 164
Mandelbaum, Seymour, 31, 57
Manning, Kristy, 34, 90, 170
Maps: nations/states and, 132; uses of,
    29–30
Márquez, Gabriel García, 49, 174
Marshall, Alex, 57
Matrix, 27
Mayer, Albert, 46
McFague, Sallie, 168
McHarg, Ian: ecological design, 88–89, 90,
    91–92, 116, 121, 163; humanity, 173;
    "layer cake," 80, 97, 154; living Earth,
    147; religion and nature, 168; universal
    style and, 45
McLuhan, Marshall, 153, 206n.27
Meadows, Donella, 171, 208n.19
Meine, Curt, 83
Meinig, Donald, 77
Metro, Portland, Oregon, 103
Miami Conservancy District, 112
Miami, Florida, 98, 100
Miami region, Ohio, 98, 100, 112
Milan, Italy, 99, 121–122, 172, 203n.67
Miralles, Enric, 159–160
Miss, Mary, 10
Mobility: of Americans, 53; communities
    and, 64; human habitat and, 41, 53, 54
Moore, Steven, 45
Morgan, Arthur E., 112
Morris, A. E. J., 71, 128
Morris, Elizabeth, 58–59
Moudon, Anne Vernez, 7, 28, 61
Moule, Elizabeth, 72
Mulisch, Harry, 128
Mumford, Lewis: community, 59; design,
    45, 46; regions, 96–97, 101, 111, 114,
    121
Muratori, Saverio, 7

Nabhan, Gary Paul, 8, 33–34, 40
NASA, 5, 154–155, 156
Nassauer, Joan, 79
National Academy of Science, 106–107
National Endowment for the Arts, 130
National Industrial Recovery Act (1933),
    113
National Research Council, 106–107
National Resources Planning Board, 101
Nations: boundaries of, 133–136; change

and, 139–140; culture and, 128–131; di-
    versity in, 137–138; idea of, 126–127;
    identity and, 131–133; institutions and,
    129–131; interactions and, 126,
    136–137, 141–142; language and, 20–21,
    126, 128–129; overview, 13, 14,
    125–126; war and peace, 137
Nation-states: change and, 133; culture and,
    128–131, 131; diversity in, 137; idea of,
    127–128; language and, 128–129, 129
Native peoples: adaptation by, 139; bound-
    aries and, 132, 134; language and, 129;
    regional culture of, 100. See also specific
    groups
Natural Resources Conservation Service,
    29–30
Nature: culture link, 8; interaction with, 67;
    religion and, 167–169
Navajo nation, 134, 139, 169
Navigli system, 99–100, 199n.11
Nazis, 62–63
Neighborhood, 60
Nested networks, 12–15
Netherlands: Alterra Institute, 159,
    161–163; interactions in, 136; national
    identity of, 131, 132; Zuiderzee reclama-
    tion works, 81, 111, 115
Newcourt, Richard, 71
New Deal, 101, 111–115, 126
New ecology, 3–4
New Jersey Pinelands Commission, 117,
    119–120
New Urbanism, 72–73
New York-New Jersey-Connecticut regional
    plan, 121–122
Ng, Fae Myenne, 50
Niche, 41–42
Niebuhr, Reinhold, 47, 193n.25
Nolen, John, 72, 91, 114, 201n.43
Nongovernmental organizations, 164
Noosphere, 147, 153
North American Free Trade Act, 135, 146
Northwest Ordinance Act (1787), 83, 139,
    140
Norton, William, 128–129
Noss, Reed, 8, 41
Nuclear testing, 8

Odum, Eugene: carrying capacity, 164; di-
    versity, 33; ecosystems, 23–24; ecotones,

28; habitat vs. niche, 41; watershed regions, 106, 111–112

Odum, Howard W., 101, 106, 111

O'Keefe, Georgia, 93

Olin, Laurie, 10, 91–92, 160

Olmsted, Frederick Law, 65, 72, 91, 97, 122

One Hundred Years of Solitude (Márquez), 49

Ophuls, William, 23

Opie, John, 7

Order Out of Chaos (Prigogine and Stengers), 10

Palazzo, Danilo, 146

Palladio, Andrea, 52, 53, 70, 72, 82–83

Parasitism, 31

Parc Diagonal Mar, 159–161, 163

Park, Robert, 58, 59

Parks, Tim, 136

Patch, 27

Paterson, Douglas, 67, 73–74, 173

Paton, Alan, 7

Patterson, John H., 112

Peace Corps, 137

Peck, Sheila, 12

Pedosphere, 147–148

Penn, William, 70–71, 79

Penone, Giuseppe, 10

Philadelphia: design of, 70–71; Mill Creek neighborhood, 79–80; West Philadelphia Landscape Project, 79, 80

Phoenix LTER, 11

Photographers and regions, 105

Piazzas, 66, 175

Pijawka, David, 171

Pinelands Protection Act (1979, NJ), 119

Planning: community and, 58; ecological design, 88–92; hierarchies and, 14; history/future of, 158; landscape ecology and, 9; regenerative design, 159, 170–171; significance of, 28. *See also* Regional planning

Plater-Zyberk, Elizabeth, 72

Plato, 13, 69, 96, 128, 129

Plowing the Dark (Powers), 54

Pluralism, 34

Poets and regions, 105–106

Poland: diversity of, 172; Kraków, 62–63, 168, 172

Polders, 81, 82, 115

Political economy, 22–24

Politics: nation-state and, 127–128; regions and, 102–103; state and, 127; technology and, 151

Polyzoidis, Stefanos, 72

Population dynamics, 150–151

Powell, John Wesley, 83–84, 100–101

Powers, Richard, 54, 145–146

Predation, 31

Preservation vs. conservation, 163

Prigogine, Ilya, 10, 185n.43

Proctor & Gamble, 51–52

Psychosphere, 147

Pulliam, H. Ronald, 3

Putnam, Robert, 66–67

Pyne, Stephen, 7

Quakers, 32–33

Quarries, travertine, 22–23

Quayle, Moura, 57

Ransom, John Crowe, 101

Rappaport, Roy, 20, 187n.2

Reading the Landscape: An Adventure in Ecology (Watts), 40

Reagan administration, 120

Rees, William, 73

Refuge (Williams), 7–8

Regional Plan Association (RPA), 117, 121

Regional planning: descriptions of, 116; human ecology and, 95–96; natural-science approach, 116, 119–121; overview, 110–111; social sciences and, 116, 117–118, 121; in U.S., 111–115, 115–122. *See also* Ecological planning/design

Regional Planning Association of America (RPAA), 101, 102, 103

Regions: adaptation and, 110–111; agricultural regions, 104–105; biophysical divisions of, 103–104, 106–107; boundaries of, 106; climate divisions of, 103–104; culture and, 98–100, 101–102, 104, 105, 122–123; definitions/descriptions of, 95–96, 126; discrimination and, 107, 108; diversity and, 105, 109–110, 122–123; economic regions, 104; idea of, 96–97; identification of, 102–107; identity and, 108–109; institutions and, 109; integration and, 107–109; language and, 98; overview, 13–14, 95–96; political regions, 102–103; "regional city," 101–102; sociocultural regions, 104; as urban form,

13; water and, 99–100; watershed divisions of, 103, 104, 106–107
Reiniger, Clair, 106
Religion: as institution, 32–33; nature and, 1, 167–169
Remote-sensed information, 5–6
Renaissance, 68, 70, 72
Reps, John, 70
Republic, The (Plato), 128
Resettlement Administration, 114
Resource exploitation, 21–24, 42
Restoration, 159
Rivers and boundaries, 135–136
Rivers and Harbors Act (1937), 113
Roethke, Theodore, 80, 93
Rome, Italy, 22–23, 65, 69, 164, 172, 174–175
Roosevelt, Franklin D., 111, 112, 126
Rust Belt, 69, 104

Sale, Kirkpatrick, 106
Sanders, Russell Scott, 96–97
San Pedro watershed, 135–136
Satellite uses, 5, 6, 148
Sauer, Leslie, 91–92
Schama, Simon, 7, 88, 131, 132
Schengen agreement, 134
Schmandt, Michael, 61
Scully, Vincent, 45
Sears, Paul, 1, 41, 147
Segregation: *apartheid*, 138; in community, 62, 64, 194–195n.24; economics and, 64–65, 138
Selznick, Philip, 59, 74
Seminole Indians, 98
September 11 attacks, 138, 141, 145
Sforza, Duke Lodovico, 100
Shepard, Paul, 2, 82, 83, 181n.4
Shetter, Kim, 171
Singer, Michael, 10, 161, 207n.41
Sinton, David, 5
Smithson, Robert, 10, 90, 92
Smuts, Jan, 36
Snelson, Kenneth, 61
Snyder, Gary, 105–106
Social sciences: ecology and, 2–3; regional planning and, 116, 117–118, 121
Society of Friends, 32–33
Socrates, 128
Soil Conservation Service, 29–30
Soleri, Paolo, 59

Sontag, M. Suzanne, 35, 42, 50
Southwest Center for Environmental Research and Policy (SCERP), 135–136
Spain: Barcelona, 159–161; regions of, 108, 109; Toledo communities, 68–69
Spirn, Anne, 79–80, 91–92
Sports and regionalism, 123
Sprawl, 73, 74
States: civilized states, 127; idea of, 127; interactions and, 126, 136–137, 141–142; language and, 20–21, 128–129; as organization level, 13, 14
Stegner, Wallace, 7, 69, 93
Stein, Clarence, 72, 114
Stein, Gertrude, 110
Steinitz, Carl, 91–92
Stem families, 50
Stengers, Isabelle, 10, 185n.43
Steward, Julian, 21
Stilgoe, John, 7
Street/block, 13
Structure: of communities, 61–63; deep structure, 80, 123; of Earth, 147–148; in human systems, 26–28, 170; institutions and, 32; of landscapes, 82–84; physical elements of, 27
Suburbs, 65, 66
Sun Belt, 69, 104
Survival, 30
Sustainability: of communities, 74, 171; designs/plans for, 35, 159–163; foundation of, 121; of homes, 171; significance of, 11–12, 170; trend in, 89–90, 92
Symbiosis, 31
Symbols and identity, 138
Systems: definitions/descriptions, 21, 23–24, 188n.5; open vs. closed, 3–4; resource exploitation and, 21–23

Tagliabue, Benedetta, 159, 160
Tahoe Regional Planning Agency, 117, 119, 120
Taoism and nature, 169
Tate, Allen, 101
Taylor, Carl E., 61
Taylor-Ide, Daniel, 61
Teaford, Jon, 31
Technology: climate information from, 5, 6, 148–149; communication and, 156; community and, 60, 62; global processes and, 146, 149–150, 151; habitat and, 42,

44, 46, 51; landscapes and, 88; nation-states and, 129, 130–131, 133; overview, 24, 25–26; politics and, 151; settlement and, 25–26, 87–88; significance of, 4–6, 153–154
Technosphere, 153
Telesis group, 101
Television networks, 130–131
Tennessee Valley Authority (TVA), 111–113
Tensegrity, 61
Tertullianus, Quintus Septimius Florens, 164
Texas, 122–123, 140–141
Thoreau, Henry David: human nature, 173; nature, 66, 91, 96–97, 146, 165
Tijuana watershed, 135, 136
Tillich, Paul, 167–168
Timaeus (Plato), 13
Tissue: of the city, 7, 183n.17; of the community, 61
Tito, Marshal, 141
Transcendentalists, 72, 90–91, 170
Tuan, Yi-Fu, 35, 86
Tugwell, Rexford Guy, 114
Twatwa native people, 98, 100

United Nations, 156, 157
Universal Forum of Cultures-Barcelona 2004, 160, 161
Urban ecology, 4, 11. *See also* Human ecology
Urban form: hierarchy of, 13–14; history and, 28
Urbanization and change, 150–151
Urban morphology: overview, 3, 6–7; physical elements of, 27; urban ecology link, 11
U.S. Army Corps of Engineers, 100
U.S. Bureau of Reclamation, 113
U.S. Department of Agriculture, 103
U.S. Environmental Protection Agency, 103, 135
U.S. Interior Department, 120
U.S. National Park Service's Rivers, Trails, and Conservation Program, 120

Valéry, Paul, 46
Values and habitat, 52–53
Van der Lieck, Tilo C. Driessen, 57
Van der Wal, Coen, 115
Vaux, Calvert, 91

Venturi, Robert, 45
Verma, Niraj, 24
Vernacular regions, 104
Vernadsky, Vladimir, 147
Via Tiburtina, 22
Visualization and landscape, 86, 172
Vitek, William, 68
Vitruvius, Marcus Pollio, 39, 52, 69–70

Walpole, Horace, 84
War and peace, 137
Warren, Robert Penn, 101
Washington, George, 109
Water management: Columbia Basin Irrigation Project, 113–114; disease and, 102; in Italy, 99–100, 199n.11; Miami, Florida, 100; Miami valley of Ohio, 100, 112; Tennessee Valley Authority (TVA), 111–113; by watershed, 106–107; Zuiderzee reclamation works, 81, 111, 115
Watersheds: divisions by, 83–84, 103, 104, 106–107; planning and, 135–136
Watts, Alan, 169, 208n.16
Watts, May Theilgaard, 40
White, Lynn, Jr., 168, 207–208n.8
Whitman, Walt, 66, 80, 96–97, 105, 125
Wild and Scenic Rivers Act, 120
Williams, Terry Tempest, 7–8, 96–97
Williams, William Carlos, 105
Wilson, E. O., 157–158
Wired, 60
Wojtowicz, Robert, 96
Wolfe, Tom, 45
Wright, Frank Lloyd, 39–40, 59, 80
Wright, Henry, 72, 114
Wu, Jianguo, 15

Yeang, Ken, 9–10
Young, Gerald: habitat, 46; holism, 14, 36, 147–148, 153, 154; institutions, 31–32; interactions, 108; transcendentalism, 170

Zedong, Mao, 139
Zelinsky, Wilbur, 104
Zen Buddhism and nature, 169
Zimmerer, Karl, 3
Zonneveld, I.S., 36
Zoological parks, 130
Zuiderzee Act, 115
Zuiderzee reclamation works, 81, 111, 115